IMAGES
of America

Dennis Township

On the Cover: Three generations of Belleplain, New Jersey, patriots gather on Memorial Day in the 1950s to honor their community's heroes who died in combat. Leading the ceremony is Rollen Mason (standing in the center, to the left of the flag), a prominent local business owner, farmer, and landowner. He also served as a committeeman in Dennis Township for 39 years. (Courtesy of Thomas Champion.)

IMAGES
of America

DENNIS TOWNSHIP

Thomas Champion and Ray Rebmann

ARCADIA
PUBLISHING

ISBN 978-1-4671-1632-9

Published by Arcadia Publishing
Charleston, South Carolina

Printed in the United States of America

Library of Congress Control Number: 2016931072

For all general information, please contact Arcadia Publishing:
Telephone 843-853-2070
Fax 843-853-0044
E-mail sales@arcadiapublishing.com
For customer service and orders:
Toll-Free 1-888-313-2665

Visit us on the Internet at www.arcadiapublishing.com

Contents

Acknowledgments

Unless specifically credited, the photographs used in chapters 3 through 7 and in chapter 9 belong to the Old School House Museum, located in Dennisville. Most of these photographs were originally provided to the museum by Dennis Township resident George Brewer. In addition, unless otherwise noted, the photographs in the first and second chapter were provided by Thomas Champion, and those in the eighth chapter are courtesy of Alma Van Gilder Waltz George.

The authors would like to thank the following for providing specific assistance with our book: the Association for Retarded Citizens (ARC) of Cape May County, Joan Berkey, George Brewer, Cape May County Historical and Genealogical Society, Jack Connolly, New Jersey state senator Jefferson Van Drew, Dennisville Historic Home Owners Association, Alma Waltz George, Frank Hoff, Gerry McManus, Janet McShain, Turner Enterprises, and the Turner family.

Ray Rebmann would remiss if he did not thank his wife, Alicia, for putting up with him and all his papers and photographs while this book was coming together.

INTRODUCTION

Dennis Township is an in-between place, appearing as no more than a swampy desolate locale travelers endure while heading to vacation resorts along the Jersey Shore.

The Great Cedar Swamp, running 17 miles across the Cape May peninsula, dominates the geography of Dennis Township, essentially splitting it in two. It was once a formidable obstacle to overland travelers heading to the coast and, until the latter half of the 18th century, the most reliable way to reach Cape May was by water, via clipper down the Atlantic coast or by steamboat along the Delaware Bay. Stagecoach travel eventually offered an uncomfortable alternative, with routes passing over the swamp by way of ancient Indian trails. The coming of the railroad, with two lines crossing the township by the end of the 19th century, expedited travel and encouraged the development of the barrier islands with resorts like Sea Isle City, Avalon, Stone Harbor, and the Wildwoods.

Finally, the automobile roared across the south Jersey landscape, opening up the cape to the millions who now visit the area each summer.

Yet still, enduring through all those changes, there is that in-between place that travelers endure before reaching the beaches and boardwalks. Instead of the physical hazards of a sea journey or the bumpy hardships of an uncomfortable stage ride, today's traveler grumbles about red lights and traffic jams that cause bottlenecks on Delsea Drive or Route 9, typical on summer weekends in Dennis Township.

That is how most people see Dennis Township these days—as an annoying delay of anticipated vacations.

But there is so much more to this place, where Indians once camped and pirates buried treasure, and where pioneer families settled long before the American Revolution and generations of their descendants still call home.

Dennis Township is actually eight communities, each unique in its own right, consolidated in 1827 as one entity for administrative purposes. A diverse area, stretching west from the Garden State Parkway to Delaware Bay, Dennis Township offers productive farmland, expansive forests of oak and pine, and vast watery meadows teeming with wildlife—all minutes away from busy beaches. These features permeate and invigorate those eight hamlets, towns that still exist, like Dennisville and Belleplain and South Seaville as well as others, such as Eldora, Clermont, South Dennis, and Ocean View, which were formerly towns but are now regarded more as clusters of homes and signposts along the traveler's way. People still live there, as they have lived there for generations.

From the viewpoint of antsy tourists eager to vacate their cars and hit the beach, the landscape seen from passing cars starts with a monotony of trees. That would be the more than 20,000 acres of Belleplain State Forest, much of which is located inside Dennis Township. Interspersed among the trees are bogs, marshes, ponds, and lakes—a proliferation of evidence that Dennis Township is a watery place. The lakes, by the way, are man-made, created over a century ago by settlers exerting control over nature, erecting mills to manufacture an assortment of wood products from the surrounding forests.

The driver screeches to a stop, grumbling at a red light. If possessed of any of that sense of adventure that motivated the area's original settlers, he would turn left, off the highway and back in time to the early 1800s. It was once one of the busiest places in southern New Jersey, but today's Dennisville is a historically significant village of more than 50 structures listed in both the New Jersey and National Registers of Historic Places.

Leaving Dennisville, the shore-bound traveler crosses a small bridge over a stream winding bayward through a vast meadow. This is Dennis Creek; once a major shipbuilding center in Colonial America, it is now a scenic quick glimpse for passing tourists.

Having crossed the creek, the traffic stops at another red light. This is South Dennis, home to some of the state's oldest cedar trees on record. It is also the location of Union Cemetery. There, the interested seeker will find tombstones memorializing original settlers and prominent citizens across years of local history.

A left turn here not only brings an intrepid explorer out of the stalled line of traffic, but also presents a view of another still-wild area, Beaver Swamp. The swamp boasts few beavers now, but wildlife still abounds. Bald eagles nest there.

The back road proceeds across the township, passing the South Seaville Methodist Camp, which is over 150 years old; its outdoor services are still a popular summer gathering place. The driver then reaches Magnolia Lake and the original home of John Townsend, built in 1690 and the oldest house in Cape May County.

Here, he enters Route 9 and rejoins the slow-moving line of traffic inching toward the beach. But having stepped back for a glimpse of a special in-between place, he might not be so annoyed at being delayed.

One

Belleplain
A Family Community Tucked inside Forest

Set apart from other Dennis Township hamlets by the vast forest that shares its name, Belleplain is today what it has been since its beginnings: a tight-knit community of families employing a variety of skills to utilize available natural resources to maintain an independent lifestyle.

When the Cape May & Millville Railroad established a station there in 1863, its first superintendent, Jeremiah Van Rensellar, named it Belle Plain in honor of Annabelle Townsend. Daughter of one of the wealthiest men in the area, Annabelle was reputed to be the loveliest woman in Cape May County.

Before the era of trains, land travel through southern New Jersey was by carriage. The coach route was the only reliable overland way to cross the Great Cedar Swamp to reach Cape May. That route passed through what would become Belleplain, where a stopover for weary travelers was at the Tarkiln Tavern, operated by a family whose descendants still call the area home.

With the arrival of the railroad, houses were built in a cluster around what became the center of town, Broad and Chestnut Streets. The station became a community focal point. The first church service in Belle Plain (then spelled as two words) was conducted at the station. The railroad also brought settlers, with many of them coming from southern Europe, especially Italy.

Belle Plain grew to the point that the postal service opened an office here in 1887. George Blinn was the first postmaster.

From its early days, Belle Plain was home to members of a self-reliant family community, tilling the soil, working in native forests, and developing cottage industries, including charcoal and brick making. Other enterprising "'Plainers," as locals refer to themselves, opened small shops to service the community in a variety of ways.

At one time, Belle Plain was home to three icehouses, several gravel pits, and a number of sawmills. The railroad helped these businesses thrive, transporting their products to population centers as far away as Philadelphia.

In 1921, the town modified its name to one word: Belleplain. Other changes followed. The train station closed in 1944, and the last train to run through the town did so in 1950.

Other businesses took root and flourished. Many of these enterprises would succumb to modern economic realities and pass into memory, but families, with deep roots firmly established in the area, persevered. The rugged individualism that marks the Plainer still persists to this day.

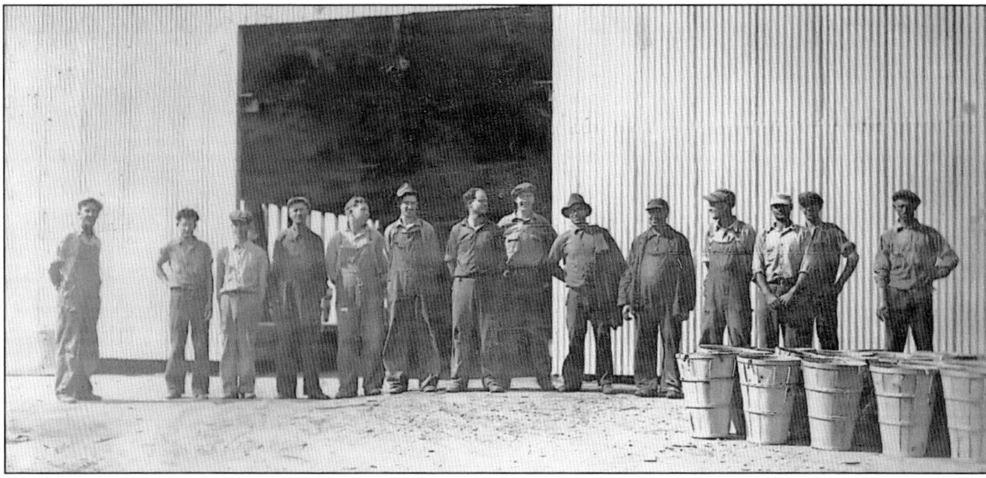

Workers stand in front of a warehouse at R.B. Mason Basket Factory in this photograph from the late 1920s. Leland Champion (coauthor Tom Champion's father) stands sixth from left. Beside him to the right is Carlton Mason, son of the factory's owner. Just before the Great Depression, Mason expanded operations, producing enough baskets to earn $100,000 in 1928.

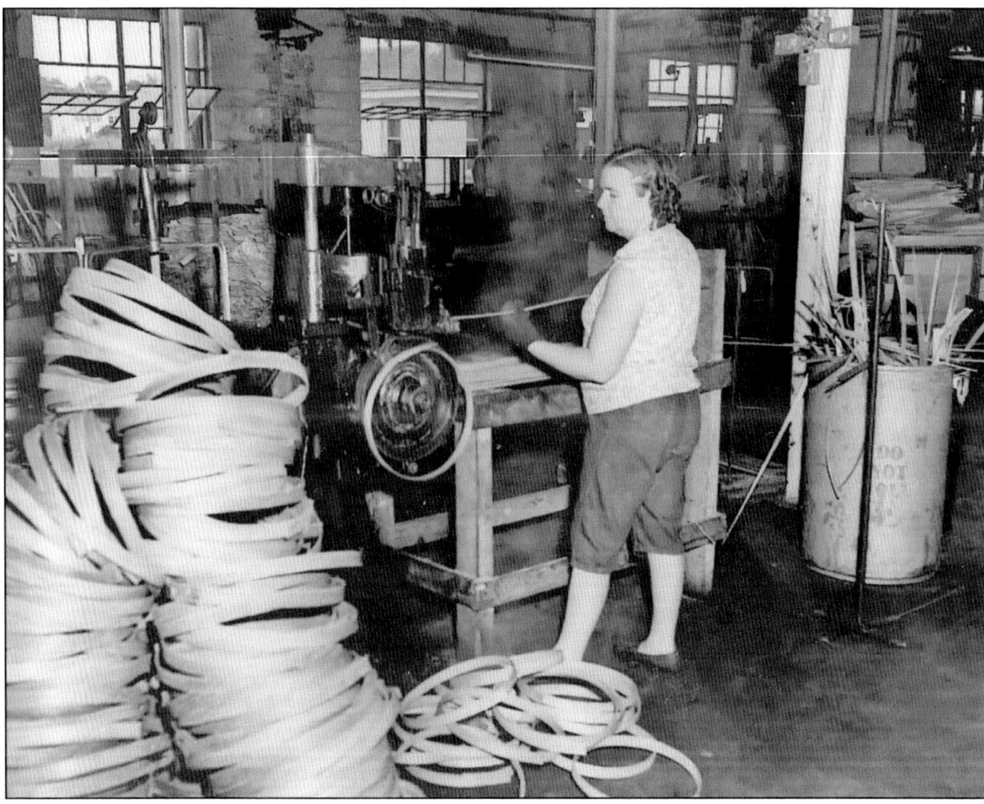

Abbie Hyson feeds material into a machine that makes basket hoops. Finished baskets were dried in outdoor sheds prior to being shipped. During the winter, baskets were stored in three warehouses, each extending a full city block. A longtime local resident, Hyson is a member of the Harris family, a large extended family in Belleplain. The factory employed more than 60 people, almost all of them locals.

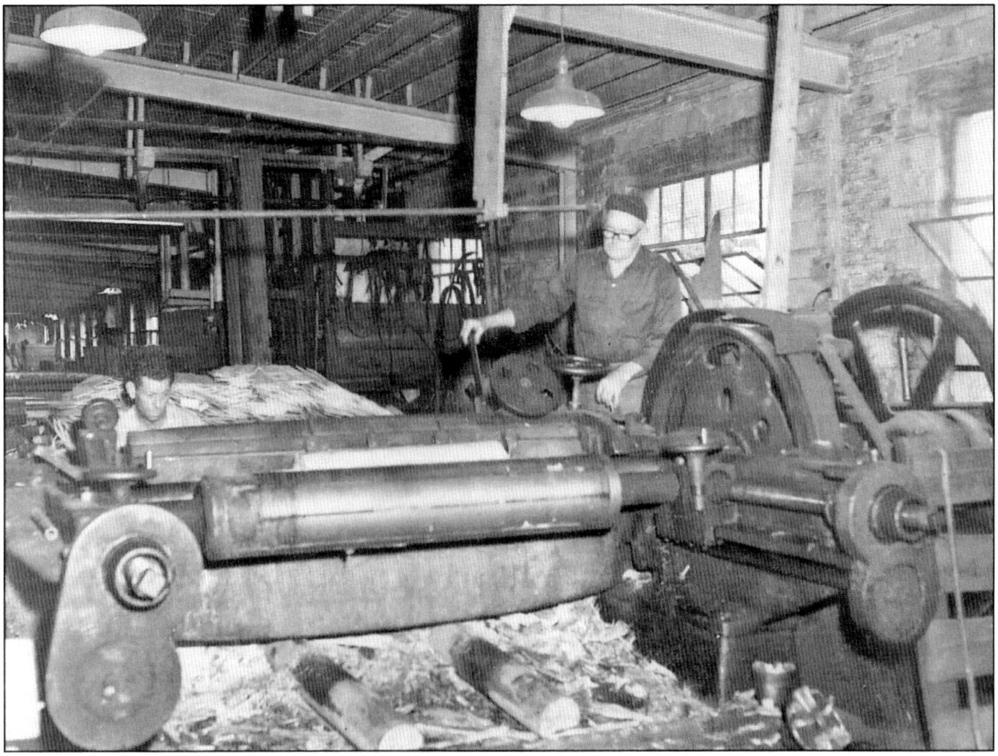

Raymond Bailey operates a veneering machine at R.B. Mason Basket Factory. All stages of the basketmaking operation were completed under one roof. Products of a major industry in the area in the first half of the 20th century, Mason baskets were used by area farmers to ship produce and fruit to area food-processing plants.

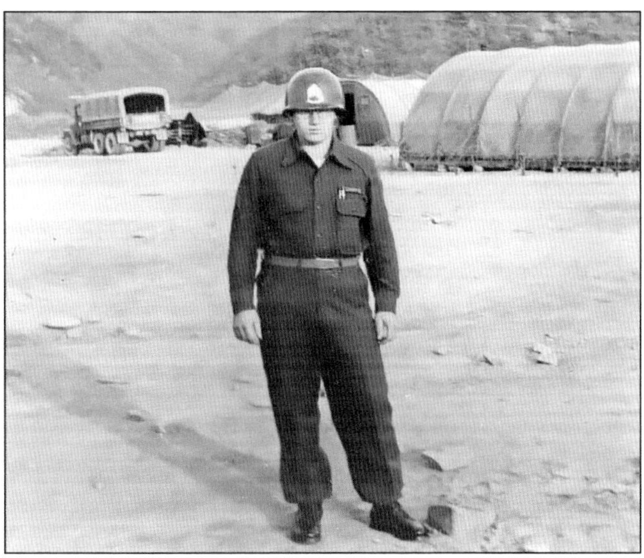

Future coauthor Sgt. Thomas "Tom" Champion enjoys a brief respite from duty in Korea, where he served 14 months as a medic with one of the "clearing outfits" mobilized along the front. It was the formidable task of men like Champion to stabilize casualties for transport back to MASH units. With no prior medical background, Champion underwent about 16 weeks of basic and medical training along with some specialized training before being deployed to Korea.

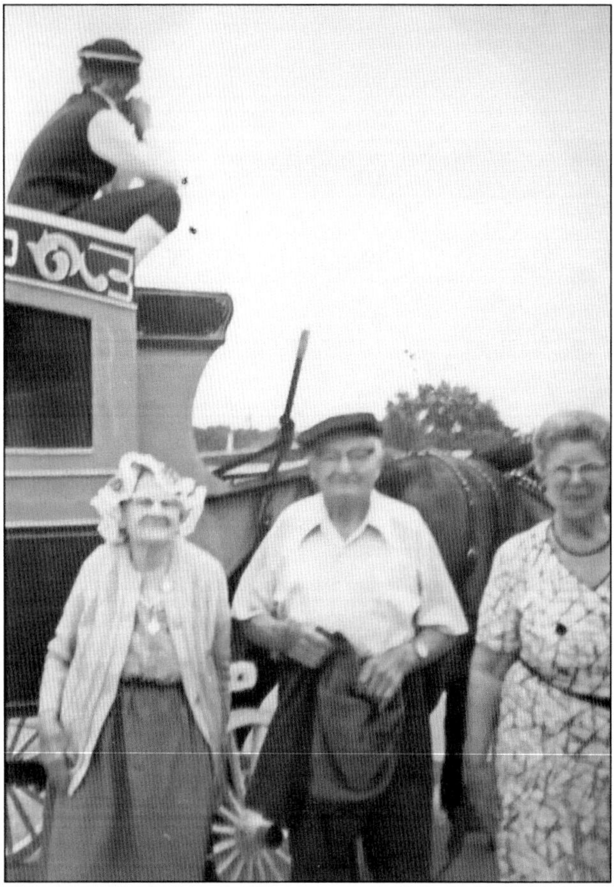

The 1976 Bicentennial Day parade in Belleplain was a generational celebration involving the entire community. Among participants are, from left to right are Minnie (Germanio) Cifoni, John Germanio, and Maryann Durell. Durell was a registered nurse and, at one time, supervisor of the nursing staff at Burdette Tomlin Hospital in Cape May Court House.

Below, Lyndall Day drives a horse cart in Belleplain's Bicentennial Day parade. To the left is the home of Tom and Emma Harris, coauthor Tom Champion's grandparents. The building behind the house is for sorting cranberries, a major crop in southern New Jersey to this day. In the rear is a chicken coop. Tom Harris huckstered eggs in lower Cape May County. The stack in the center behind Day's cart is a fueling station owned by Henry Hess (and later owned by Jesse Creamer and Ted Steenland).

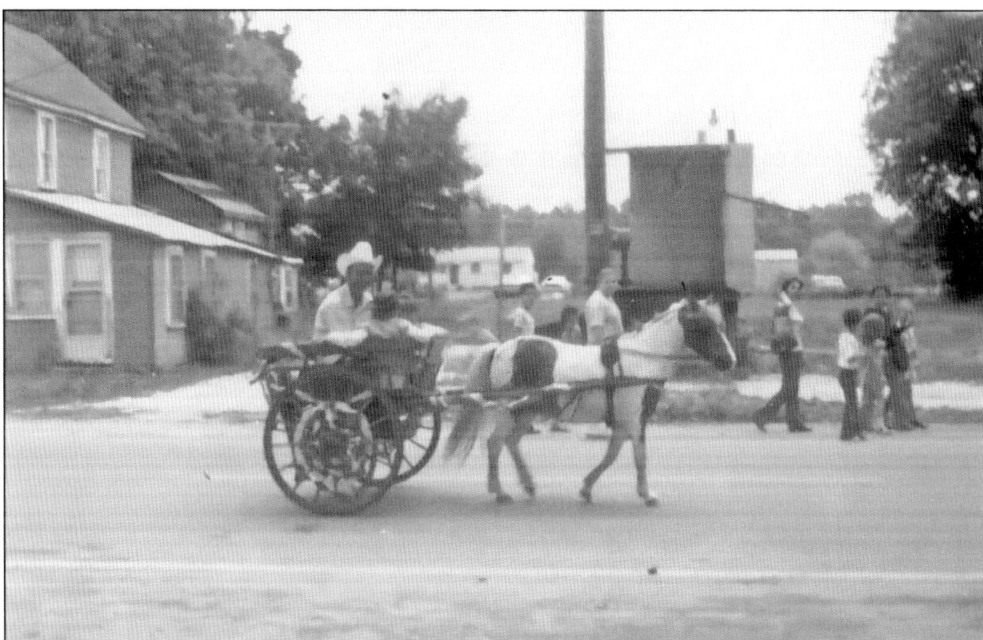

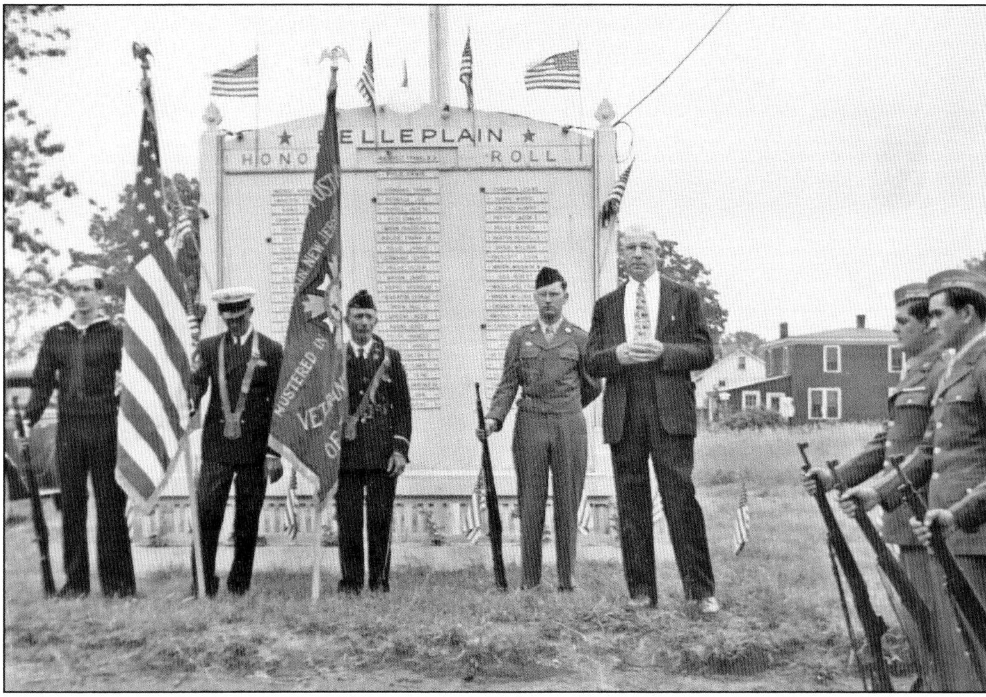

Belleplain's Roll of Honor was the center of attention on Memorial Day, an annual event at which the community gathered in the town center on Broad Street to honor its war veterans. In this 1940s photograph, Roland B. Mason addresses attendees. Owner of the basket factory, Mason was also a Dennis Township committeeman for 39 years. Pictured are, from left to right, Ashbury Batchelor, Norman Nichols, two unidentified men, Mason, John Lorenzo, and Tommy Caprioni.

A gathering of generations celebrates the heroism of Plainers who served in World War II at this Memorial Day service held at the VFW Hall. The wood memorial that stood for years near the center of town had finally deteriorated and was replaced with a field of crosses. Roland B. Mason stands to the left of the doorway. Belleplain's World War II–era population was around 200. Fifty-eight men served, and four died. Frank Polise Sr. had seven sons and a son-in-law serve.

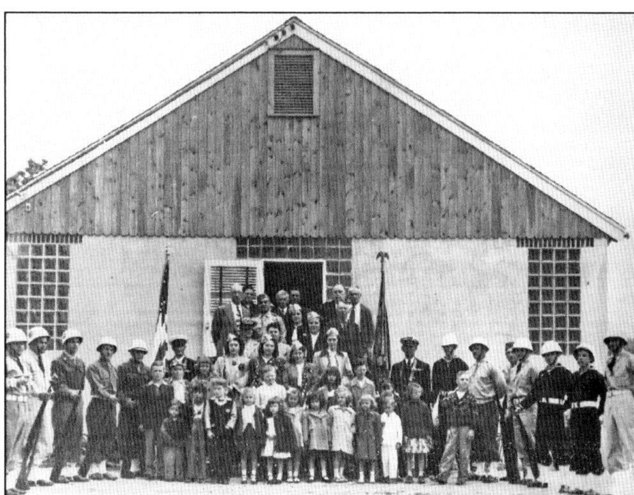

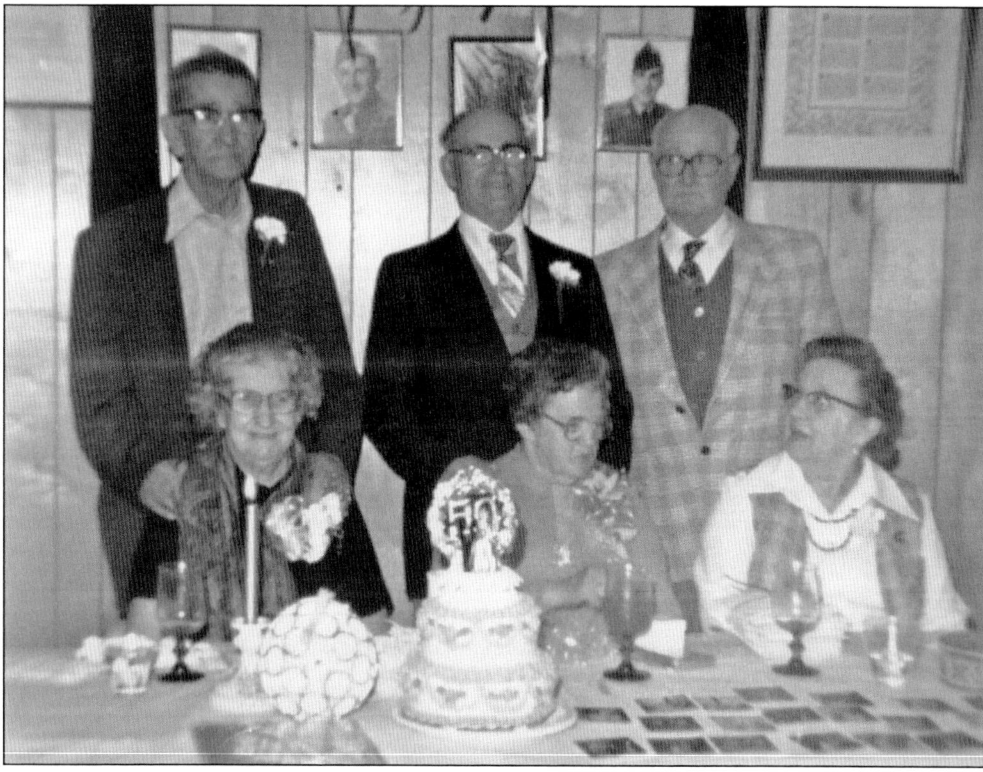

Petrella-Repici-Caprioni-Champion VFW Post 6257 serves as a community center for a variety of special Belleplain events, both public and private. This March 9, 1979, photograph shows three couples celebrating their 50th wedding anniversaries. From left to right are Evelyn and Walter Batchelor, Elena and Leland Champion, and Emma and Dan Corson. Note the photographs of the deceased vets for whom the post is named on the wall behind the celebrants.

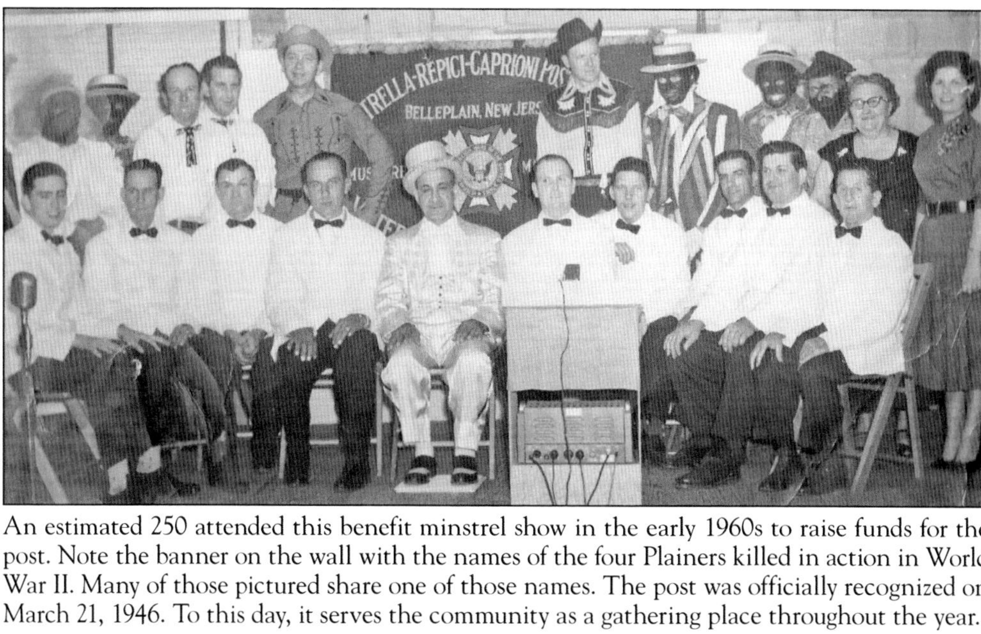

An estimated 250 attended this benefit minstrel show in the early 1960s to raise funds for the post. Note the banner on the wall with the names of the four Plainers killed in action in World War II. Many of those pictured share one of those names. The post was officially recognized on March 21, 1946. To this day, it serves the community as a gathering place throughout the year.

Members of VFW Post 6257, helped by volunteers from the Belleplain Emergency Ambulance Corps, prepare and serve lunch to guest veterans and family members from the Vineland Veterans Memorial Home. The ambulance corps also provides free transportation for wheelchair-bound vets in need of that service.

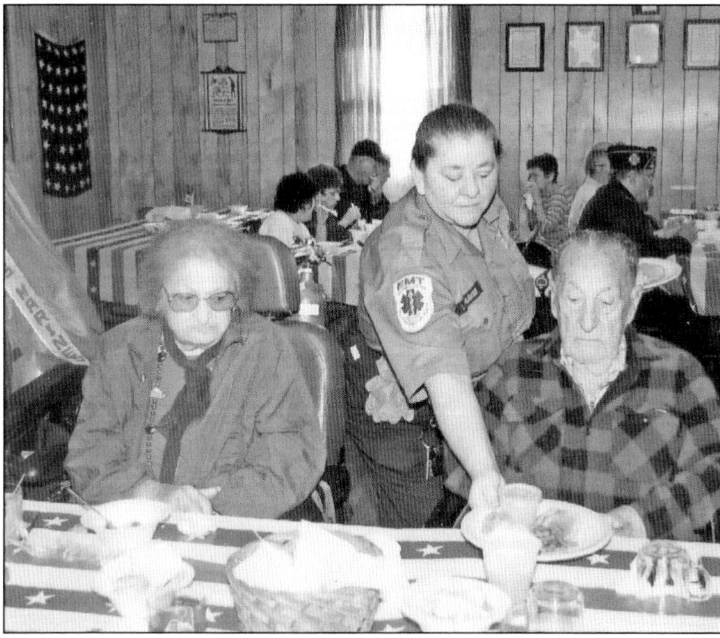

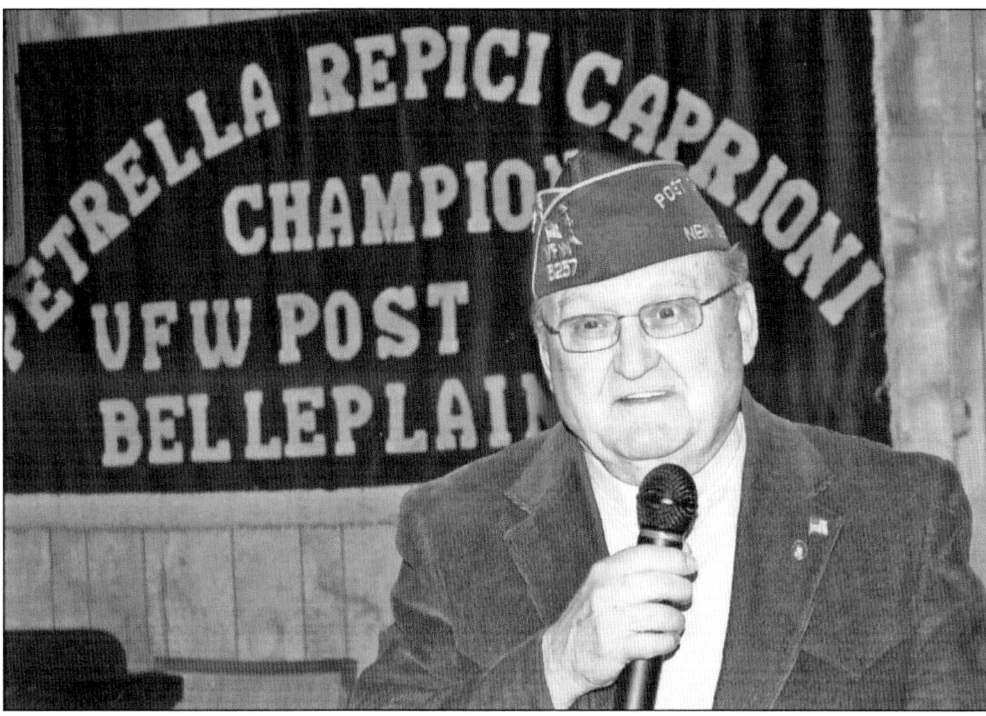

Plainers remember those who served their country in uniform. Rev. William Foster gives the invocation at the VFW post during the annual appreciation luncheon the post holds for service veterans living at the nearby Vineland Veterans Memorial Home. The post has hosted the luncheon for about 50 years. In addition, each year at Christmas, local housewives bake as many as 200 dozen cookies to deliver to the home.

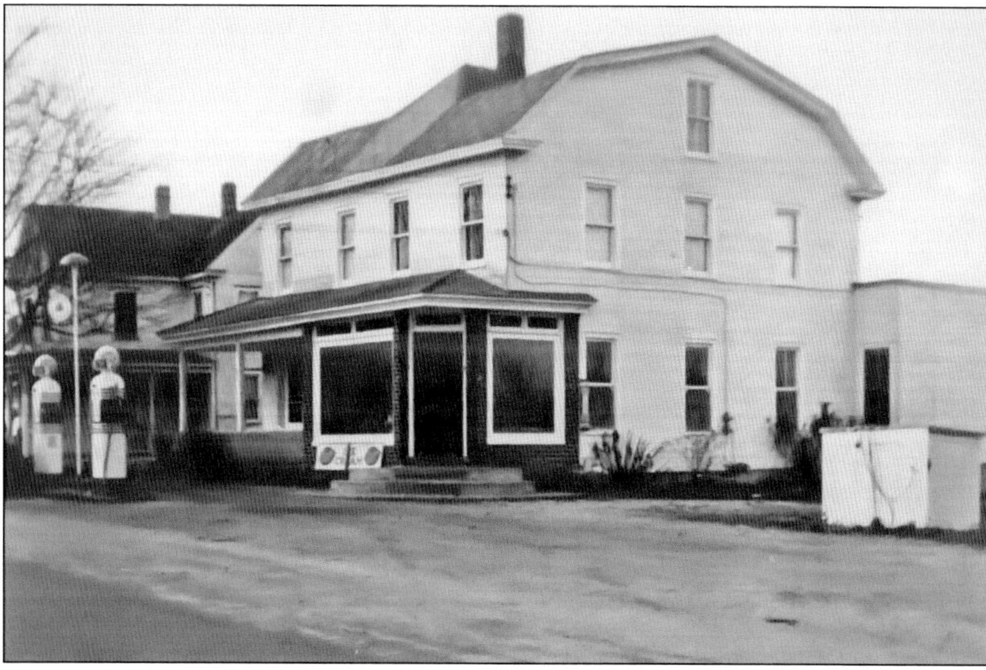

Hess store was one of many mom-and-pop stores that operated in Belleplain in the mid-20th century. This November 1954 photograph shows the gas pumps in front of the store. To left is the home of John Harris. The store was later owned by Frank Stanley.

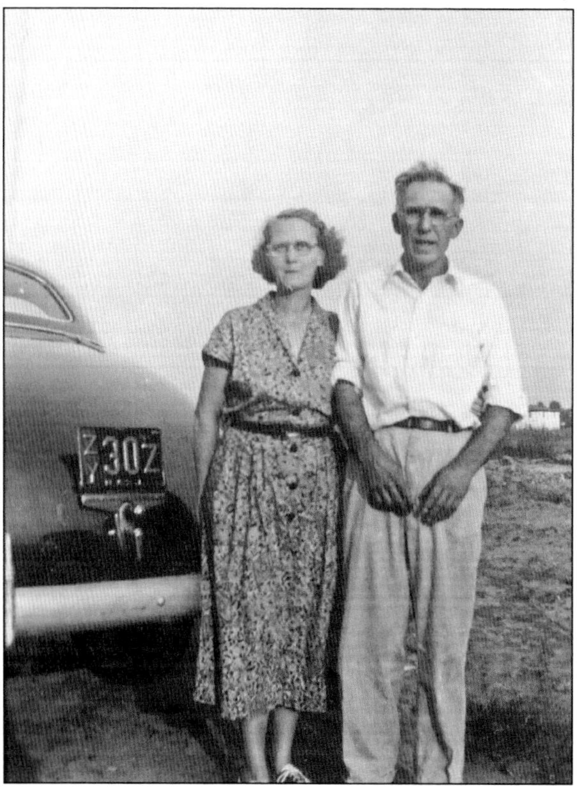

Maude Hess and her husband, Rupert, owned the store. Hess was also co-owner of a local sawmill. The Hess family had the first oil distributorship in the area. This eventually went to another prominent local, Jesse Creamer, and today, it is owned and operated by the Steenland family.

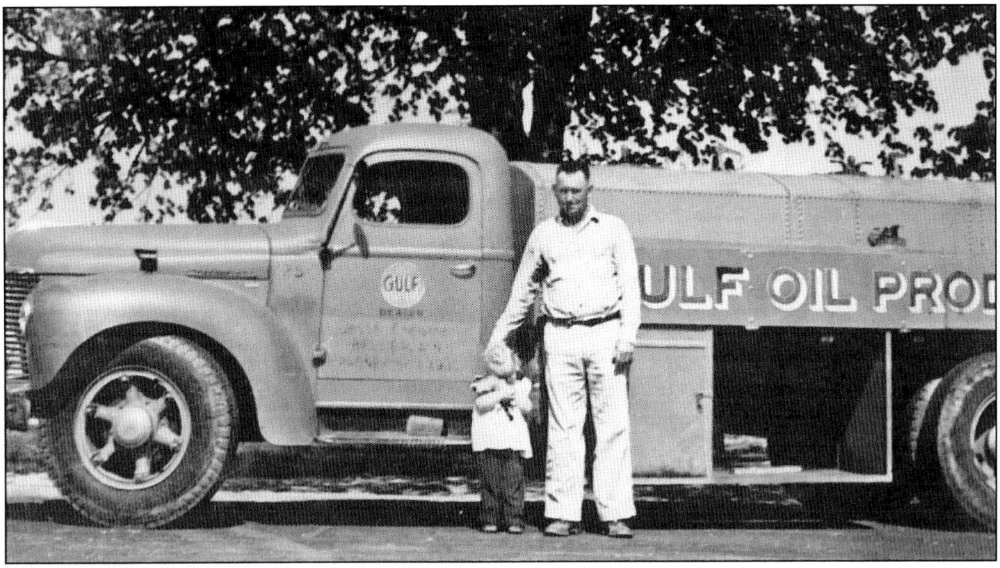

Jesse Creamer not only owned an oil business—he also drove the delivery truck as well. In addition, he operated a luncheonette and poolroom and still managed to find time to drive a bus for the township school. This late 1940s photograph shows him with daughter Darlene, who later married into another large "Plainer" family: the Saduks.

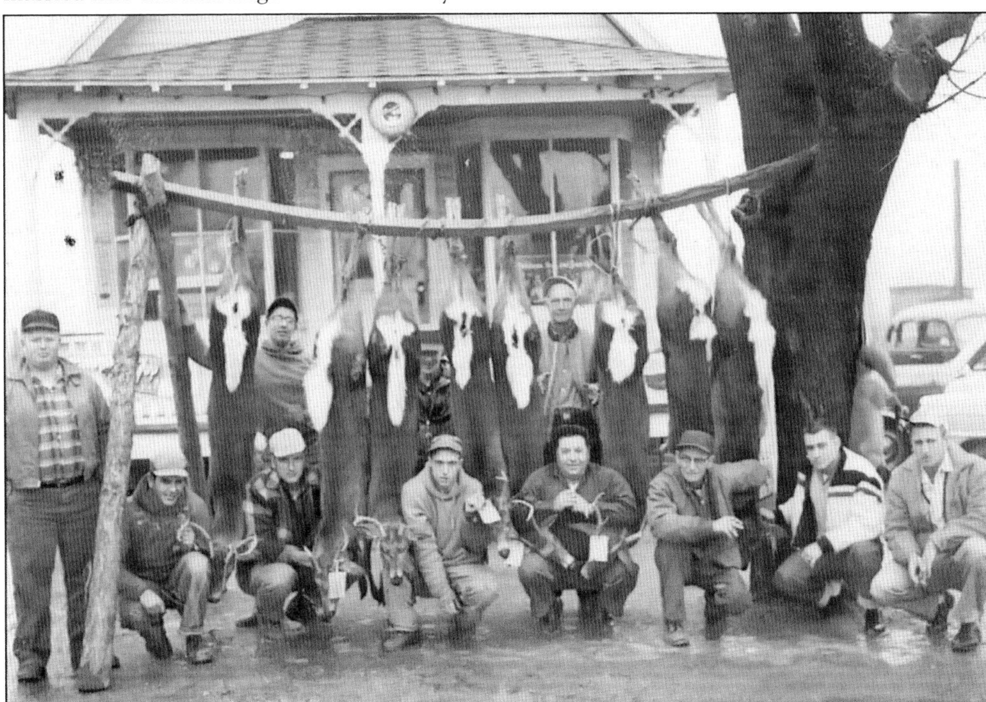

Rewards of a successful deer hunt season hang outside Jesse Creamer's store. Creamer is pictured in front of the tree. He was well known in the community. In addition to his business interests, Creamer was a charter member of the ambulance corps and served as chief of the Belleplain Fire Company. He died fighting a fire. The location pictured is now the home of the Belleplain Emergency Corps.

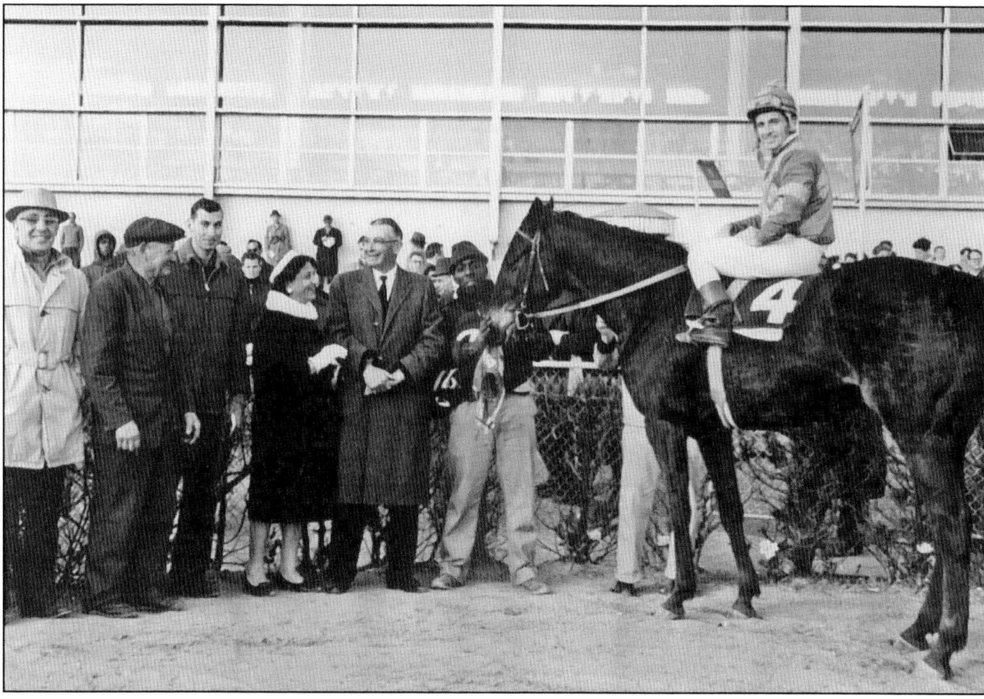

Mr. Nino, the Germanio family's prizewinning horse, poses after a successful run at Bowie, Maryland, in this 1963 photograph. Celebrating the victory are, from left to right, Ben Germanio's son James; Ben's father, John Germanio (wearing cap); unidentified; Ben's wife, Anne Germanio; Ben; an unidentified groom; Mr. Nino; and an unidentified jockey.

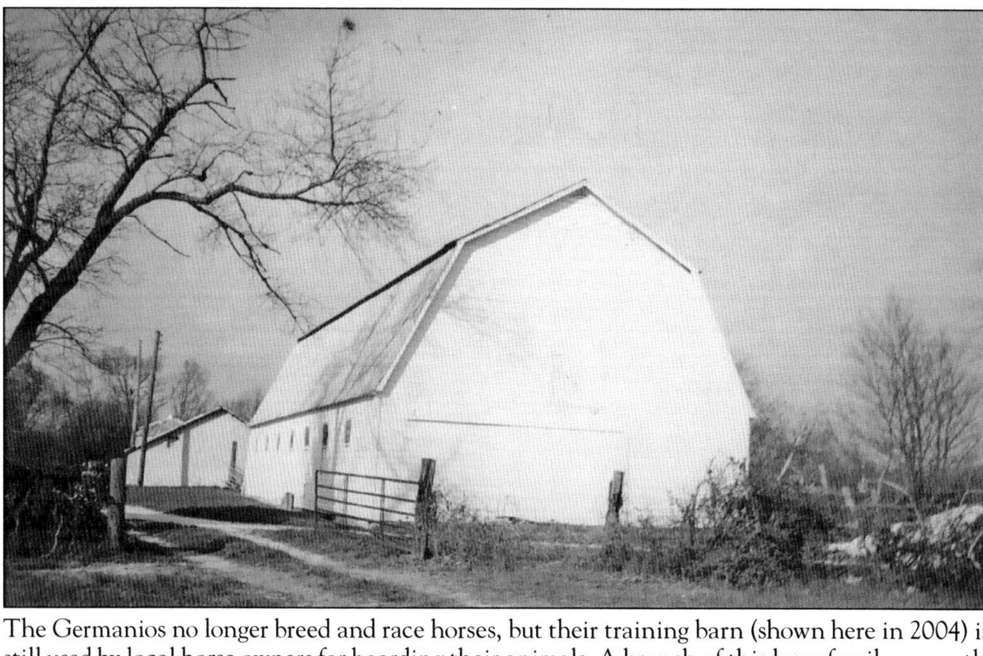

The Germanios no longer breed and race horses, but their training barn (shown here in 2004) is still used by local horse owners for boarding their animals. A branch of this large family currently operates the Belleplain Supply Gun Center, which caters to the many sportsmen who live in and visit the area.

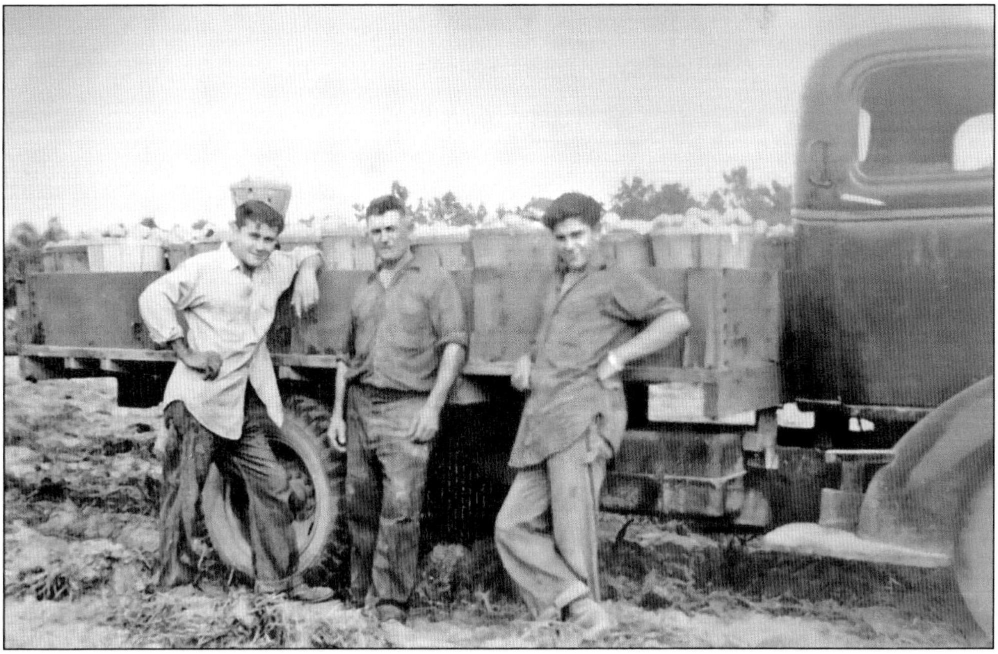

From left to right, Jake and Dave Caprioni and Tommy Repici load potatoes for shipping in this pre–World War II photograph. In addition to huckstering local produce to nearby barrier island tourists, Belleplain farmers shipped to processing plants in neighboring Cumberland County and as far as Philadelphia.

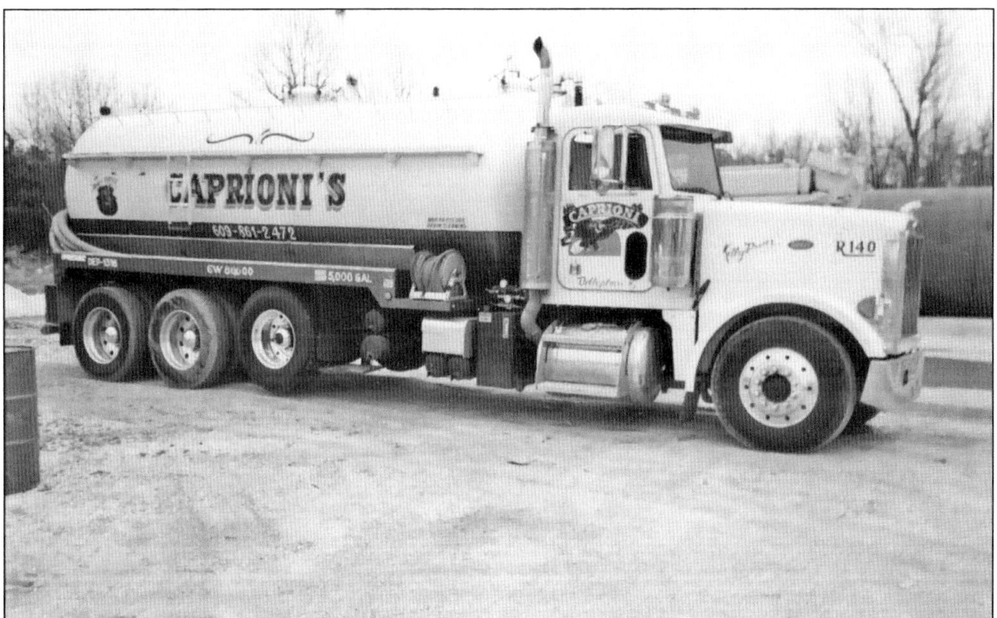

Dave Caprioni's grandson Thomas currently operates one of the largest septic treatment companies in southern New Jersey. This 2003 photograph shows a Caprioni service truck hauling sludge to a Chester, Pennsylvania, landfill. Dennis Township residents depend on businesses like that of the Caprionis, as there is no public sewer service.

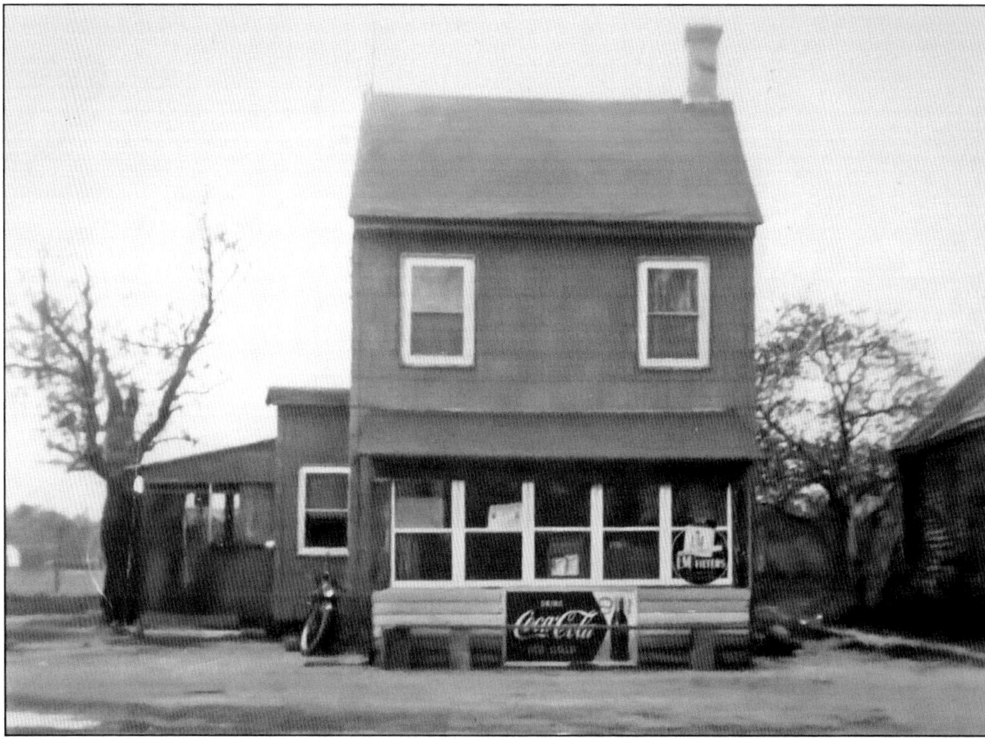

This photograph shows Gus Trippett's store in downtown Belleplain. A mom-and-pop store, Trippett's mostly sold penny candy, cigarettes, and cold soda and somehow managed to survive in the late 1950s. Trippett's was one of numerous such stores operating on Broad Street in those days in what was a small but thriving business district.

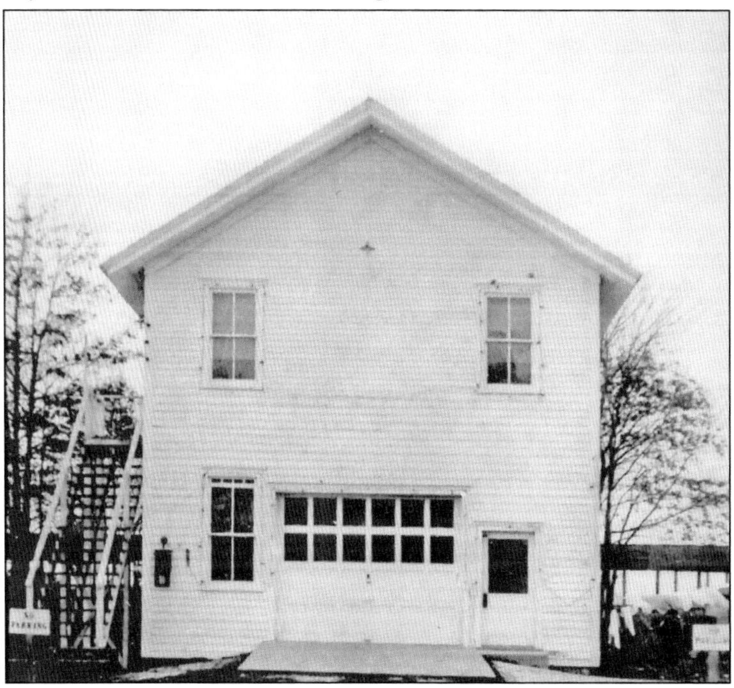

It looks nondescript from the street, but this building served Belleplain well. It was a school, a fraternal lodge, and a firehouse. In addition, the upstairs hosted many a gathering of Plainers celebrating various events in their lives, a function now assumed by the VFW post. The building no longer stands, except in the memories of older residents.

The original Kubiak family gathers around patriarch Stephan and his wife, Bernice, in this turn-of-the-century photograph. Like most Plainers, the Kubiaks were farmers, but they were small business entrepreneurs as well. At one time, a beauty parlor operated in the rear of their spacious farm home. (Ann Kubiak Radzietta.)

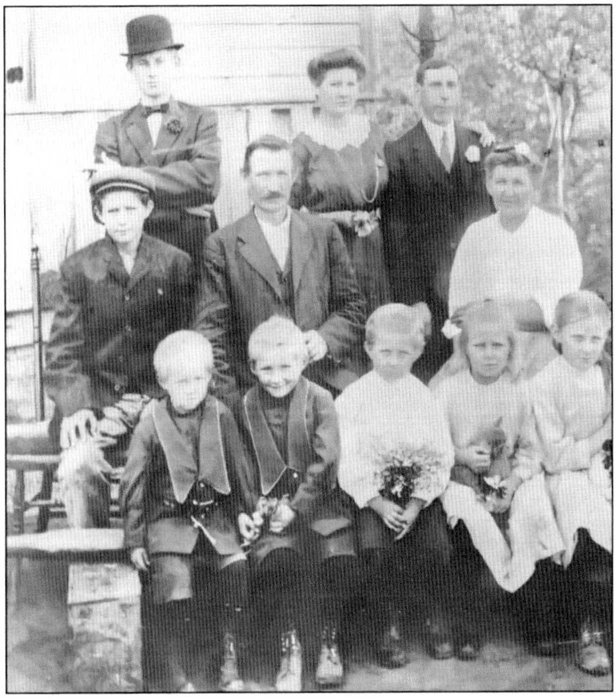

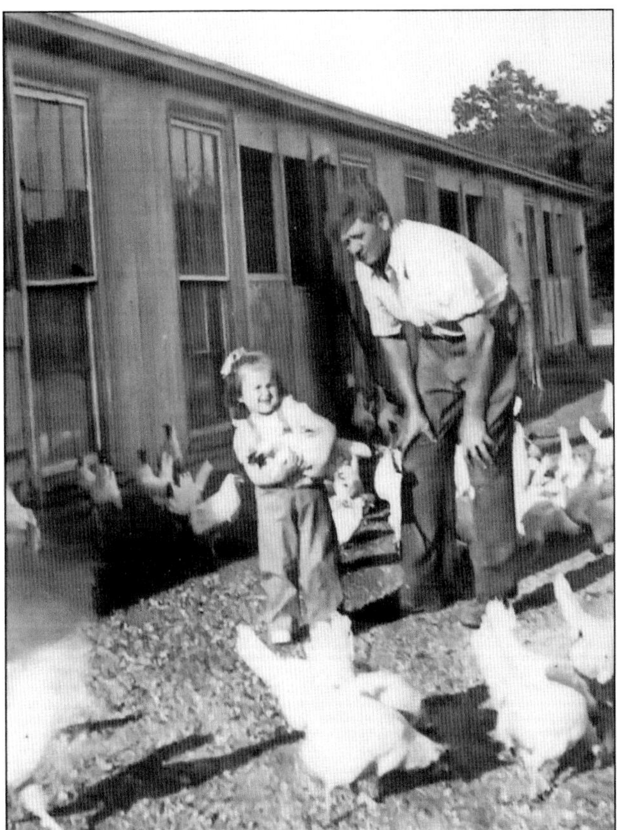

Ann Kubiak Radzietta feeds chickens at her family's farm. The abandoned coops still stand. Ann still lives in Cape May County and is married to John Radzietta, who owns a funeral home in Cape May Court House. (Ann Kubiak Radzietta.)

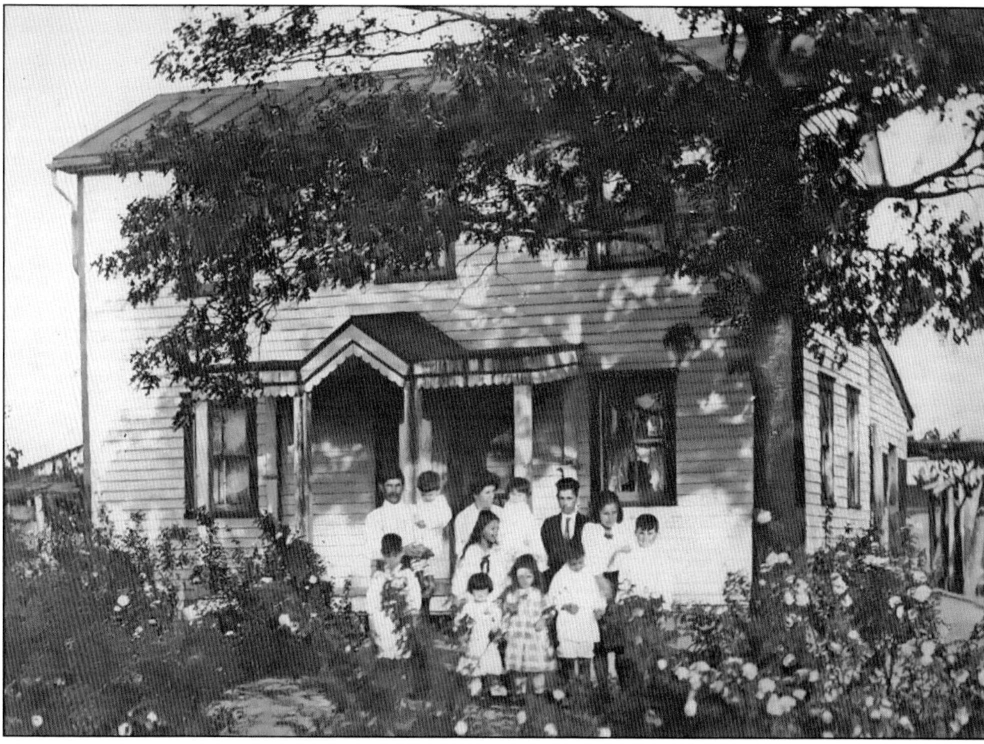

The Repici family poses in front of the family homestead in 1920s. Rose, standing in the foreground, is now in her 90s. She continues to live in the house as of this book's publication. The Repicis owned extensive farmland and were known for their strawberries. They huckstered produce at Ocean City and other island resorts.

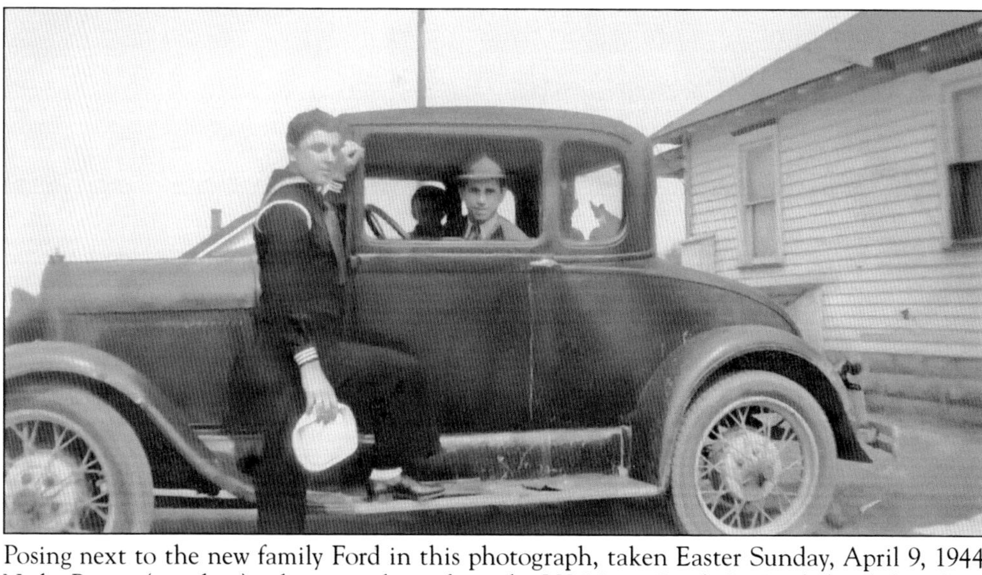

Posing next to the new family Ford in this photograph, taken Easter Sunday, April 9, 1944, Nicky Repici (standing) is home on leave from the US Navy. "Little Joe" is behind the wheel, and son Donald sits in the passenger seat. Joe worked at a shipyard in Dorchester, a town in Cumberland County. Another member of this extended family, Frank, was killed in action on August 28, 1944.

Jake and Matilda Pettit pose in front of their home on Broad Street. The Pettits were farmers and lived for generations in Belleplain. They had eight children. Their grandson James served on the Dennis Township Committee. Georgeanne, wife of grandson Joseph, also served on the committee, as well as mayor of Dennis Township. For several years, Jim and Georgeanne served together on committee—Jim as a Republican and Georgeanne as a Democrat.

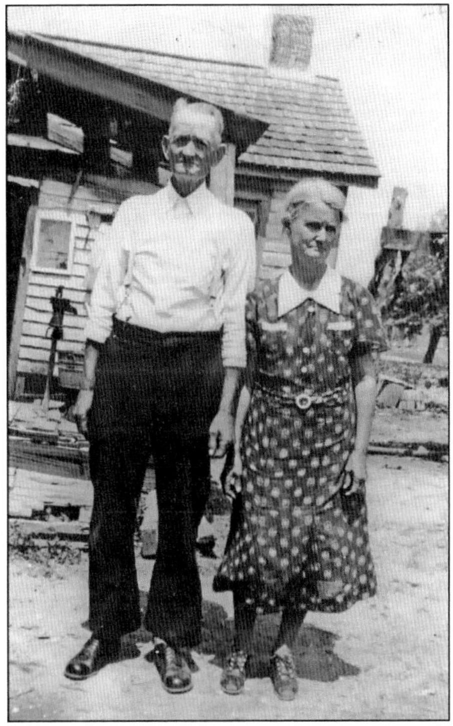

The extended Pettit family (with a few neighbors thrown in) gathers to celebrate the birthday of Matilda (center, behind the cake) on the firehouse's second floor. The firehouse was an unofficial community center for Plainers in the years before the VFW post was built in 1946. A number of people pictured still live in Belleplain. Matilda passed away in 1971, thirteen years after her husband, Jake. She lived to be 88 years old.

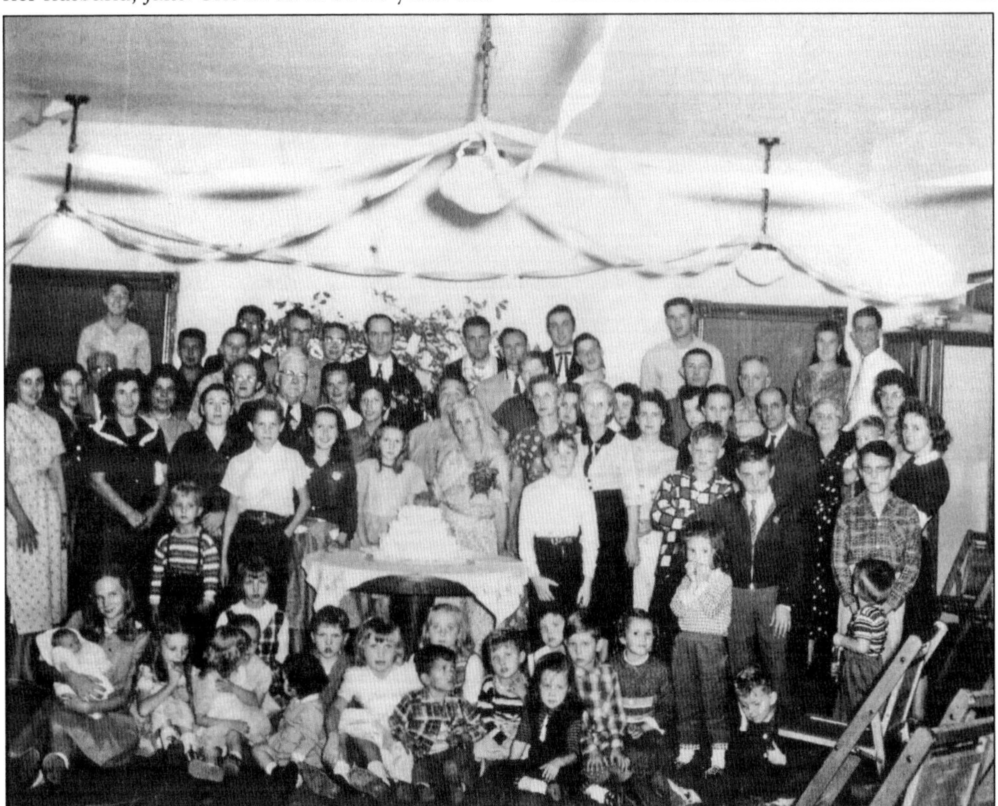

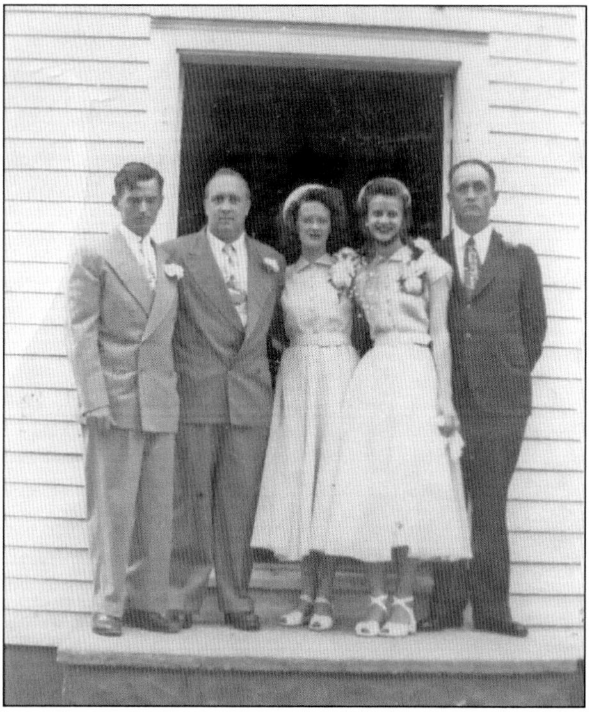

It is a wedding day at Belleplain Methodist Church. From left to right, Ed Creamer, Lawrence Dixon, Clara Pettit, Thelma Pettit, and Tom Pettit pose for Lawrence and Clara's wedding. Tom is Clara's father; he and his wife, Sarah, lived near Tom's parents, Jake and Matilda Pettit. Creamer, a World War II vet, is the son of Jesse Creamer, who owned a store in Belleplain as well as other small businesses.

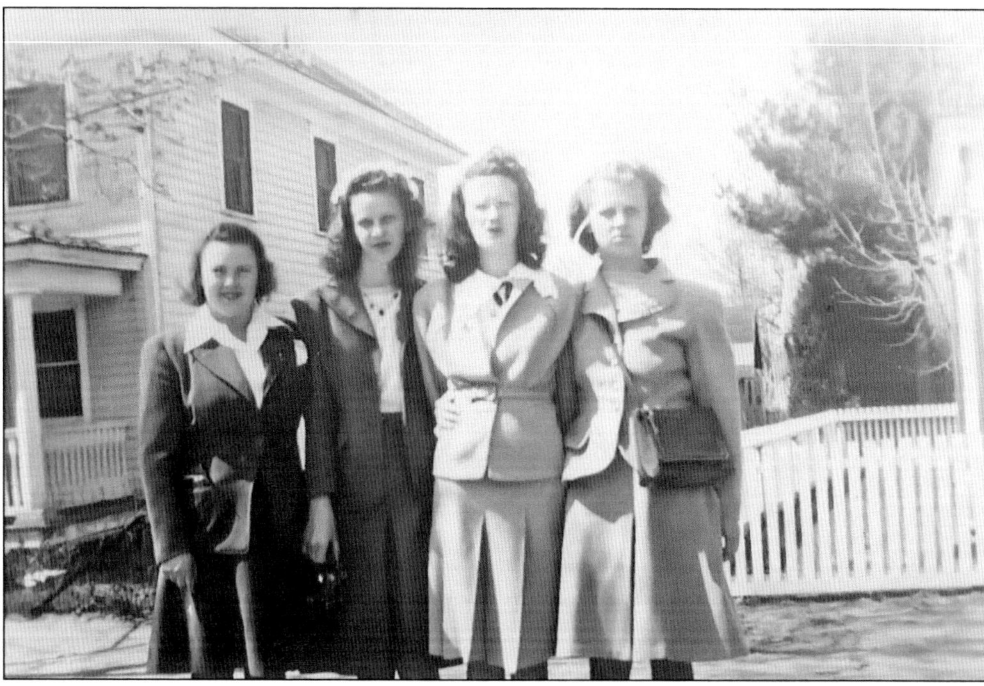

The Pettit girls are out for a Sunday stroll. Mary Harris (left) joins, from left to right, Thelma, Clara, and Danny Pettit. Wayne Harris lives in the house to the left. Partly shown on the right, the Pettit house served as office for the New Jersey State Forest Service before being moved to Belleplain State Forest. Clara and her husband, Larry, built a new home on the vacated lot after they married. Grandchildren Lucille and Alex Petit still reside on Broad Street.

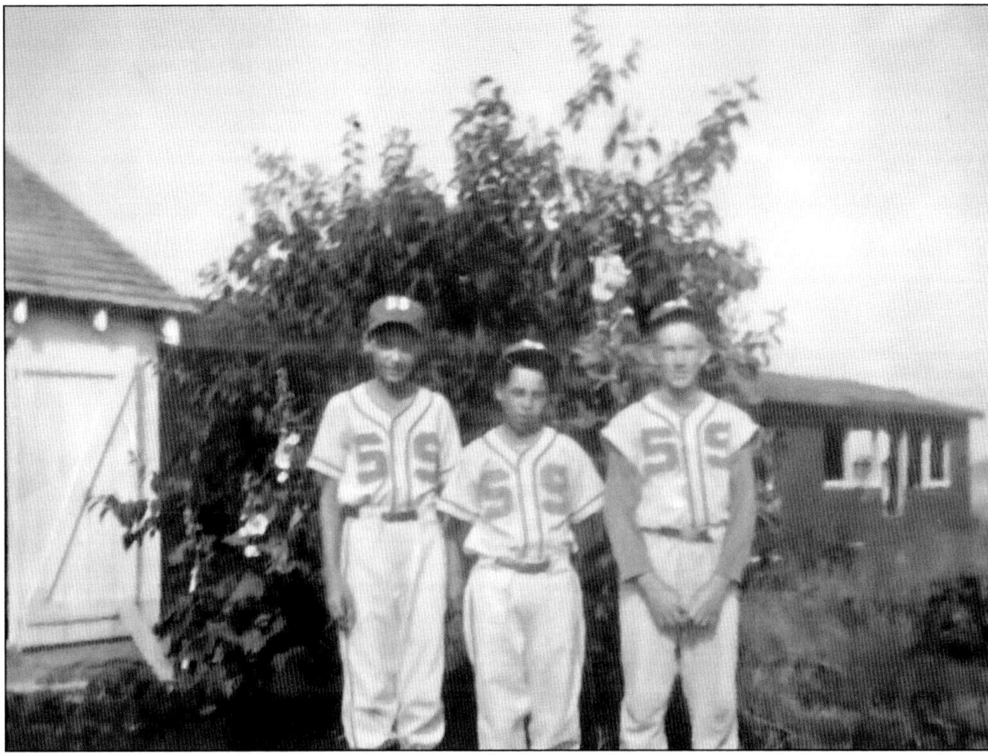

Home team players are shown here before a big game. Carlos Pettit (center) stands with George "Inky" Wheaton Jr. (right) and an unidentified member of the Batchelor family near the chicken coops (right rear) at the Wheaton place. In addition to raising chickens, the Wheatons rented horses to campers at the nearby state park and operated a horse-cart ride there during the summer. Wheaton was also one of many locals to operate a small store.

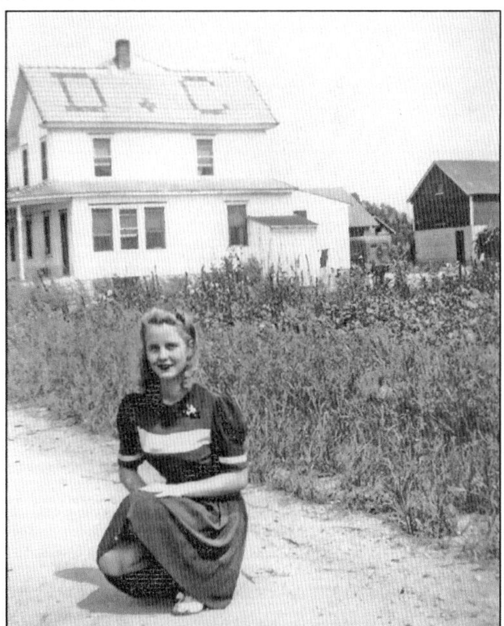

Edna McCormick Batchelor kneels in the road by the Caprioni home. The "D + C" on the roof stands for Dave Caprioni. The Batchelor family still calls Belleplain home. Tom Champion's son James married Mary Batchelor, and they live at the Batchelor homestead. The first McCormicks in the area were charcoal makers, living on what is now Joe Mason Road. Edna was married to Ashbury Batchelor for 63 years.

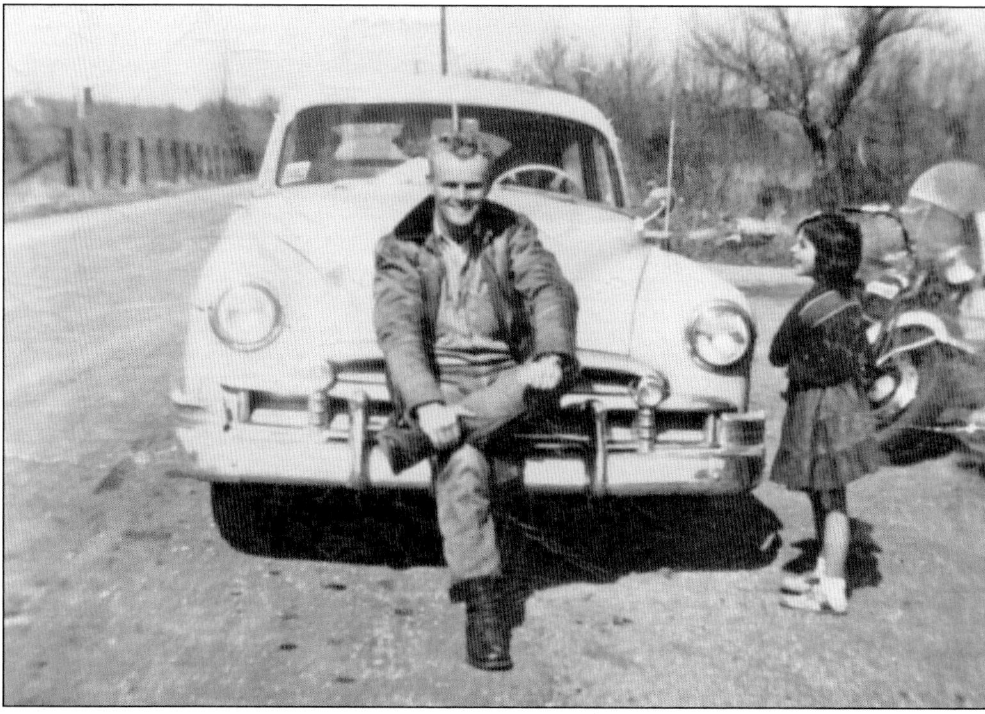

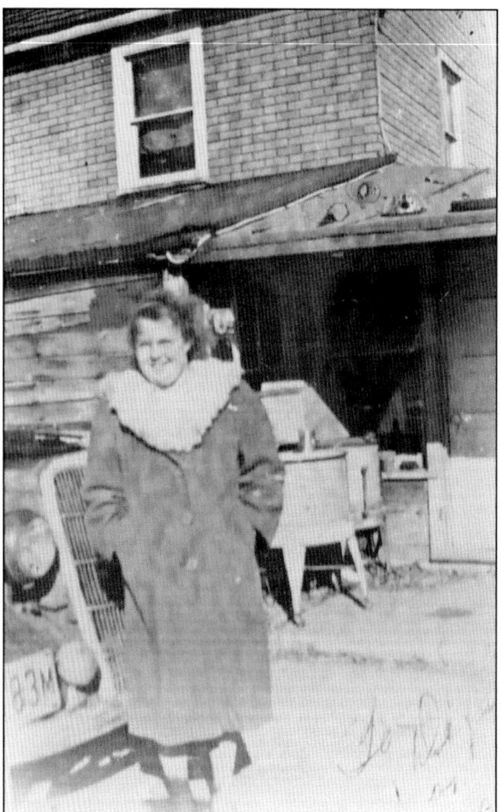

Pete Kuhns poses on the bumper of his car in this 1950s photograph. For 45 years, Kuhns worked at Whibco Brothers, a sand and gravel plant in Cumberland County, eventually becoming a foreman. His original home no longer stands; however, his wife still lives in nearby Upper Township.

Mary Harris stands in front of the Harris homestead in this photograph from the late 1940s. She married, raised a family, and lived her entire life in Belleplain. Also coauthor Tom Champion's aunt, she lived in a house built on a section of farmland owned by the Harris family.

The term "lifelong residents" applies to many Plainers, including Nelson "Butch" Creamer, shown riding his bike. A mechanic by trade, Butch worked for the township. His father, Jesse Creamer, owned a luncheonette. Butch was one of 10 children, several of whom married into other Belleplain families.

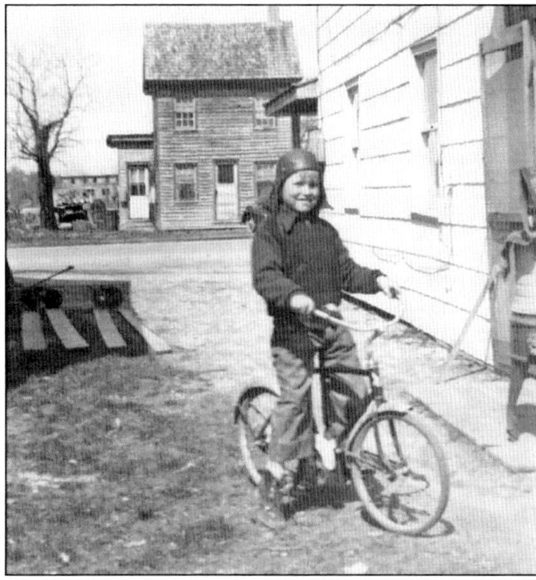

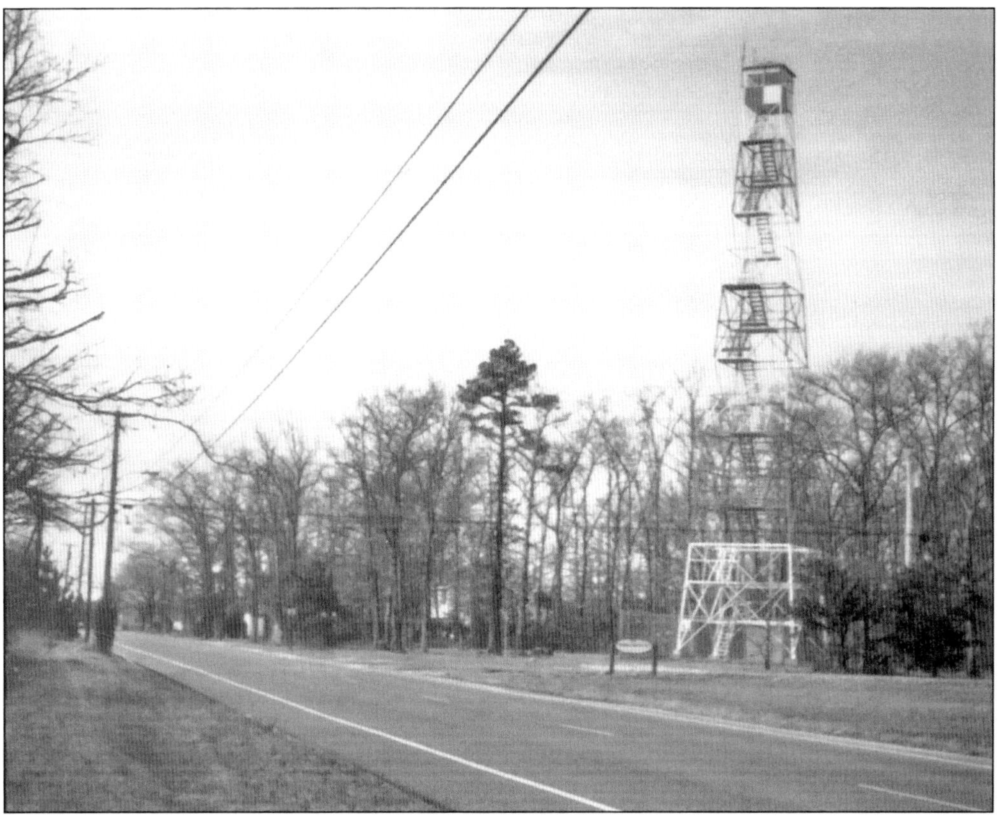

A fire tower watches over Belleplain, surrounded by thousands of acres of state forest that shares its name. For years, Plainers manned the 60-foot-tall tower overlooking almost 6,000 acres. The tower is located on the Old Cape Road, formerly an Indian trail. Later, stagecoaches between Cape May and Philadelphia passed through, stopping at nearby Tarkiln Tavern. Many descendants of today's Plainers arrived in the area via that road.

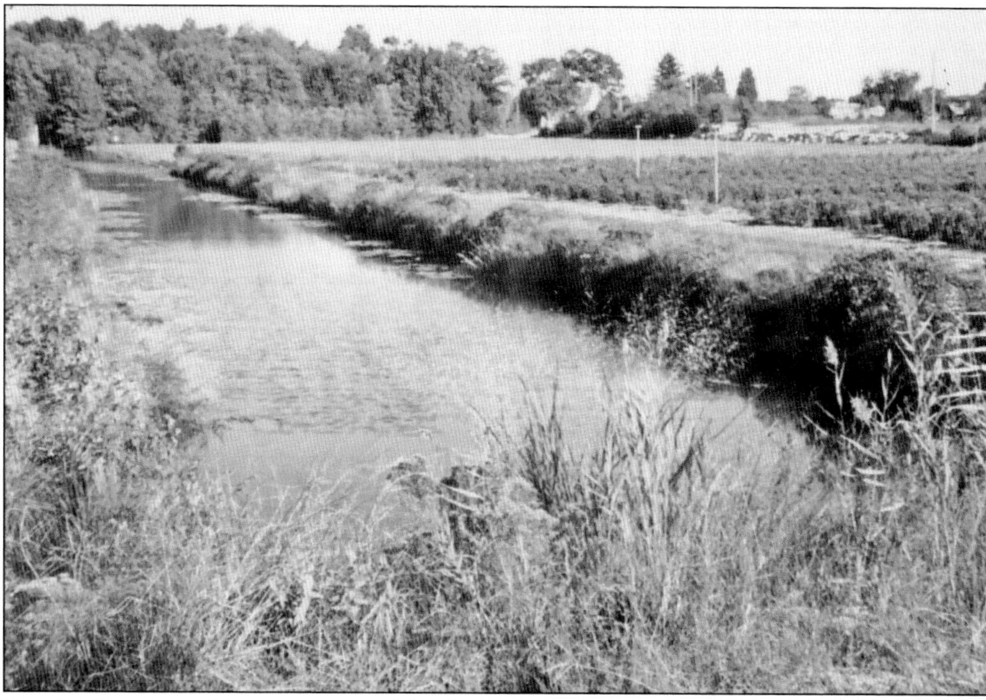

Durell's Cranberry Farm was one of the largest cranberry growers in southern New Jersey. A Princeton graduate, Thomas Durell served as principal at Belleplain's school and then as superintendent of Cape May County Schools. In 1941, he became New Jersey assistant commissioner of education. Starting with 90 acres in 1866, Durell's grew to over 4,000 acres, complete with warehouses and housing for workers. The Durell family was the first in the community to have a telephone line and own a Ford Model T.

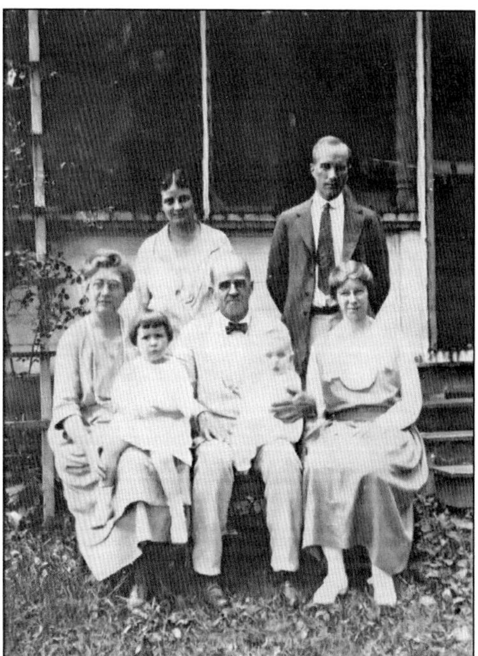

This is a 1922 photograph taken of the Fletcher Durell family. From left to right are (seated) Laura Jackson (with Virginia on her knee), Fletcher Durell (with John, eldest of Thomas and Marian Durell's, on his knee), and his sister Marian Durell; (standing) Marion Dudley Durell and Thomas Jackson Durell. Virginia Durell was Elizabeth's mother. (Photograph courtesy of Elizabeth Way Marinelli.)

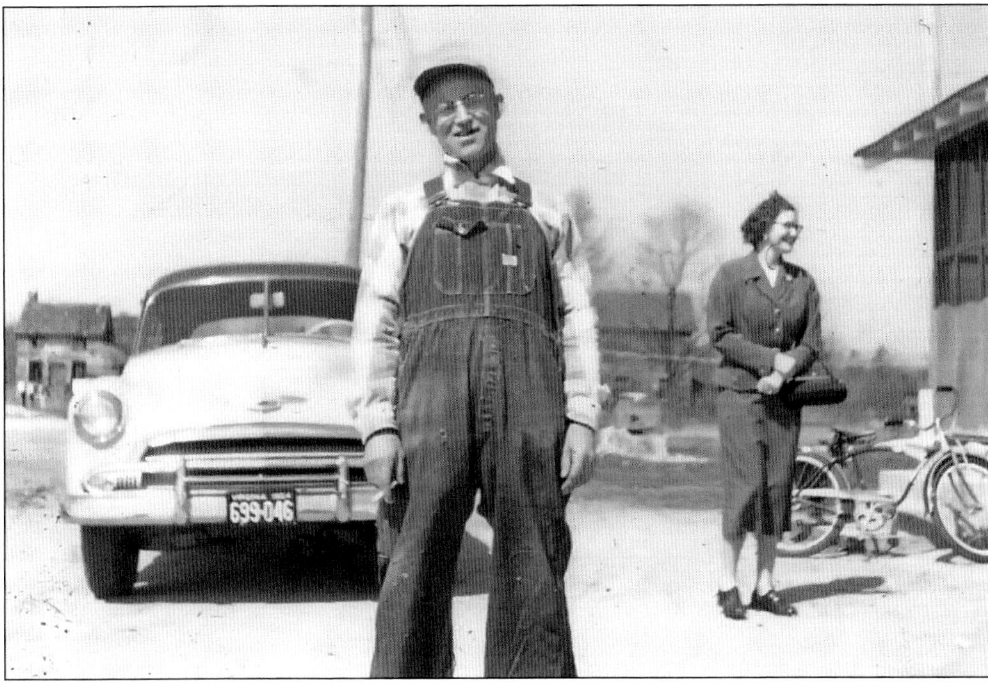

Leland Champion stands in front of his house (right) to greet visitors from Virginia in this 1954 photograph. Watson Horton (right) is son Tom Champion's mother-in-law. The house in the right background is that of Jake Pettit. The building in the left background was bought by Tom and torn down to make room for his new home. Tom had just returned from active duty in Korea at the time of this photograph.

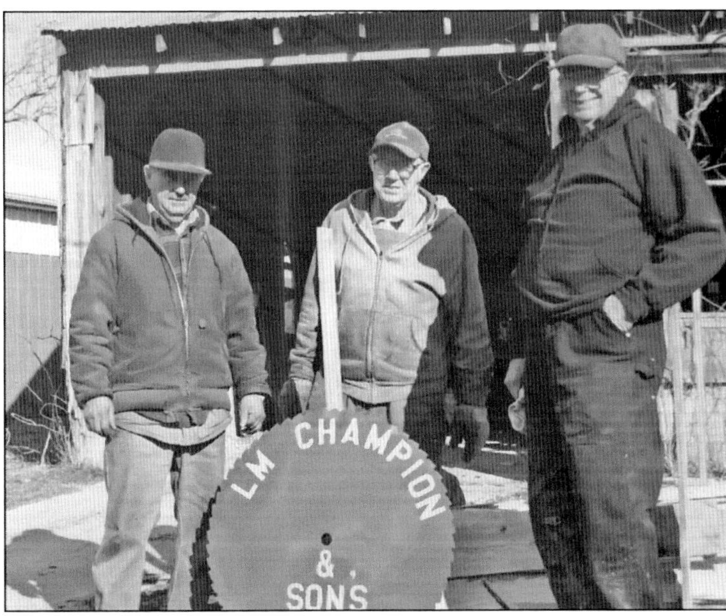

Leland Champion's sons Paul (left), Tom (center), and Walt take a break from their work at the family sawmill. Their father started the mill in 1937. It operated for more than 75 years and, as of this writing, still produces pallets used to hold shipments of sand from local mines. The saw blade shown here has retired; however, it is now on display at the Old School House Museum in Dennisville.

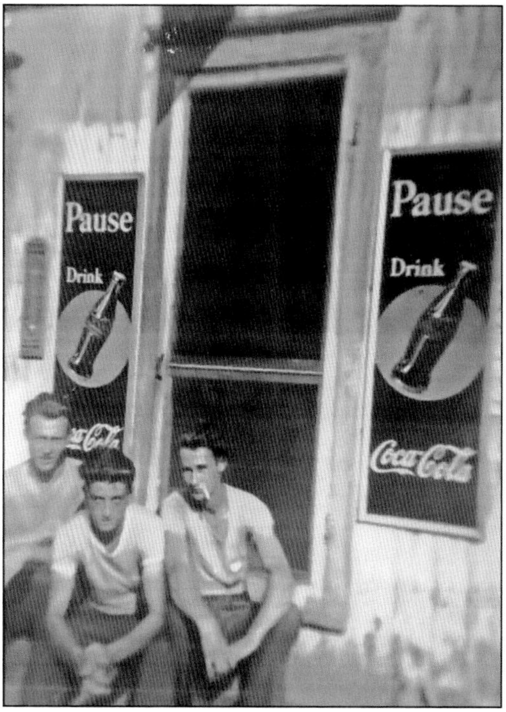

Friday night meant hanging out at Belleplain's "action" spot: Frank Barnes Pool Hall. Barnes's hall boasted two regulation-size tables and all the Coca-Cola one could drink. From left to right, Leland Champion Jr., Frank Kuhns, and Lawrence McCormick pause to catch a smoke in the early 1940s before the war, when many of the area's young men answered the call to military duty. McCormick served as a sergeant in the Army Air Forces during World War II.

Standing fourth from the left, with his cap back on his forehead, Leland Champion Jr. waits with fellow crewmen to go into action during World War II. Leland Jr., a tail gunner for the *Kickapoo Gal*, died when his plane exploded on takeoff during a mission. His memory is honored as part of Belleplain's VFW Post 6257 as well as on display at the Old School House Museum in Dennisville, with memorabilia donated by Plainers.

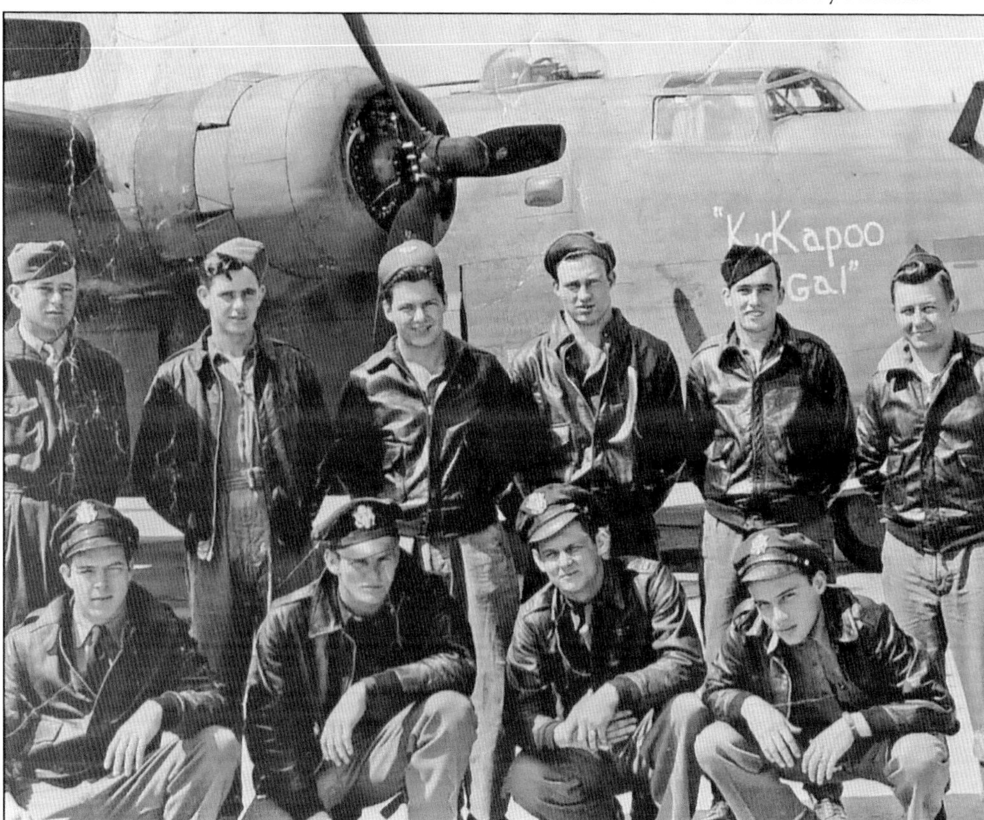

Two

Belleplain State Forest
Creating a Natural Playground

While not officially part of Dennis Township, Belleplain State Forest is centrally located within the boundaries of the township. Its presence plays a large role in the lives of local communities, especially in the western half of the township. No book about Dennis Township is complete without a look at this significant area.

The idea for a state forest in this part of southern New Jersey started in 1928 with land purchases from private owners in Eldora, North Dennis, and, particularly, Belleplain. Over 5,600 acres were acquired. With the arrival of Civilian Conservation Corps (CCC) labor crews in 1933, major work began to create a recreational area in the heart of this wilderness.

The CCC's first major task was to create a lake. How does one make a lake? Start with a water source—in this case, a stream and a bog. Apply the shovel work of young men eager to earn a living and, eventually, one gets a lake.

Over an eight-year period, CCC crews built more than lakes, and today, whether swimming in the lake, camping under a canopy of green, or merely passing through on a hike or a bike over some of the 40 miles of trails meandering throughout the region, the efforts of those workers are everywhere to be seen in the sturdy buildings and invigorating nature that makes Belleplain State Forest a special place.

Today's forest spans over 22,000 acres. It offers activities throughout the year from ice fishing and cross-country skiing in the winter to swimming and camping in summer. Fall visitors enjoy the forest's colorful foliage and birders make the forest a routine stop as part of their visits to world-famous birding venues farther down the Cape May peninsula.

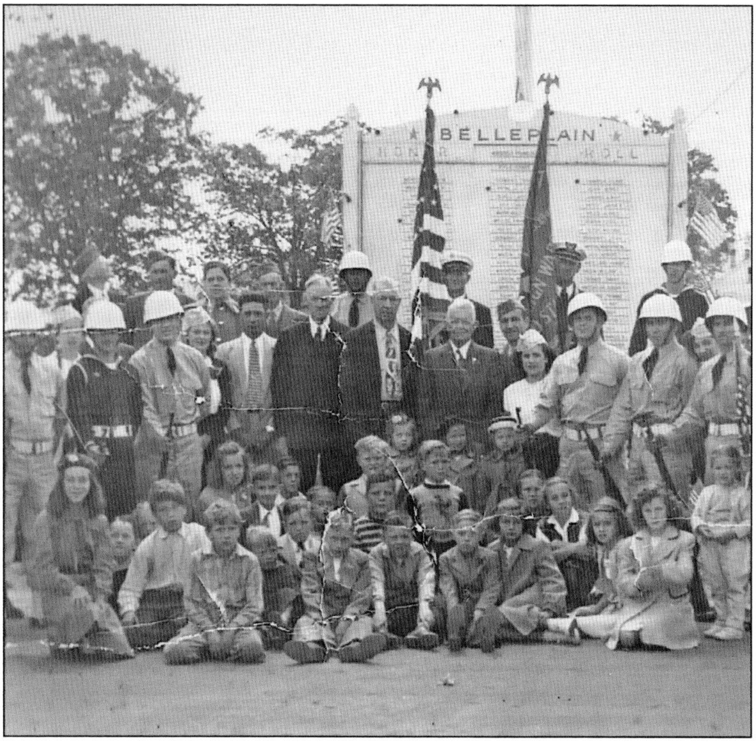

Work begins as crews carve a park out of wilderness. Roland B. Mason (right of the American flag), a Belleplain businessman and local government official, was instrumental in organizing land purchases for Belleplain State Forest. Among landowners selling 5,564 acres were Ogden Gandy, George Meisle, S.G. Mason, B. Hess, Stephan Kubiak, and Aimee Faure. The total price paid was $46,879.77, or $8.42 per acre.

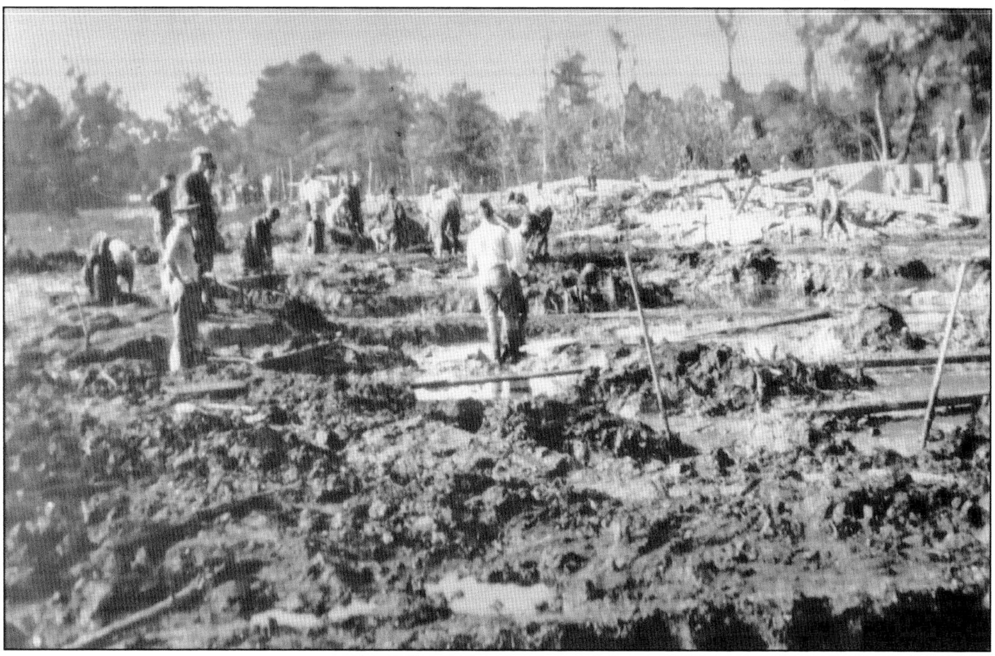

Civilian Conservation Corps workers get muddy on the job. It required 10,456 man-days (eight-hour shifts) of mostly manual labor to carve out a lake from a former cranberry bog. Workers were paid $1 a day plus food, shelter, and clothing, and they lived in barracks they built on-site. Later, during World War II, the barracks were used by New Jersey National Guard 113th Infantry. Some of the barracks foundations can still be seen.

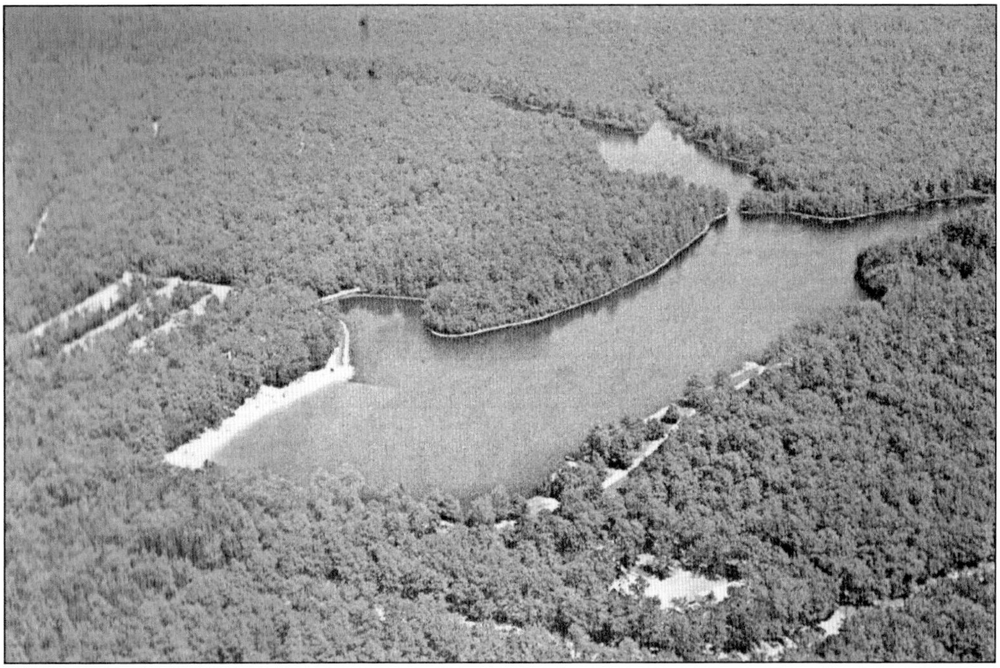

This late-1960s photograph offers an aerial view of Lake Nummy. Originally called Meisle Lake, it was renamed to honor the last Lenape chief to live in Cape May County. Indians frequently camped in the area to hunt. The CCC camp opened in June 1933 and began work creating a park. The resulting 26.2-acre lake opened for swimming in 1936.

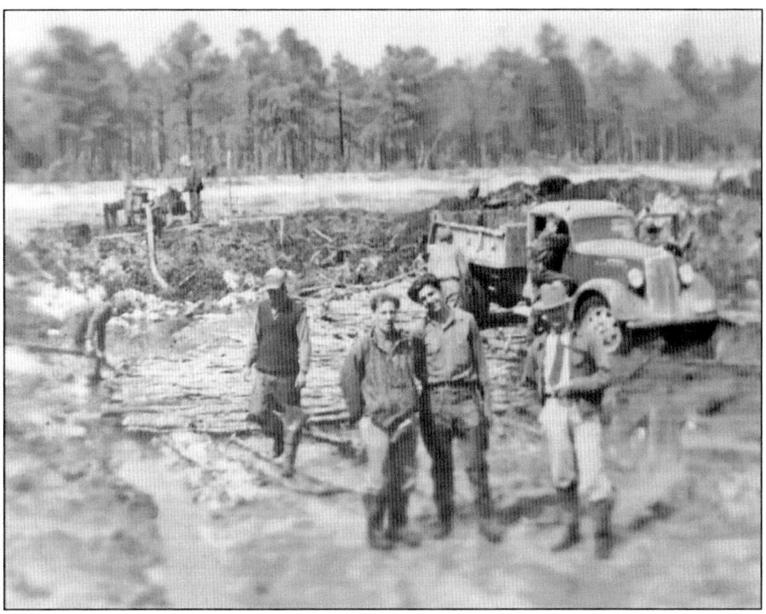

CCC workers also built or dug boathouses and bathhouses, pumps and dams, power lines, docks, water wells, sewage treatment facilities, and fireplaces. They constructed roads, seven bridges, assorted garages, offices, and storage and maintenance shops. Many of these structures are still in use.

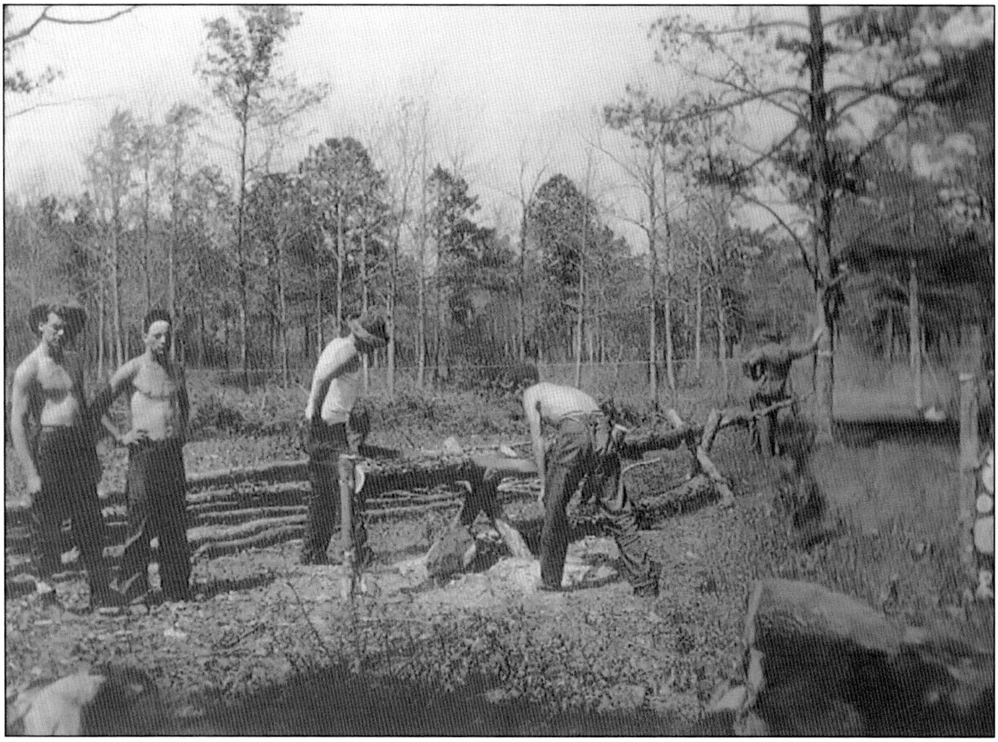

When they were not changing the land to facilitate human use, CCC workers planted trees—over 525,000 seedlings—on almost 1,200 acres. They planted mostly white cedar and pine and red oak. In 1942, Congress decided that the work of the CCC was finished, and all camps were closed.

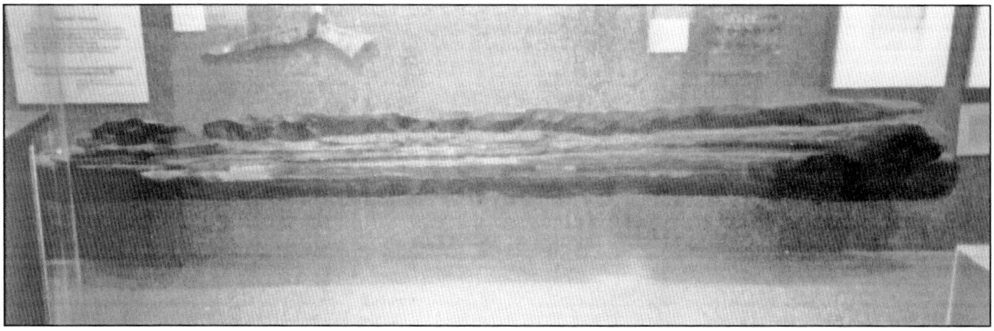

While excavating the area for the lake, workers uncovered the well-preserved remains of an Indian canoe buried in thick muck. The canoe had been made in traditional Lenape fashion, using fire to hollow out the trunk of a tree, leaving a seamless hull. The canoe was given to the New Jersey Historical Museum in Trenton.

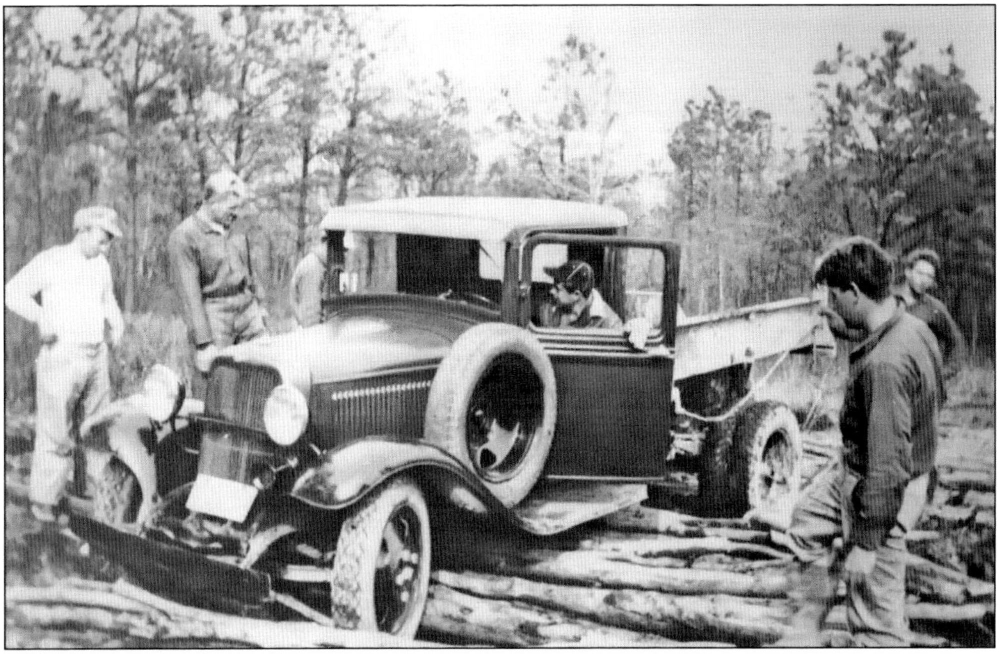

CCC workers lay out a corduroy road, which was a log road employed typically over swampy areas. Much of the ground on which they worked was formerly George Meisle's cranberry bog, hence the first name given to the lake that was created in its stead.

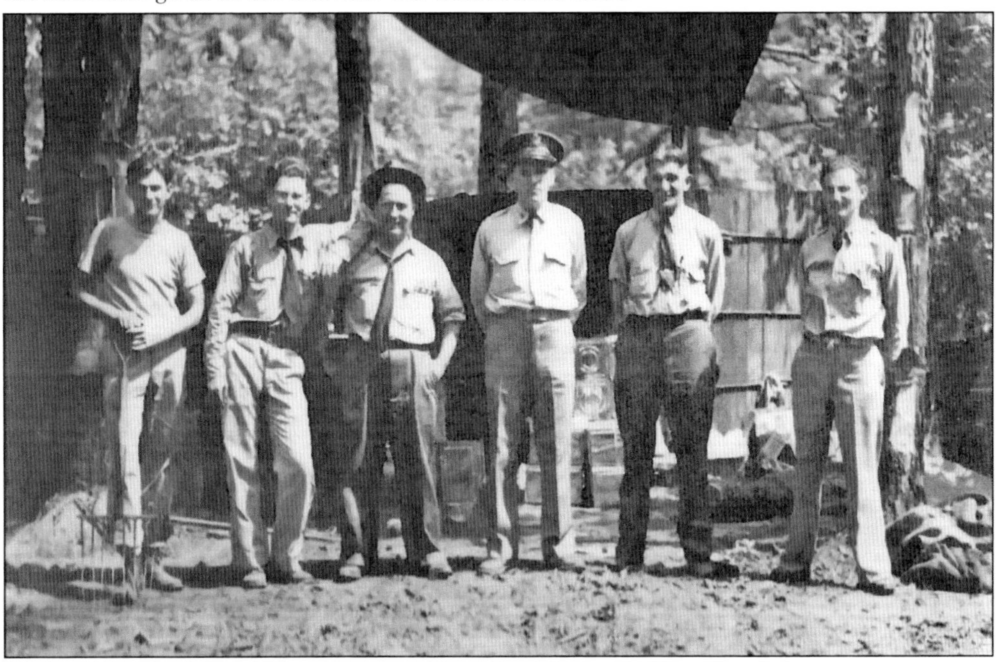

Long after Prohibition was repealed, moonshiners continued to manufacture "Jersey Lightning" in desolate parts of the state, including the deep woods of Belleplain State Forest. In this 1940s photograph are successful law enforcement officials posing before a still; from left to right are Joe Pacona, Luke Gray, Bob Peck (forester), Captain Sapora, Freeman Truman (US Army), and unidentified.

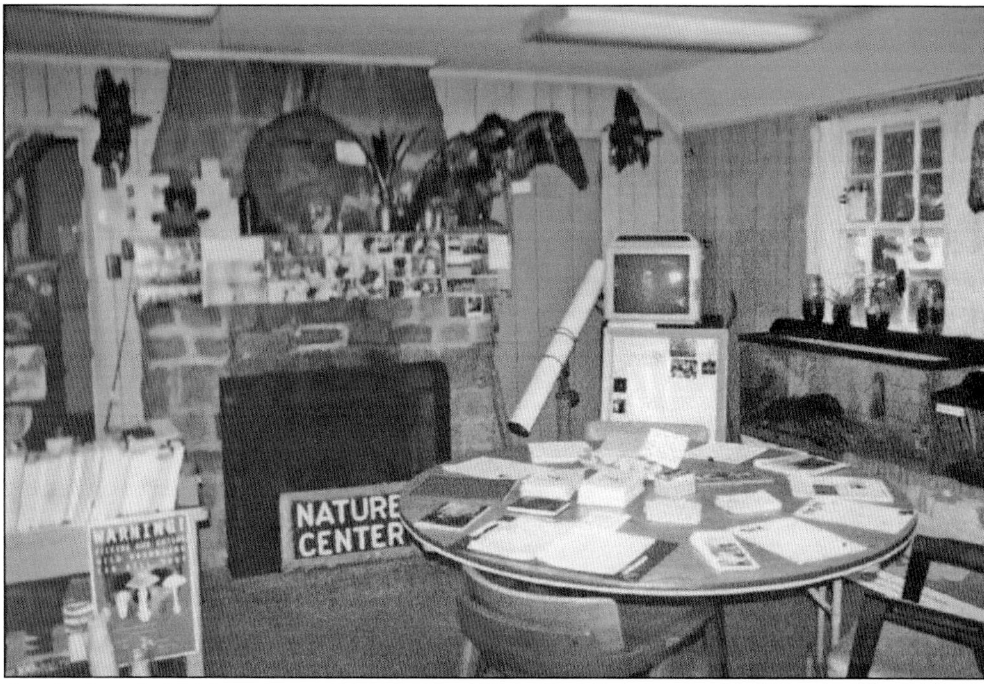

Overlooking Lake Nummy is a CCC building that formerly served as headquarters for the park. It is now an interpretive center, filled with artifacts and specimens found in the forest. On-staff teachers offer assorted nature and history programs for campers, especially during the busy summer season.

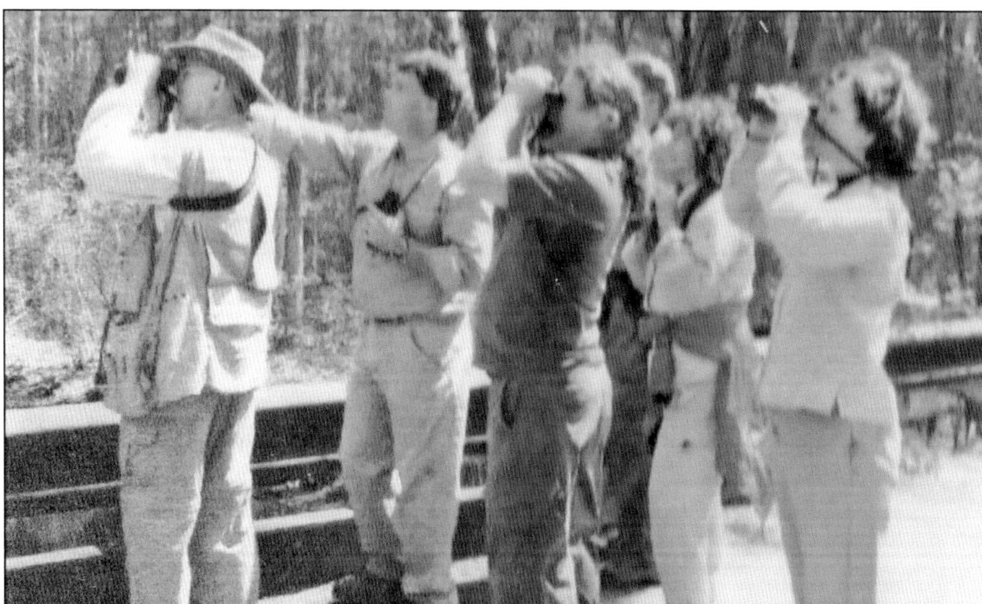

The Jersey Cape peninsula is a world-renowned venue for bird-watching. Situated in the center of the flyway, Belleplain State Forest is one of the stops during the World Series of Birding, during which teams of birders compete to count the most species. This group is probably focused on the bald eagles that routinely visit the area.

One of many CCC success stories, Orville Harris from Belleplain poses in uniform. Harris was a camp laborer from April 1935 until he was honorably discharged on September 22, 1937, when he found other employment.

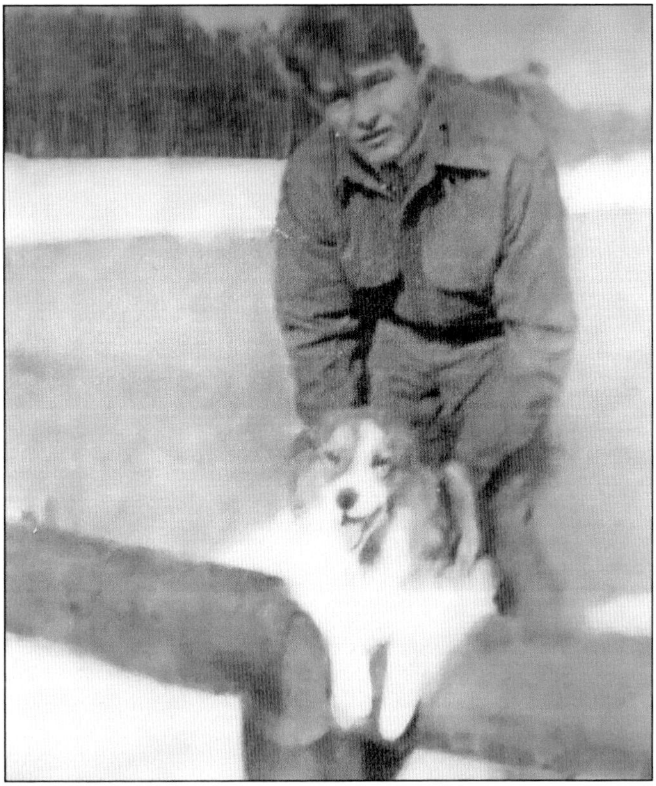

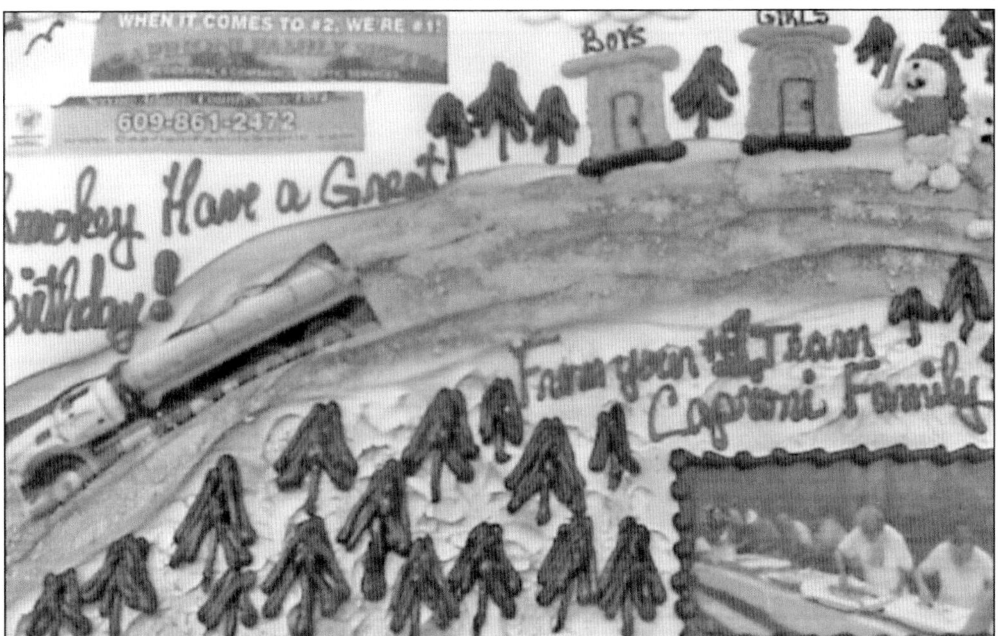

Each year, area businesses donate cakes to help Smokey Bear celebrate his birthday. The cake in this photograph came from the Caprioni family of Belleplain. The year this book was written was that of Smokey's 71st birthday—and he's still on the job.

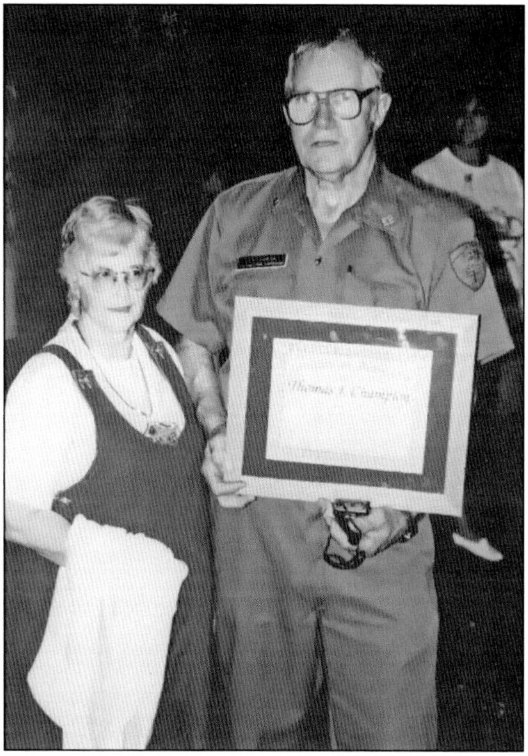

In 1980, Belleplain State Forest first celebrated Smokey Bear's birthday on the Saturday of a busy Labor Day weekend. The event has become a tradition, organized by park employee Tommy Champion, who has been working summers at the park for more than 50 years. In this 2003 photograph, Tom, with wife Reba, holds a plaque celebrating his 40 years of service.

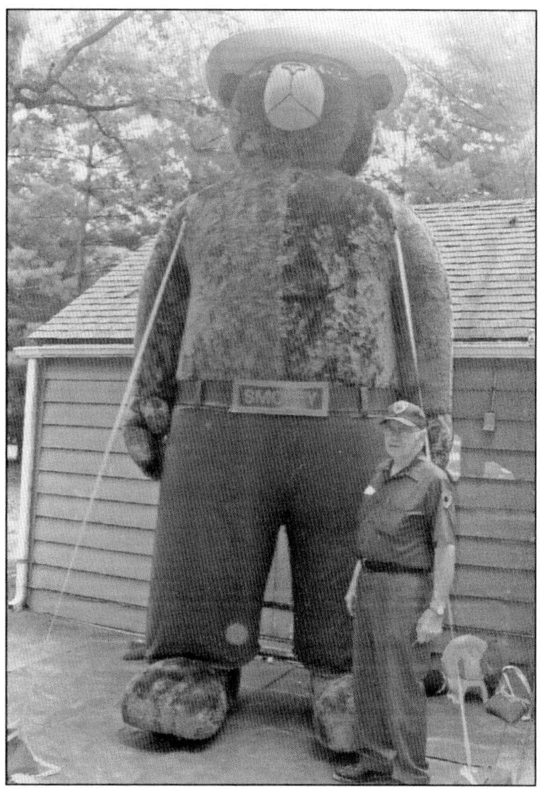

Tom Champion poses next to a king-size Smokey inflatable outside the interpretive center. Champion has been present at all but one of Smokey's birthday extravaganzas in the last 35 years. This particular occasion marks the forest service icon's 70th birthday in 2014. As he has since 1980, Champion raised funds to throw the annual shindig.

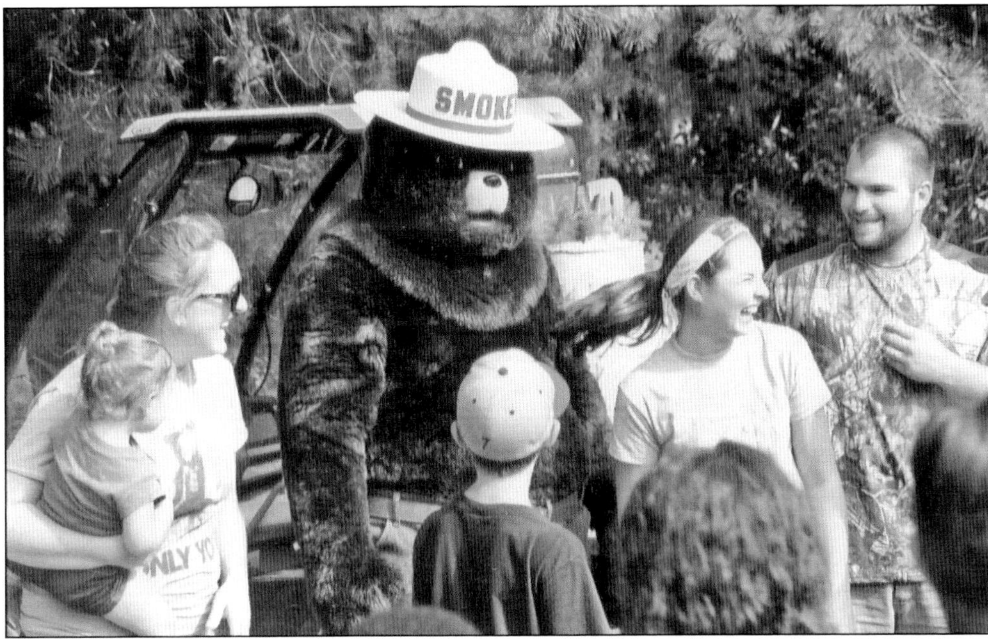

Campers pose with Smokey after he arrived by helicopter to celebrate his Labor Day Weekend party. Smokey was "born" during World War II when the US Forest Service initiated a public awareness campaign aimed at preventing forest fires. The bear first appeared in public in 1944.

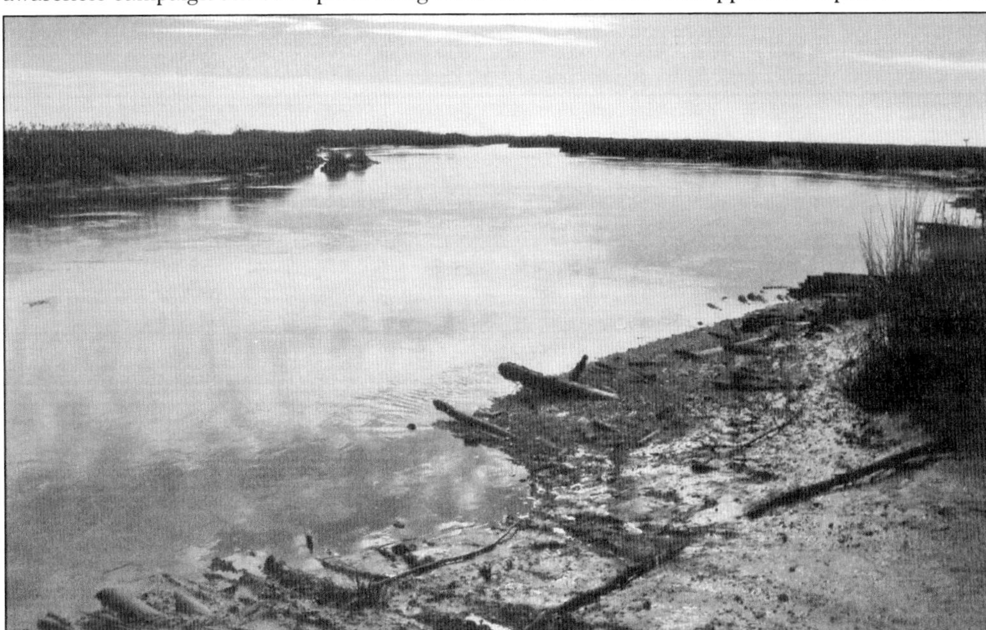

Jake's Landing, located in northwest Dennis Township, is also part of Belleplain State Forest. The banks of Dennis Creek are quiet here, but these waters hold tales of many pasts. British warships anchored off the creek in nearby Delaware Bay during the War of 1812. Pirates, seeking to conceal their ill-gotten gains, rowed up the creek under a full moon, and later, rumrunners, bearing treasure of a different kind, found their way through perfect darkness to deliver their wares at Jake's Landing. (Photograph by Ray Rebmann.)

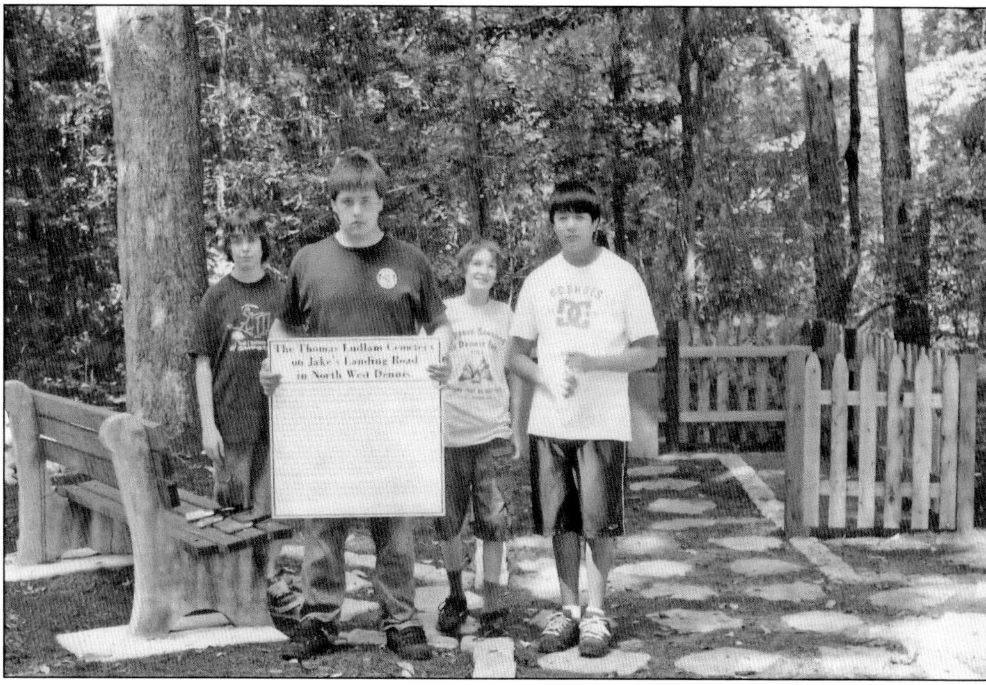

Alex Pascoe holds the sign that now marks the restored Ludlum family gravesites at Jake's Landing. The site had been neglected for years and vandalized. The small plot was owned by descendants of the Ludlum family, who once owned the entire area. The descendants granted permission for Pascoe to complete his Eagle Scout project. The acreage surrounding the site is now owned by the New Jersey Division of Fish and Wildlife. (Old School House Museum.)

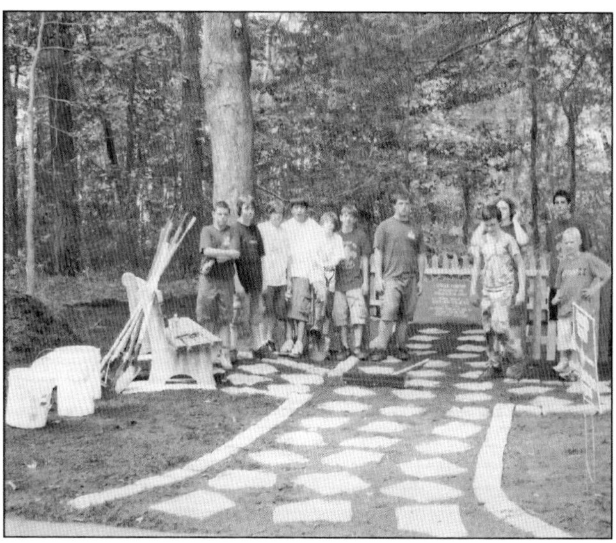

Members of Dennisville Scout Troop 56 who helped Alex Pascoe complete his Eagle Scout project pose during a work break. They are, from left to right, Nick Crippen, Raymond Haig, Ryan Haig, Nick Resigno, Nick Martino, P.J. Dietrich, Pascoe, Frank Smyth, Adan Dotts, Jonathan Thompson, and Ben Campbell. This Ludlam cemetery contains buried remains of Thomas Ludlam (father and son), wife and mother Zilpha (died in 1829), and Reuben Ludlam (died in 1823) as well as a child (name unknown) of George Lawrence. (Old School House Museum.)

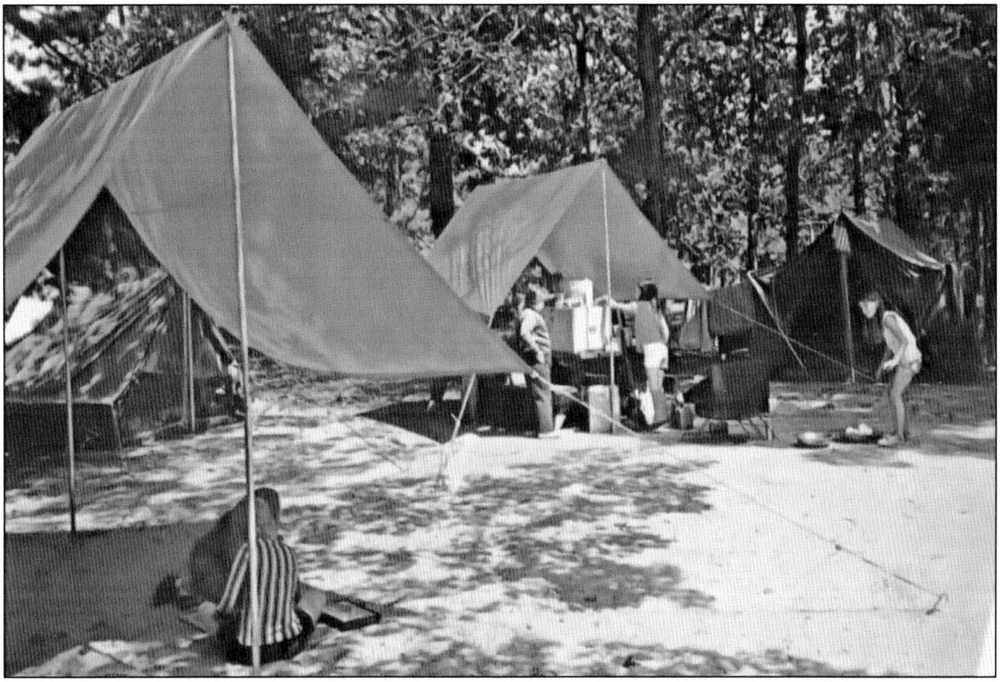

This postcard shows happy campers enjoying the great outdoors. When camping was first permitted in 1955, campers slept on platforms because of ubiquitous snakes and a site cost $1.25 per night. Today's still reasonably priced facilities include tent and group camping areas, lean-to cabins and yurts, and RV areas. Camping now include hot showers and bathroom and laundry facilities. Though they are fewer in number, the park is still home to snakes.

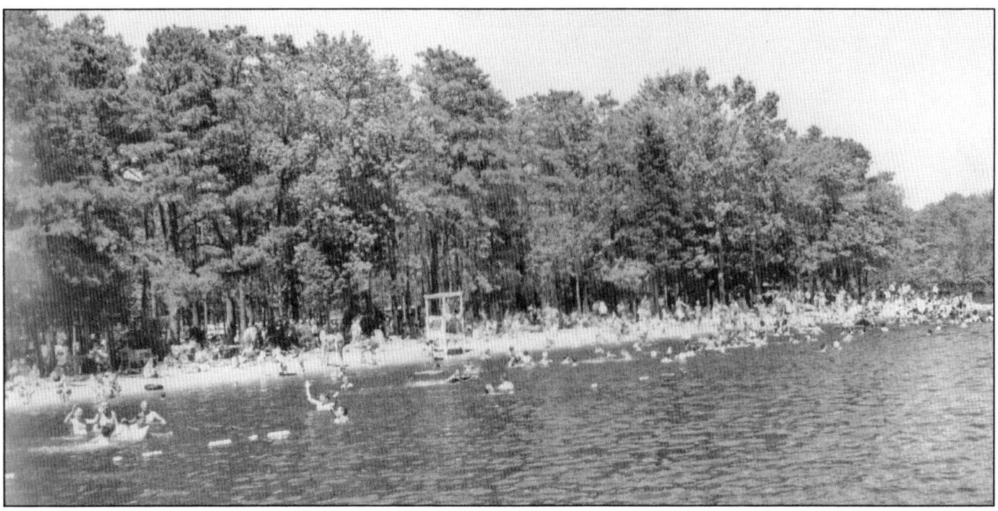

This photograph was taken during a busy Fourth of July weekend at Lake Nummy. Each year, the bottom of the swimming area of the lake is cleared of vegetation so swimmers can enjoy a smooth surface; however, that does not stop the occasional fish or turtle from joining the aquatic fun. The area where swimming is allowed is clearly marked. The lakeside offers a sandy beach and maintained swimming area with barbecue grills and picnic tables close by. Lifeguards protect the beach from Memorial Day to Labor Day. There is also a boat rental and refreshment stand steps away.

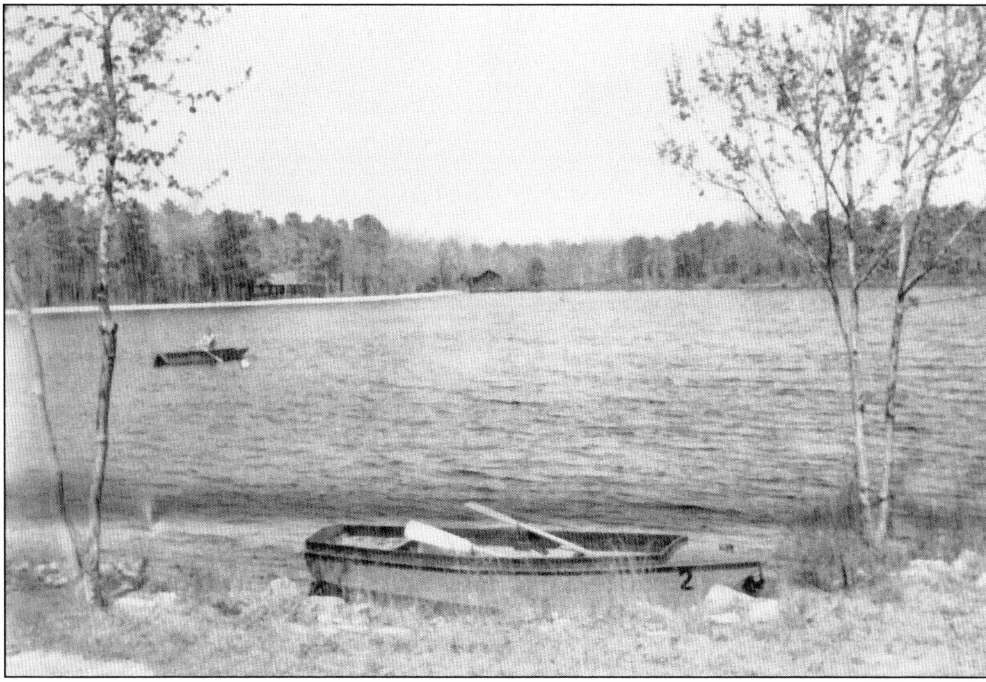

A visitor enjoys a leisurely row on Lake Nummy in this 1940 photograph. In the background are the boathouse and pavilion. Rowing enthusiasts can enjoy two long stretches in the lake's two sections, the second of which takes intrepid explorers back into marshy headwaters. The park offers canoe rentals; however, visitors can bring their own.

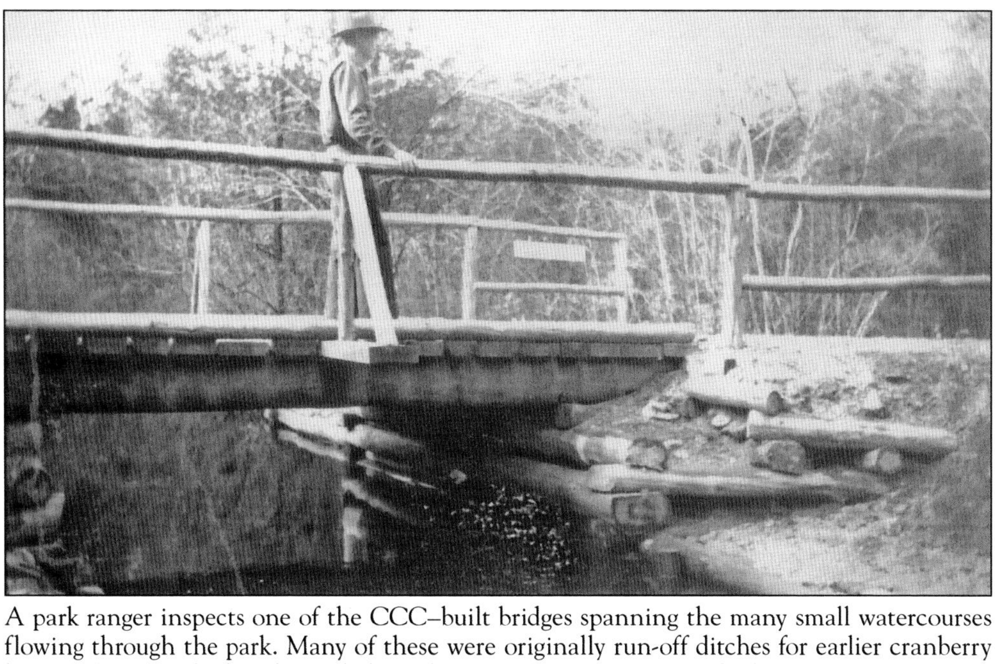

A park ranger inspects one of the CCC–built bridges spanning the many small watercourses flowing through the park. Many of these were originally run-off ditches for earlier cranberry bogs or drainage ditches dug to help with mosquito prevention in the boggier sections of the recreational areas.

Three

Eldora and North Dennis Not Just Mile Markers on the Way to Cape May

Eldora consists of salt marsh interspersed with spits of upland. The area has worn many names since representatives of English nobleman Daniel Coxe purchased land in the late 17th century—Stipson's Island, Stepson, Stuypson, Jaycock's Island, Benezet, East Creek, and West Creek to name a few. Those creeks are Eldora's boundaries.

Coxe apparently indulged in a shopping spree, buying land sight unseen in southern New Jersey, as well as thousands of acres in other parts of North America. He never set foot on this continent, yet his family's insistent claim to ownership of those lands created such resentment among settlers, it may have contributed to the agitation leading to separation of the colonies from England in 1776.

Absentee landlord or no, settlers flocked to Eldora in Colonial times, establishing themselves along the creeks. Like most settlements in the vicinity of Delaware Bay, Eldora developed an economy based on working the land, using the water to transport what it produced. Eldora shipped lumber and produce as far as Philadelphia in return for finished goods such as shoes and other necessities such as molasses.

In the 1890s, industry flourished, particularly industries whose products derived from agriculture and locally abundant natural resources. Those factories are gone now. Today, local place-names, like Pickle Pond and Paper Mill Road, serve as reminders of more prosperous times, before transportation and technology improvements rendered Eldora's factories obsolete.

The next area on a traveler's route is North (or Northwest) Dennis. While the area is best known for Jake's Landing, another landmark in North Dennis is "Five Chimneys." Now home to a professional artist, the house enjoys historical connections to such 19th-century figures as Henry Clay and Edgar Allan Poe.

Modern-day travelers, passing through on Delsea Drive (Route 47) to shore resorts, are more interested in future vacation plans than remembering the past. However, tempting reminders of that past are there. A more leisurely ride affords a memorable glimpse back in time.

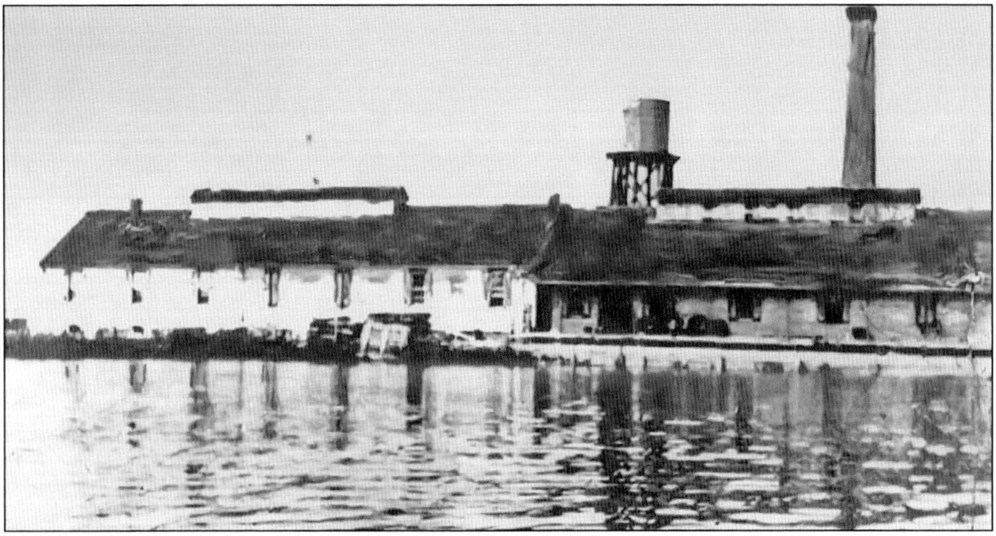

Rev. Isaac Dawson opened his canning factory in 1893. In its first year, it produced over 500,000 cans of tomatoes and employed more than 100 workers. Dawson sold the plant in 1901 to the Stevens brothers, who operated it until 1935. Today, Pickle Pond is a wildlife mecca where bald eagles pause to sample the pickerel and perch.

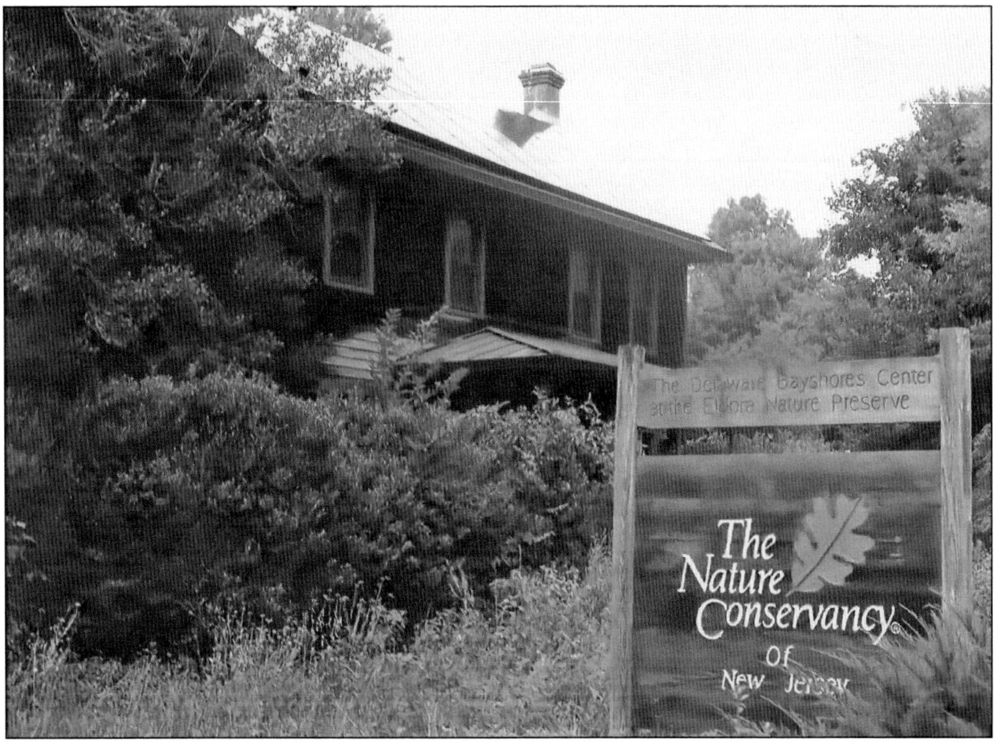

Dr. Brooke Worth was a world-renowned naturalist, teacher, and nature writer. He is author of the book *Of Mosquitoes, Moths, and Mice*. Worth purchased 177 acres because the site had never been sprayed and it offered a rare chance for him to study native moth and butterfly species. In 1981, he donated the property to the New Jersey Conservation Fund. Today, its walking paths are open to the public under the auspices of the Nature Conservancy.

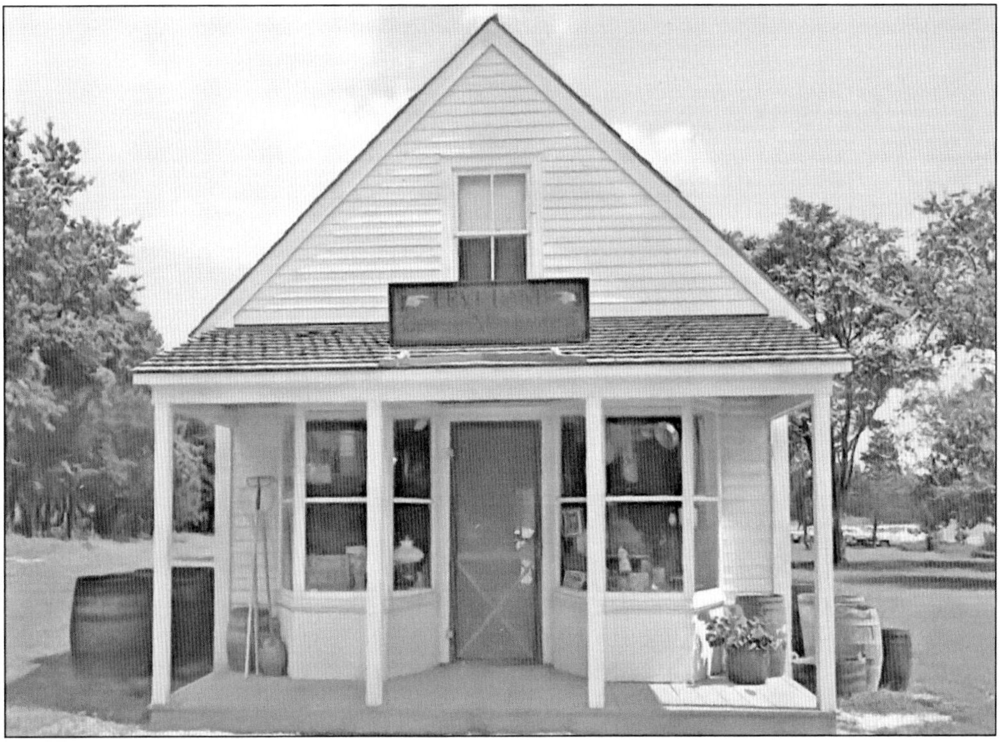

Levi Hand's general store sold everything a farm family needed and more, including blubber knives, which were used by whalers. The store was eventually relocated from Eldora to its present site, Historic Smithville Village in neighboring Atlantic County. It still serves as a general store and post office, or at least as a reminder for tourists of how a pre-mall store looked not so long ago.

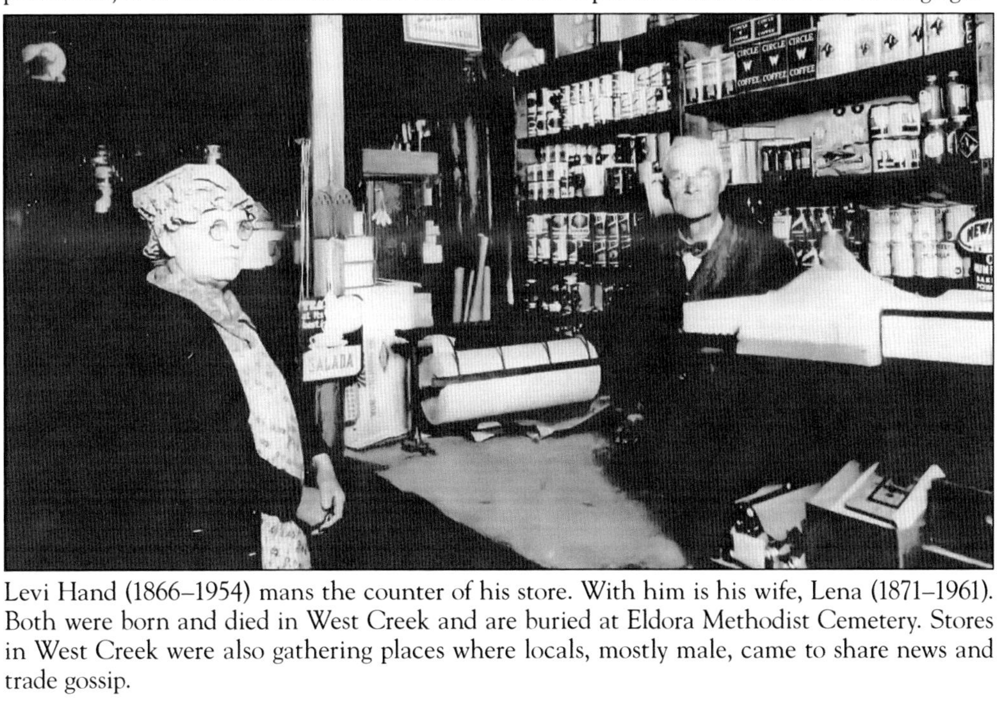

Levi Hand (1866–1954) mans the counter of his store. With him is his wife, Lena (1871–1961). Both were born and died in West Creek and are buried at Eldora Methodist Cemetery. Stores in West Creek were also gathering places where locals, mostly male, came to share news and trade gossip.

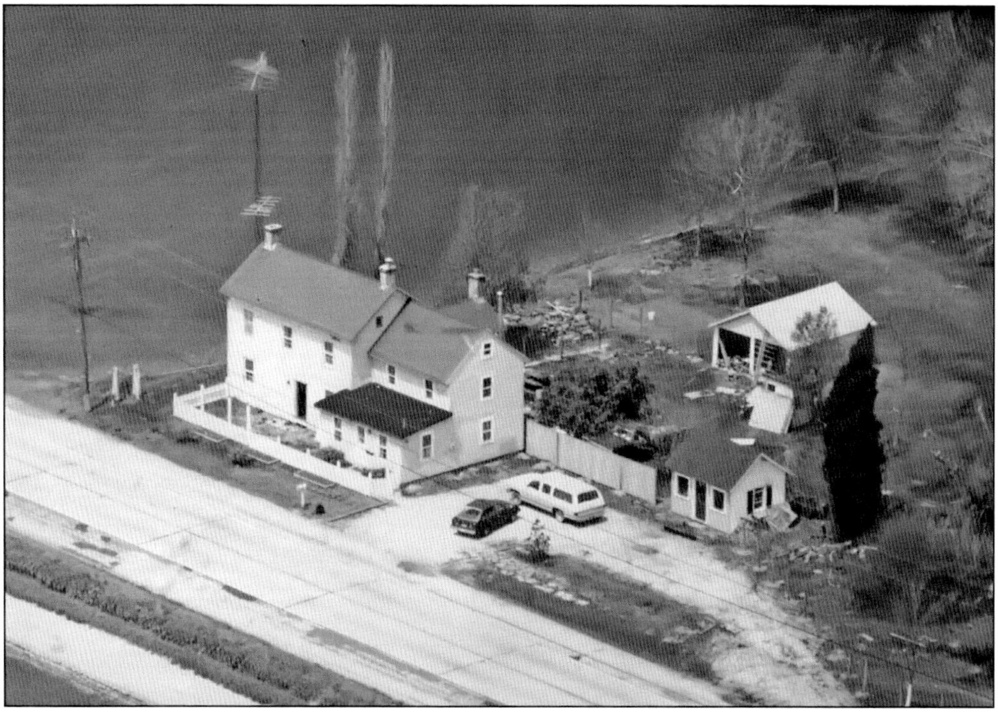

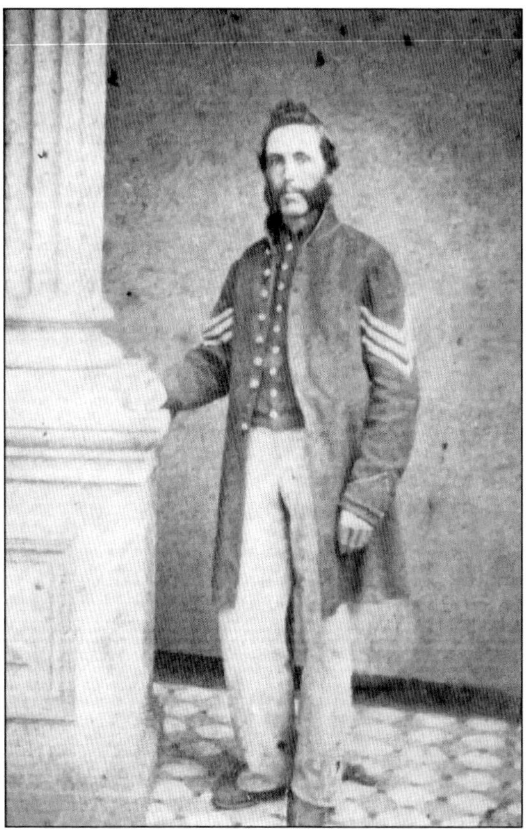

Following the Revolutionary War, Anthony Benezet, a Quaker, purchased 5,000 acres near West Creek. He built a sawmill and dam near Pickle Pond. Benezet was a well-known abolitionist and founder of the first antislavery society in North America. John Goff, born in Eldora in 1807, was a Methodist minister who established a store with a boat landing. He died in 1899, at the same location where he was born.

This 19th-century photograph shows another of the extended Goff clan that called Eldora home. Born in 1827, 1st Sgt. John F. Goff served in Company F, 25th New Jersey Volunteer Infantry. Surviving the Civil War, he returned home, where he lived until he died in 1896. He was buried at Eldora Methodist Cemetery.

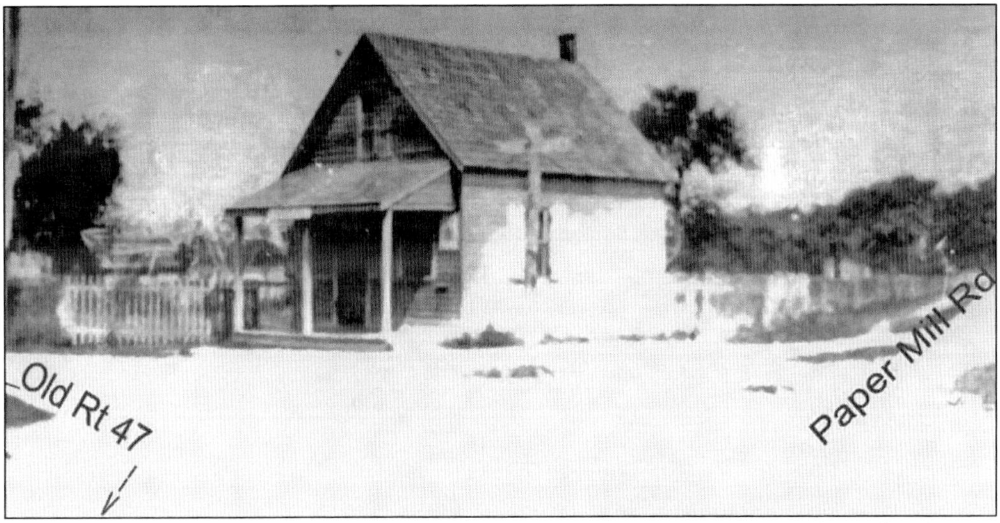

The area's first post office was established in 1842 under the name East Creek. With it having had so many names in its lifetime, residents of this community in 1892 officially named it Eldora. That post office closed in 1899. The original Eldora Post Office was located on the stage route. Later, mail was brought in by train to the Belleplain station and conveyed from there to Eldora and Delmont.

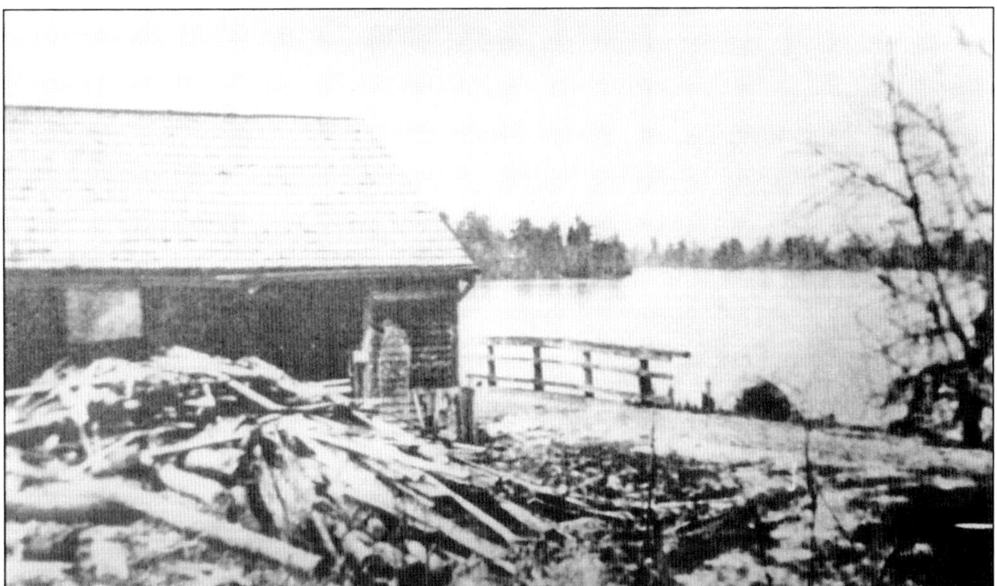

East Creek Mill was built in 1785. In Colonial times, Eldora was a thriving commercial area, thanks to mills such as this. The mill was used until 1920 and no longer stands. In the 19th century, locally cut cordwood was shipped out of Eldora, and much needed staples were shipped in. (Photograph by Tom Kinnemand, courtesy of Old School House Museum.)

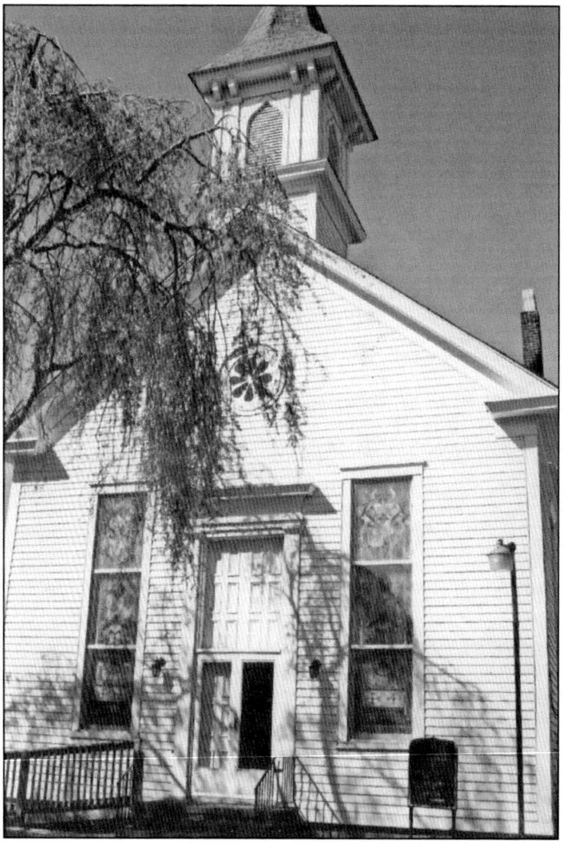

Eldora Methodist congregation organized in 1860 and built a church. A new meetinghouse, complete with belfry, was erected across the road in 1883. It stands today off Route 550. (Photograph by Ray Rebmann.)

In 1950, Larry Bohn Sr. relocated his farm from Cumberland County, where he had grown vegetables for 14 years, to the site shown in this photograph. He and son Larry Jr. initially planted sod on 15 acres here. As the farm prospered, the Bohms became one of the first sod operations in the country to automate palletizing its harvest. Today, Bohm's Sod Farm consists of over 300 acres. (Photograph by Ray Rebmann.)

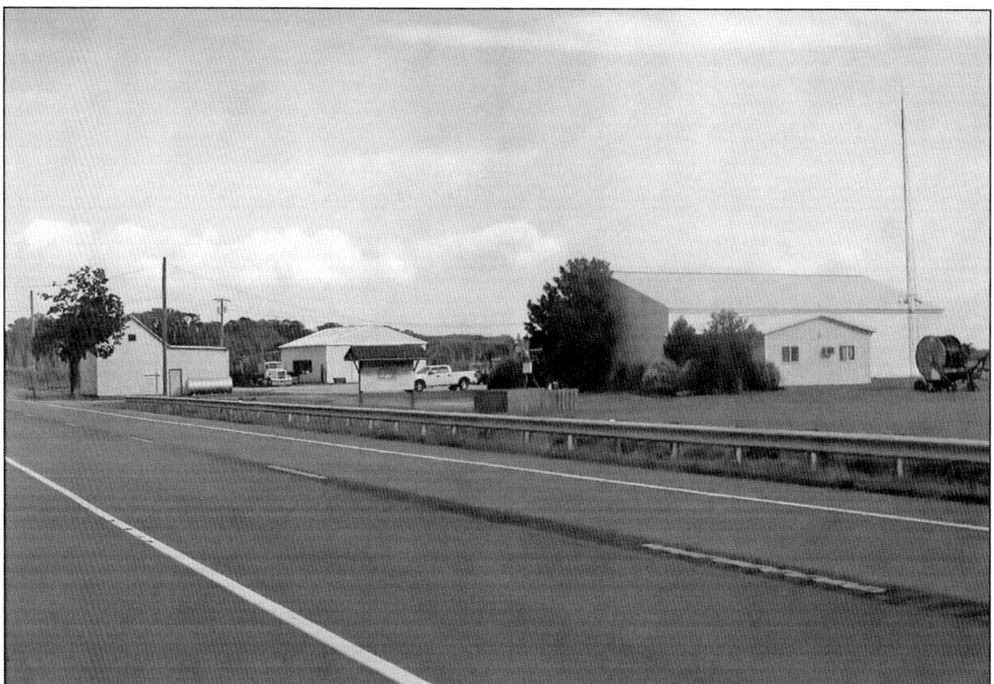

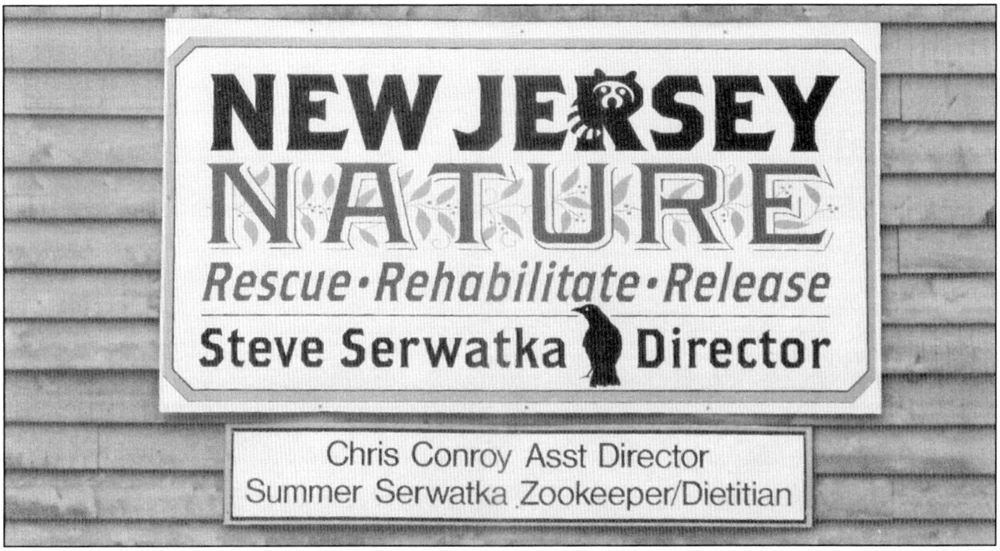

Steve Serwatka is a former educator, veterinary technician, and, as of this writing, works as an animal control officer for Dennis Township. At his home, which is also home to New Jersey Nature, he rehabilitates injured wild animals brought from all over the area. Most of these are successfully returned to the wild. Serwatka finances his work with educational programs at area schools, church groups, and special events, where he instructs the public about how best to interact with the wild.

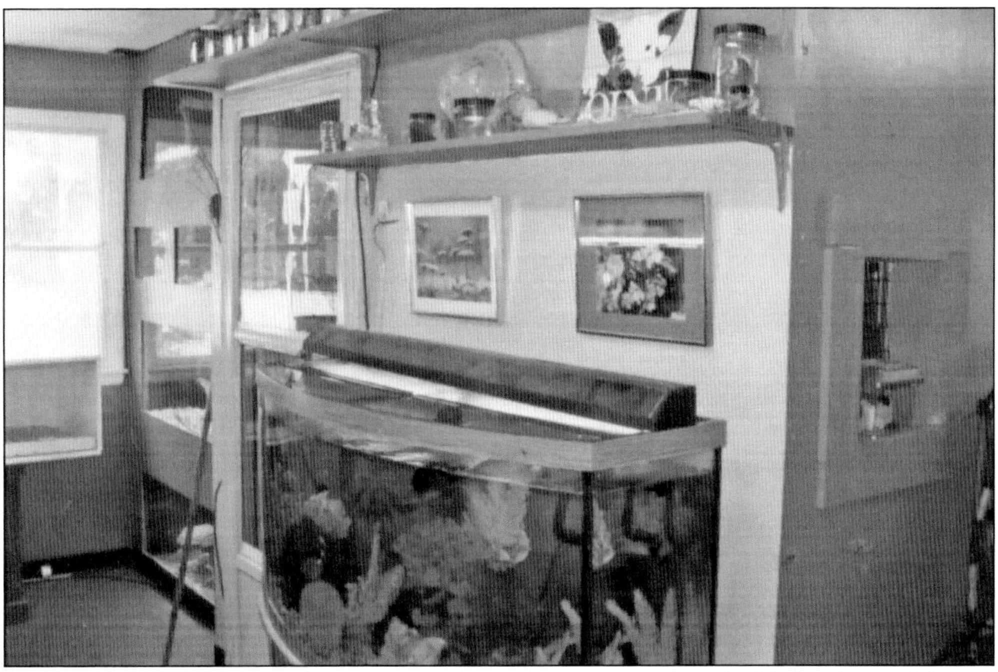

Many of the injured critters that arrive at New Jersey Nature are too disabled to be rehabilitated and returned to the wild. Steve Serwatka has provided a home to this ever-growing number of animals. He receives help from volunteers as well as donations from local businesses, such as Lenny Catanoso's Garden Greenhouse in Clermont. But the care and feeding of a range of wildlife from possums and raccoons to tarantulas and snakes largely falls on Serwatka.

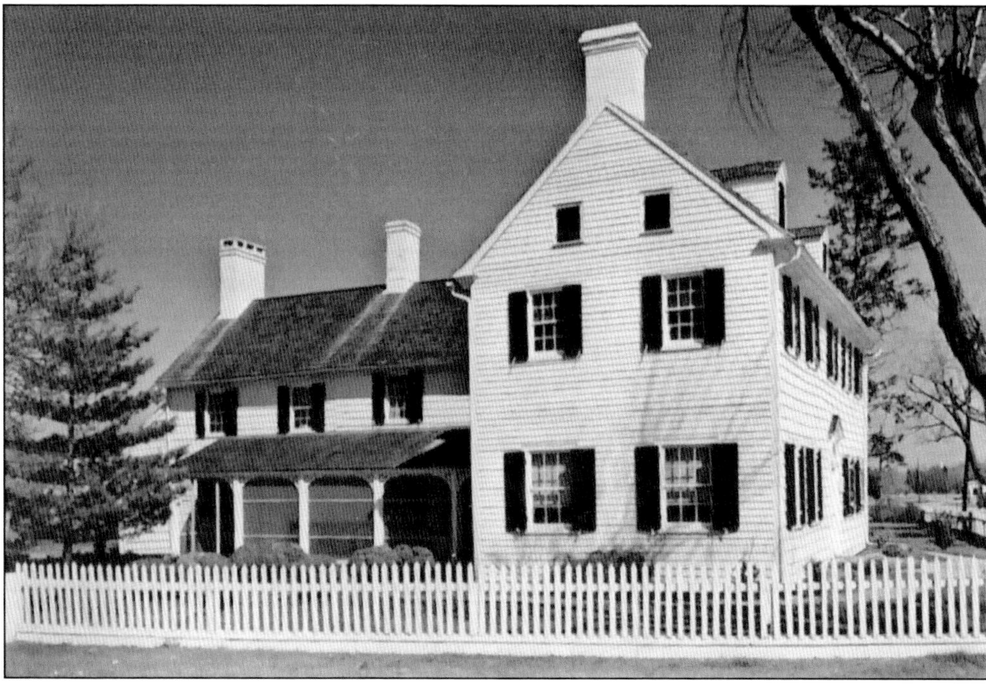

William S. Townsend (1811–1880) was a businessman, farmer, landowner, and public servant who became one of southern New Jersey's wealthiest men in his era. His home, shown in this photograph, still stands on Route 47. The prominent Ludlum family, which Townsend married into, built it in 1820. The house is typical of Federal-style architecture, with one distinction—the five chimneys, by which the house came to be identified.

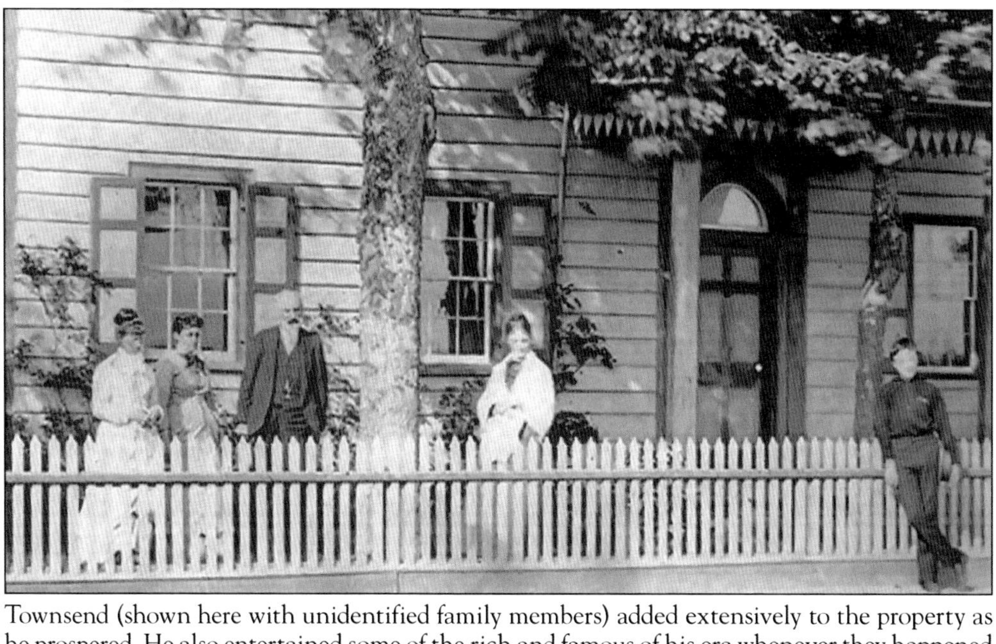

Townsend (shown here with unidentified family members) added extensively to the property as he prospered. He also entertained some of the rich and famous of his era whenever they happened to be in the area. One guest was Sen. Henry Clay, an unsuccessful candidate for the presidency several times as a member of the Whig Party.

Townsend's son Richard served with the 10th Regiment, New Jersey Volunteer Infantry, achieving the rank of second lieutenant during the Civil War. He led his Company C into battle at Gettysburg. Commissioned just three months earlier, he was killed, shot through the head, on July 3, three days after joining his new command. He is buried at Gettysburg National Cemetery.

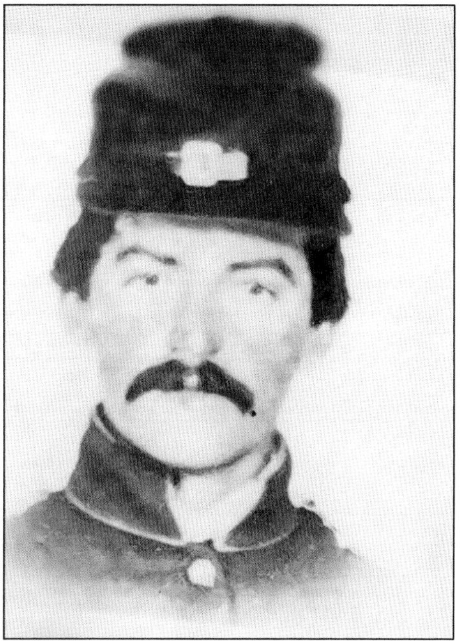

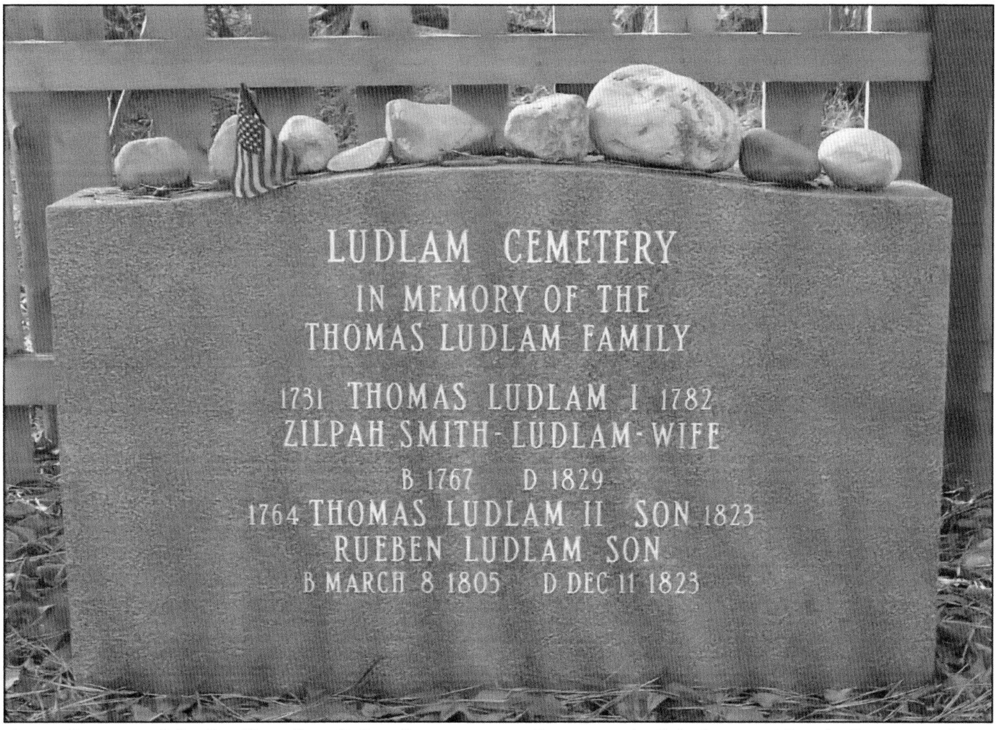

A tombstone of the Ludlam family has been restored to its rightful place in North Dennis, where the Ludlams settled extensively. The historic Henry Ludlam House is located on the busy highway. Long empty and considered to be one of the most haunted buildings in southern New Jersey by those who take interest in such matters, the house was last occupied by a bed-and-breakfast operator and operated under the name Henry Ludlam Inn. Ludlam is also a character of historical interest, having served in the Revolutionary War under George Washington.

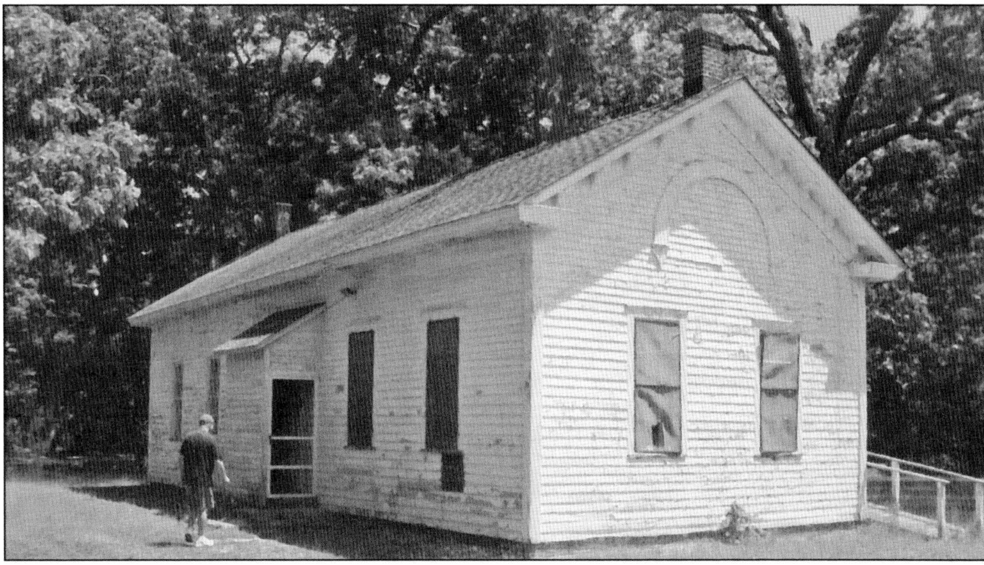

Pictured is the Ludlam School as it looks today. In 1801, local residents bought one acre from Henry Ludlam on the north side of Dennis Creek. Located on the stagecoach road, the land was dedicated to be "used for a school house forever," according to the original deed. That did not happen; however, it did serve longer than any other school in the township, for over 150 years—until 1957, when township schools consolidated. In this 2015 photograph, Dennis Township committeeman Albert DiCicco inspects the exterior.

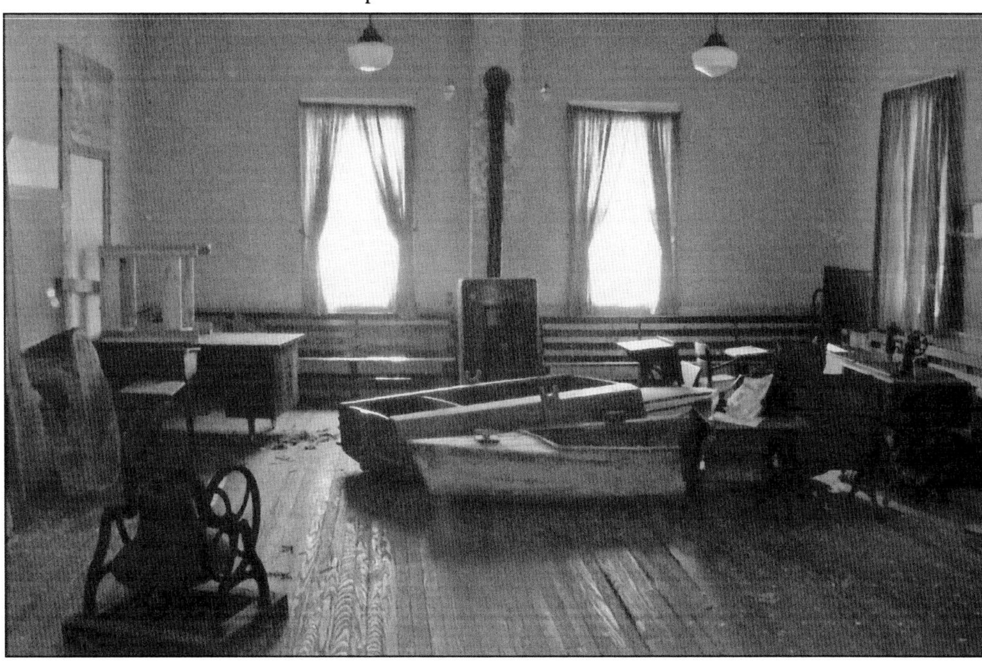

This photograph shows the interior of the Ludlam School. The building continued to serve the community after the school closed when the Northwest Dennis Community Club assumed ownership with local clubs and civic organizations, making use of the facility until 2001, when the township took title. Plans are being considered to expand the township's museum, making use of the old schoolhouse once again.

Ellsworth and Hester Robinson, longtime custodians of the Ludlam School, are pictured together. The Robinson family lived in North Dennis and were involved in numerous community activities.

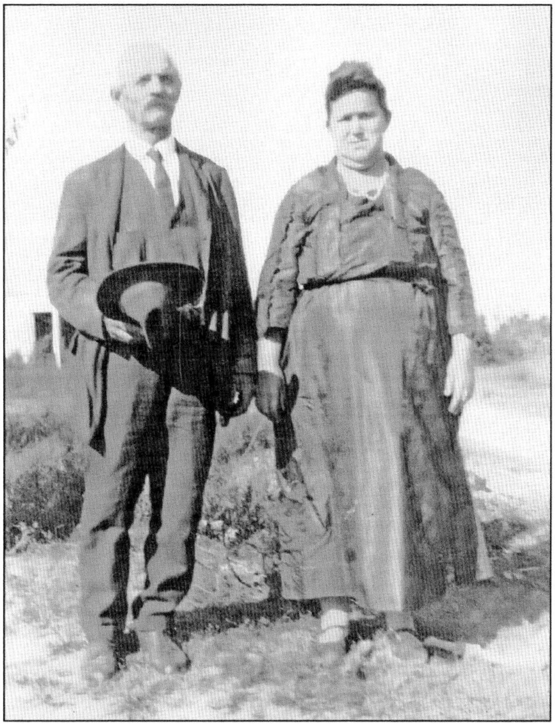

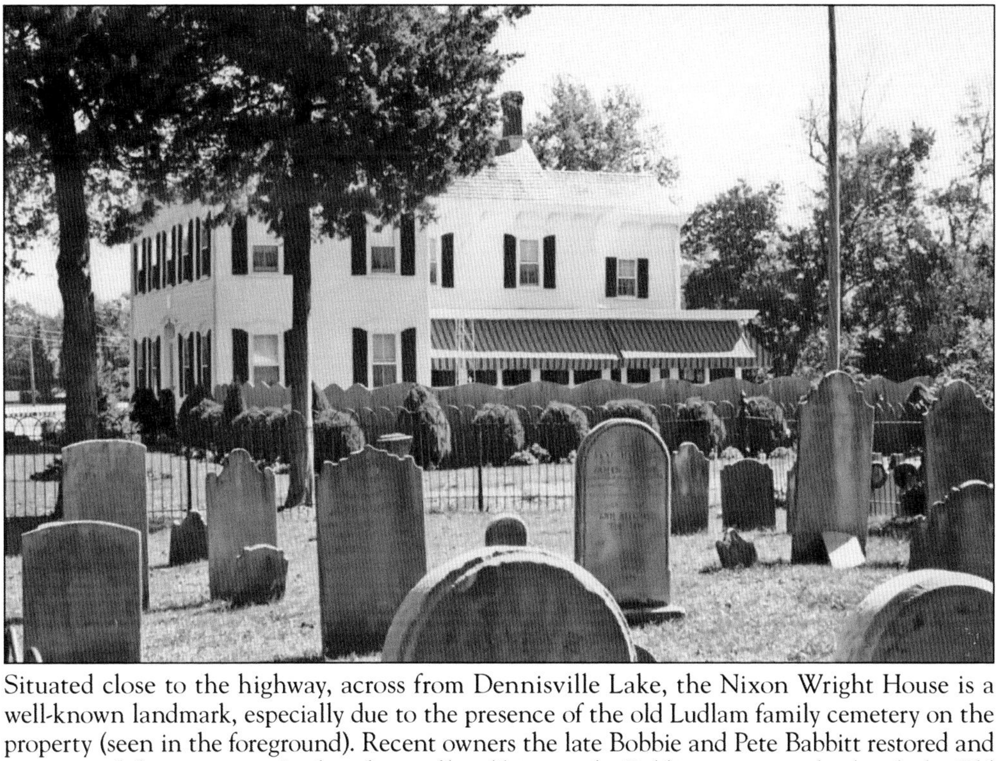

Situated close to the highway, across from Dennisville Lake, the Nixon Wright House is a well-known landmark, especially due to the presence of the old Ludlam family cemetery on the property (seen in the foreground). Recent owners the late Bobbie and Pete Babbitt restored and maintained the cemetery. Avid students of local history, the Babbitts were involved with the Old School House Museum, where Bobbie worked as curator.

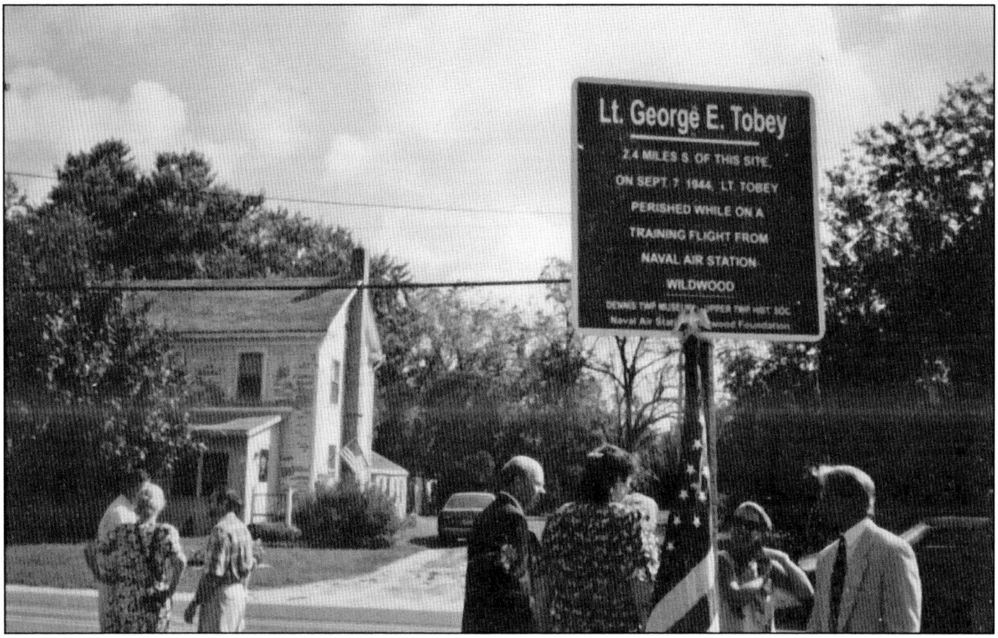

This photograph shows a moment in a program commemorating the training flight crash of Lt. George Tobey at the Eldora home of Richard E. Fowler. Lieutenant Tobey, a veteran of 35 bombing missions in the Pacific theater during World War II, was leading a dive of a six-plane division from over 11,000 feet during high winds when, due to mechanical failure, he lost the ability to control the aircraft.

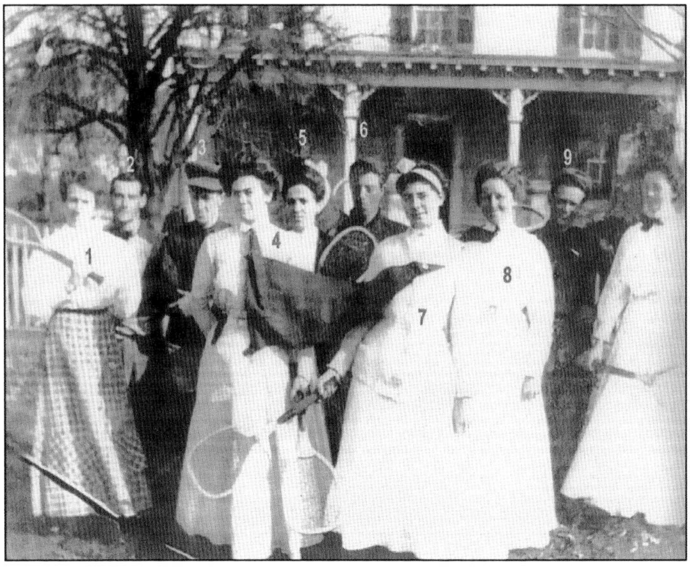

Lawn tennis was a popular sport in the early years of the 20th century. This photograph taken in Eldora shows a number of fashionably attired players. Individuals are not identified, but the group includes members of the Bingham and Chambers family. Both families are still represented in Dennis Township to this day. Helen Wolf donated the photograph to the Old School House Museum in Dennisville.

Four

DENNISVILLE
BUSTLING VILLAGE IN THE MIDDLE

Like the other hamlets of Dennis Township, Dennisville had other names before acquiring its current appellation in 1854. Originally named Dennis Creek, the area was settled around 1720. One of the first buildings to go up was a sawmill, which produced lumber for a nearby shipbuilding operation. From that beginning, Dennisville was destined to be a center for lumbering and related activities.

As European civilization took root, roads were built and communities grew on both sides of the creek. Its location, a crossroads of the north-south and east-west stage routes combined with water access to the shipping lanes of Delaware Bay, enabled Dennisville to develop as a commercial hub in southern New Jersey.

Nineteenth-century Dennisville became a village of sea captains and shipbuilders. Families accrued fortunes, taking advantage of an easily accessed supply of oak, hickory, and cedar and safe harborage along the creek. Forty-two ship captains have called Dennisville home.

As the town prospered, shops sprouted along Main Street. Farmers traveled to town to ship their produce and purchase provisions at those shops. Shipbuilding continued to be the major local industry until the 1890s, but finally, the impact of rail transportation, followed by the emergence of the automobile and truck, rendered that industry obsolete. The state's decision to bypass the town during construction of the highway spelled the end of Main Street as a commercial center.

Today's Dennisville, with its more than fifty 18th- and 19th-century buildings, is a living museum of sorts. Following World War II, a new generation of homeowners embarked upon a campaign to restore many of those buildings.

In 1985, the village was listed in the New Jersey Historical Register, and in 1987, the National Register. In 1990, local homeowners formed an association dedicated to preserving Dennisville as the special place it has always been.

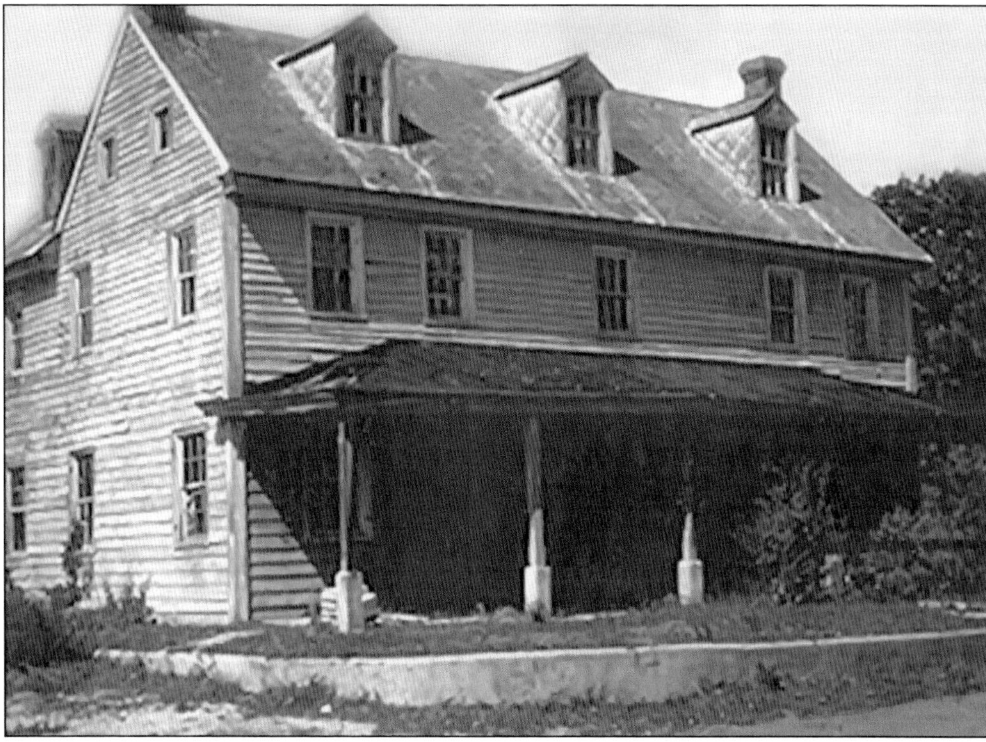

Jeremiah Johnson obtained a license for a tavern, the Dennisville Inn, in 1802. Ownership changed 13 times before the property was sold to Wawa, Inc. in 1984. In making way for the currently operating store, the inn building was relocated in two sections to Historic Cold Spring Village, where it has been restored and reopened to the public as a historical exhibit.

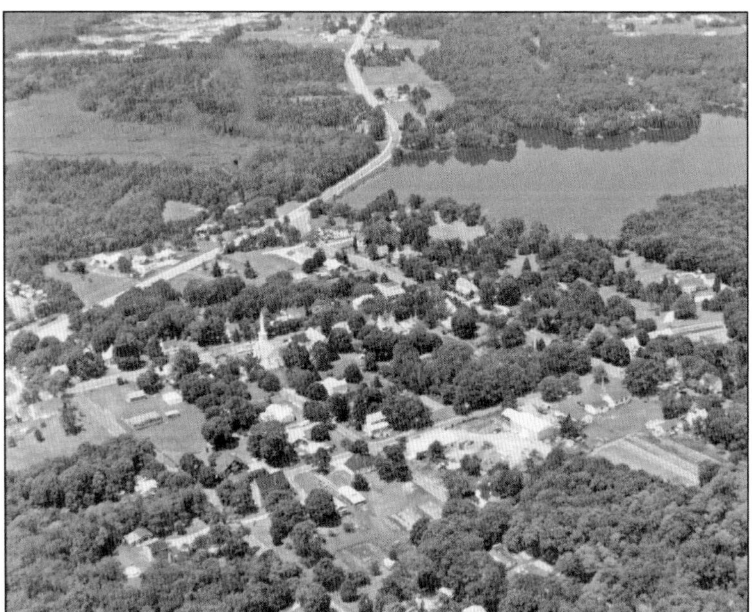

This is an aerial view of Dennisville. Johnson's Pond is seen at right. The road winding toward and through the village is Delsea Drive, the main artery for eastbound traffic heading to the barrier islands from Philadelphia and points west.

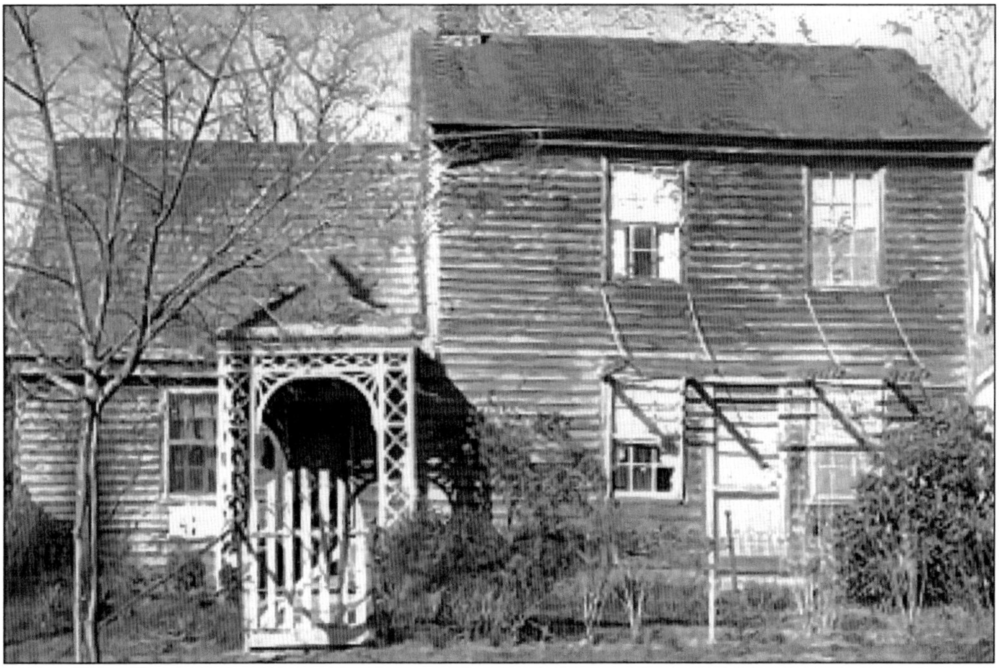

Built in the 1700s, the Belle Carroll House is listed in the National Register of Historic Places. The woman for whom the cottage is named was a member of the first graduating class of nurses from Philadelphia General Hospital in 1879. One of 10 children herself, Carroll never married. Her grandfather Thomas reportedly came to this country from his native Ireland, escaping the failed 1798 rebellion there.

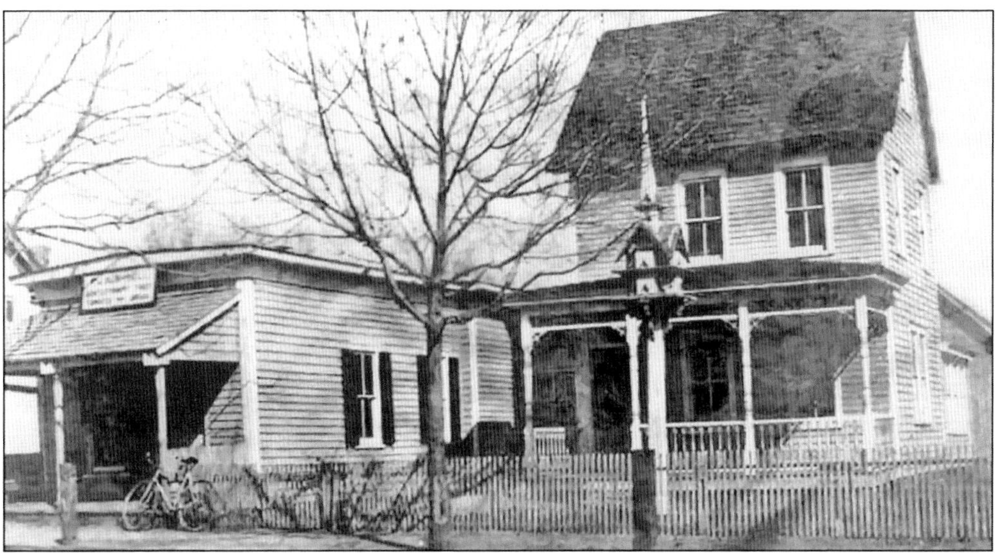

L.C. Bushnells grocery store was located in the heart of Dennisville's once-busy commercial district. The store is located to the left, with the Bushnell family home to the right. The original store sign is now on display at the Old School House Museum, donated by Arthur Lathers, a descendant of the Bushnell family.

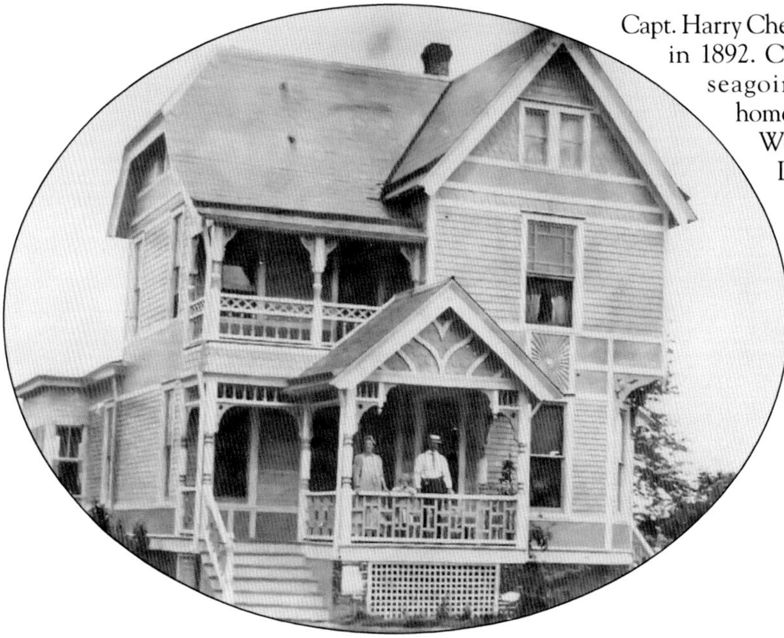

Capt. Harry Chester's house was built in 1892. Chester commanded seagoing tugboats. His home was built by Francis Wentzell, a respected Dennis Creek shipwright who worked for Leaming Shipbuilders. The house is located on the left side of Petersburg Road as one drives north through the village.

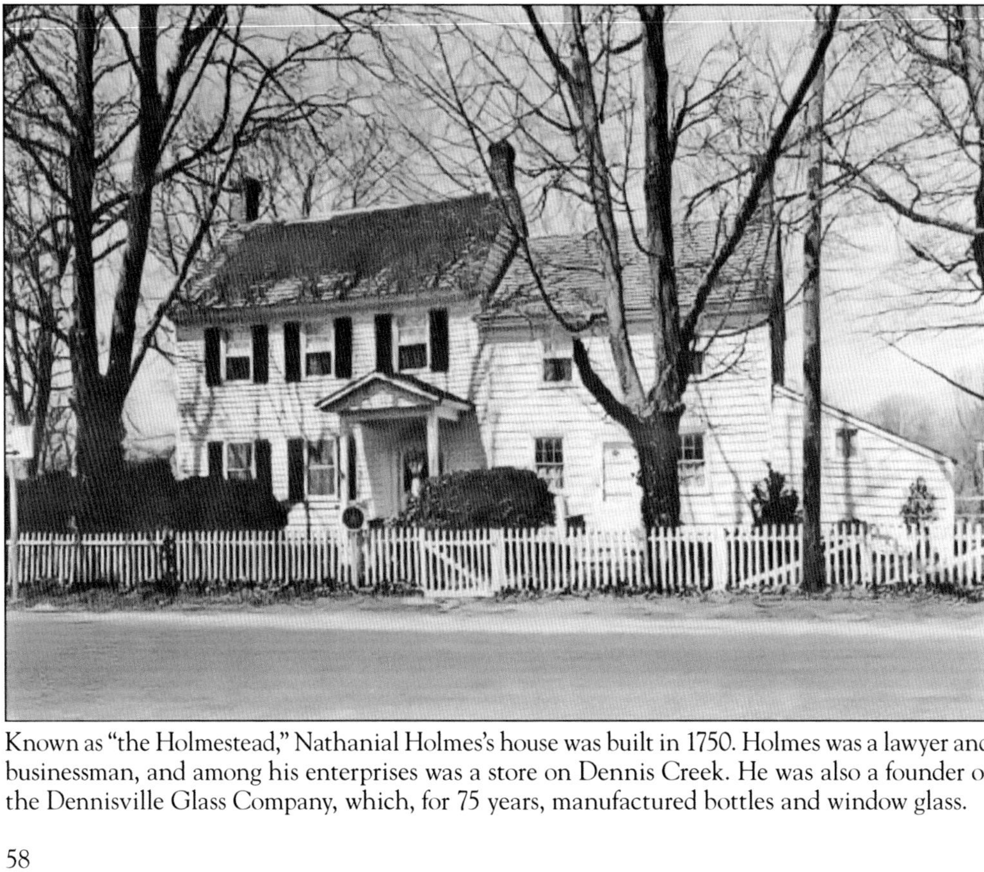

Known as "the Holmestead," Nathanial Holmes's house was built in 1750. Holmes was a lawyer and businessman, and among his enterprises was a store on Dennis Creek. He was also a founder of the Dennisville Glass Company, which, for 75 years, manufactured bottles and window glass.

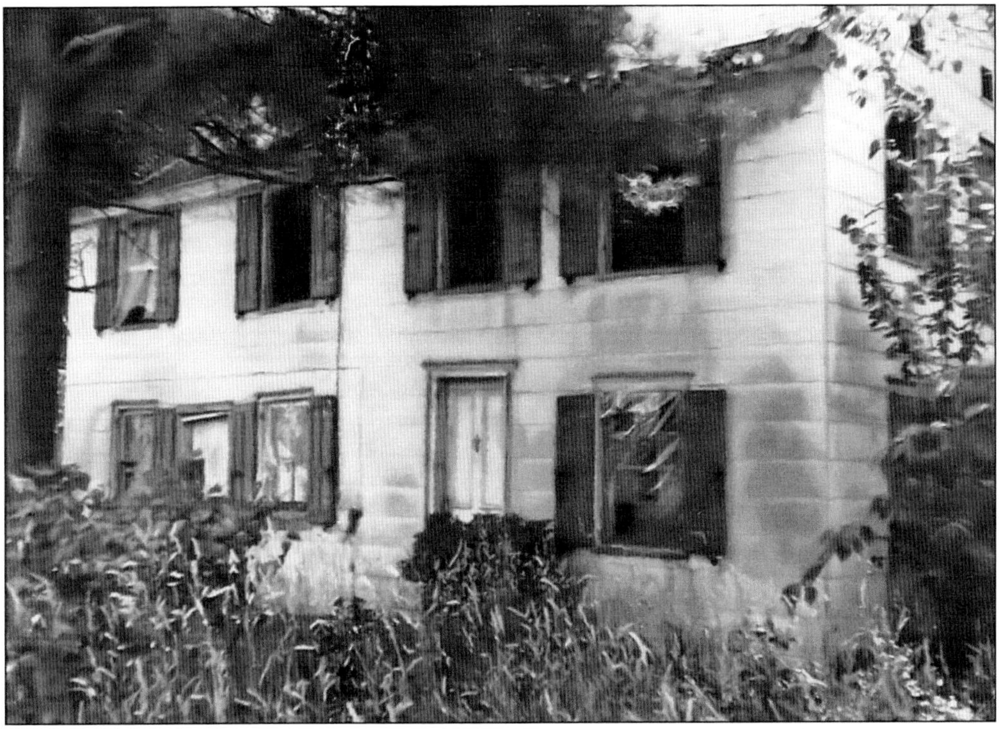

These before and after photographs provide a surface glimpse of what is involved in restoring an old house. This is the Capt. Charles T. and Lydia Crawford House. Built in 1852 by Crawford, a bay captain, the house was owned in the early 20th century by Charles Robart, known as the "last shingle maker in Dennisville." The interior, exterior, and grounds of the house have been restored by its present owners and this was the featured house for the 25th anniversary Dennisville Historic Homeowners Association Christmas House Tour in 2013. The house tour attracts thousands of visitors to Dennisville for one night each year.

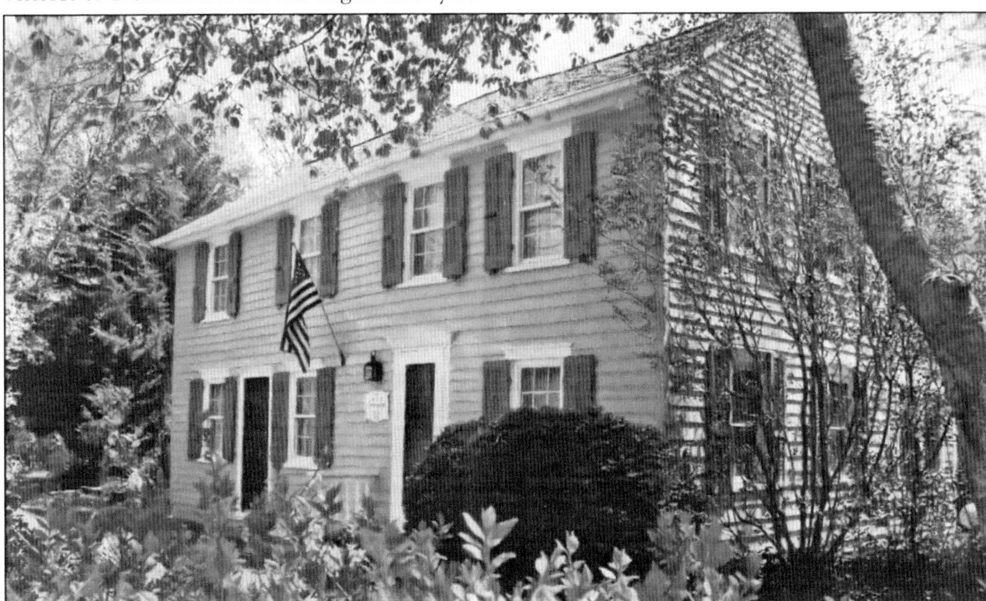

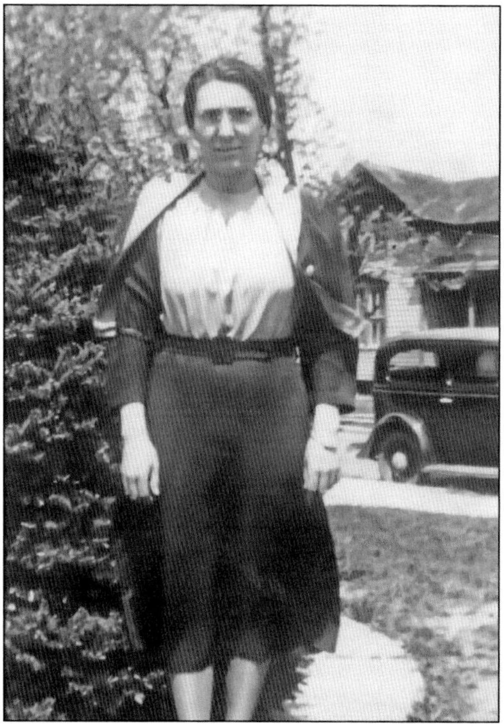

Roseann Robinson, a longtime postmistress for Dennisville, was appointed February 2, 1950. She served the community for 37 years, working out of her home. She was 73 years old at retirement. Because of its prominence in the area in the 19th century, Dennisville was granted the county's first post office in 1802. The post office, now located next to the Old School House Museum, continues to be a gathering place for local residents.

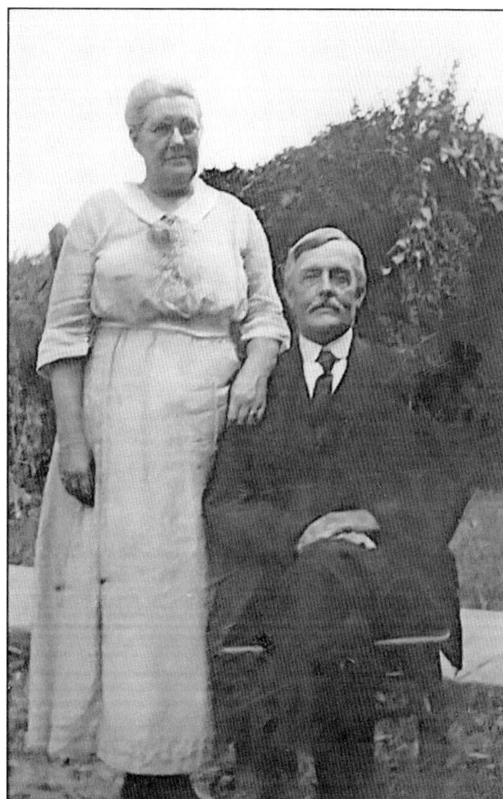

Connie and Frank Bushnell and their family owned a prominent store on Main Street. Descendants of the family still reside in Dennisville. In the mid-19th century, Main Street was one of the busiest places in southern New Jersey, with two taverns, six stores, and a gristmill, blacksmith, and sawmill that helped support a thriving shipbuilding industry along nearby Dennis Creek.

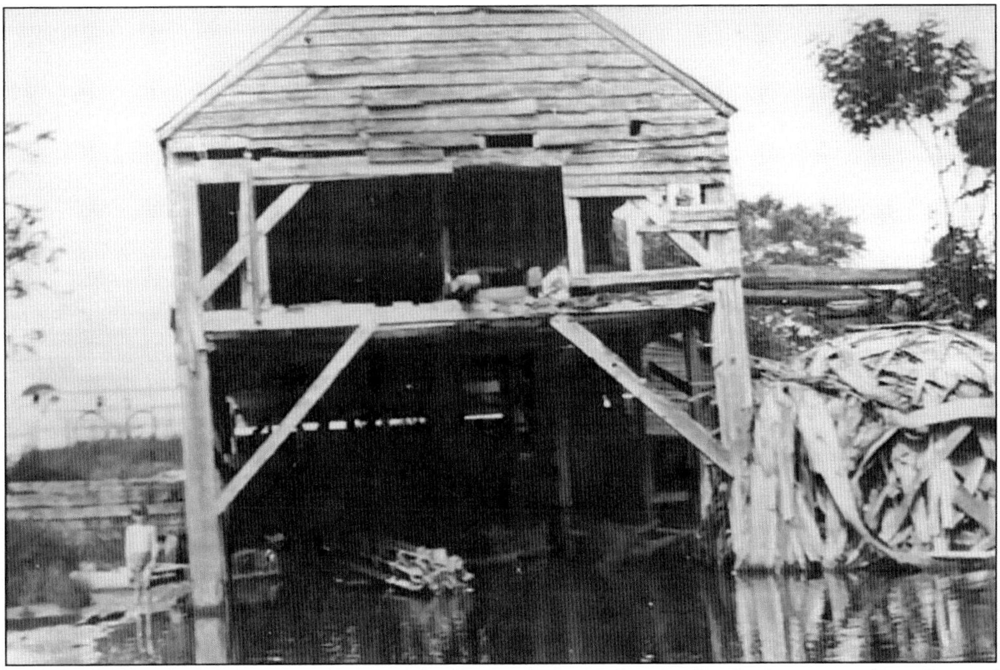

Taken in the early 1900s, the photograph shows Johnson's Saw Mill, which eventually collapsed following a storm. The mill, located on the lake bearing the same name, produced much of the lumber that built the original Dennisville while also supplying a thriving shipbuilding industry on Dennis Creek.

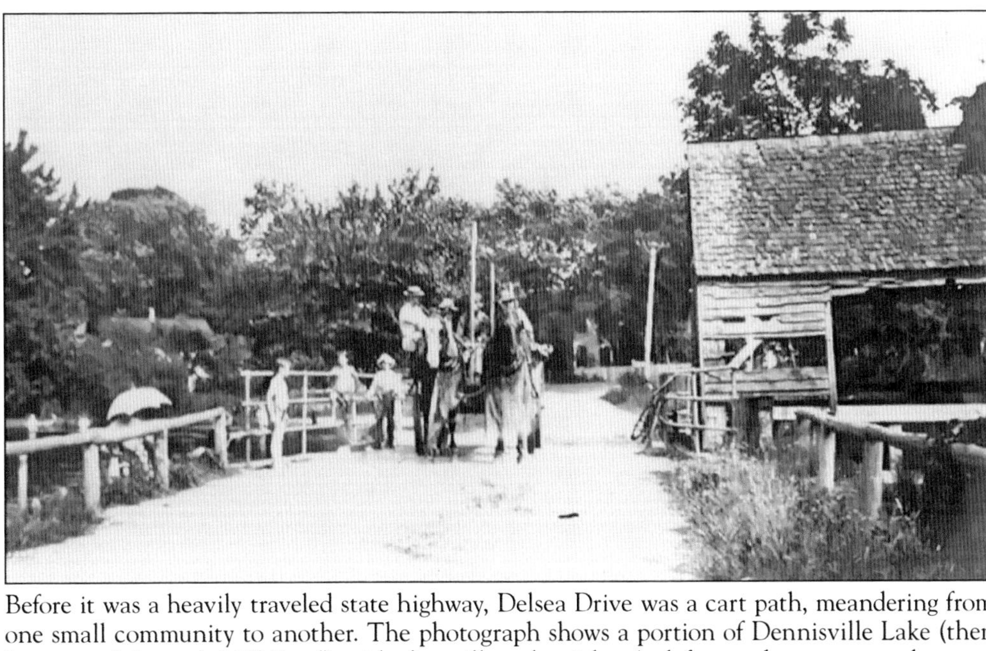

Before it was a heavily traveled state highway, Delsea Drive was a cart path, meandering from one small community to another. The photograph shows a portion of Dennisville Lake (then known as Johnson's Mill Pond), with the mill to the right. At left are what appear to be some young local swimmers.

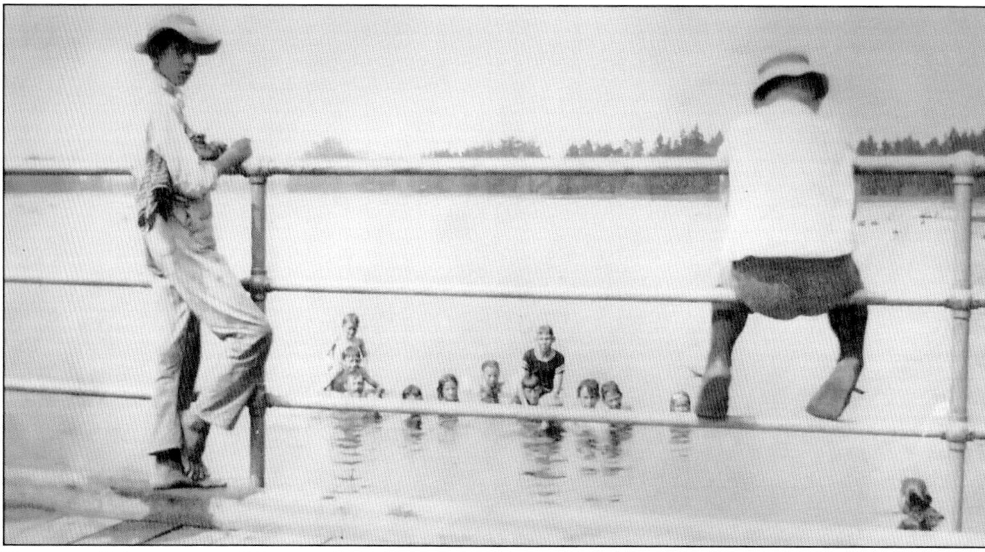

Dennisville's version of Tom and Huck enjoy a hot summer day at the pond. Local, unidentified youngsters have gathered to swim at the man-made Johnson's Mill Pond. A peculiar fact is that every lake found in Cape May County is man-made, mostly the result of damming for mills. This Norman Rockwell scene has been immortalized on postcards, titled *Sylvan Lake*.

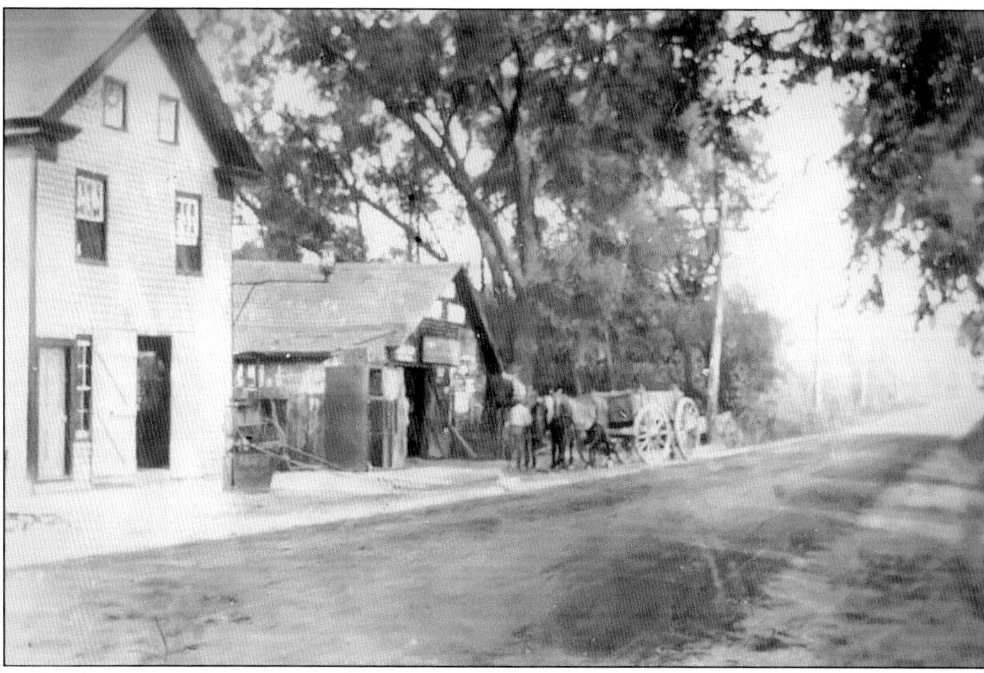

Before the advent of the automobile, real horsepower enabled overland stagecoach transportation in rural Cape May County. The local blacksmith was an important personage, hence the presence of a blacksmith and wheelwright shop in the center of town.

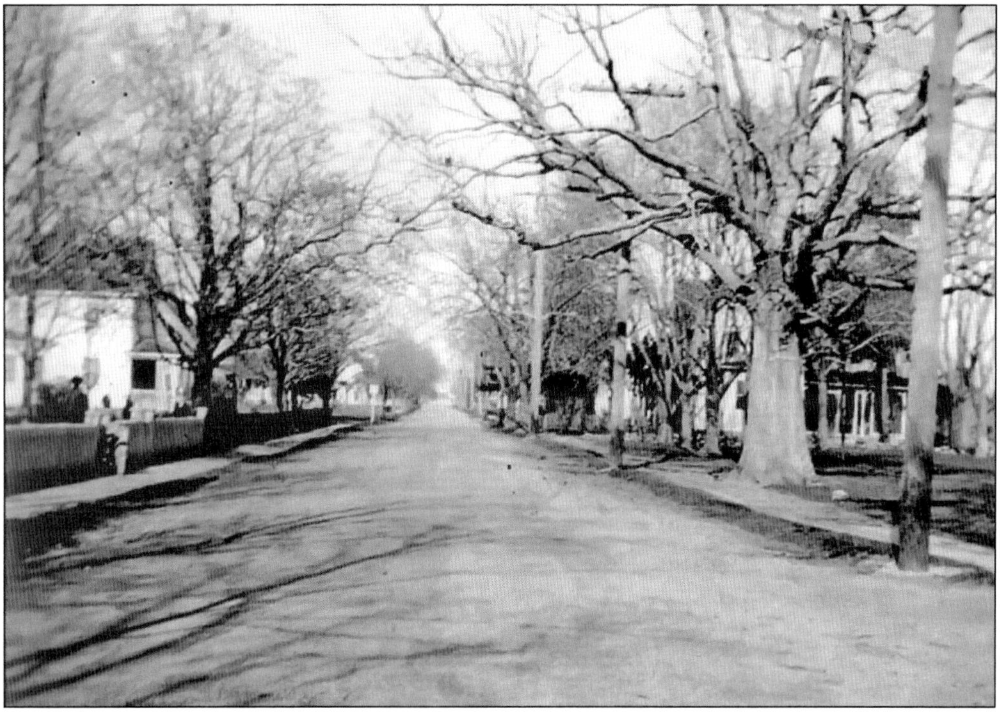

The 1900s photograph shows a more bucolic Dennisville. Today, the road through town is paved and drivers are prone to speed, much to the annoyance of locals who live in many of the same homes pictured. The gnarled-branched tree in the right foreground still stands on the property of the Old School House Museum today.

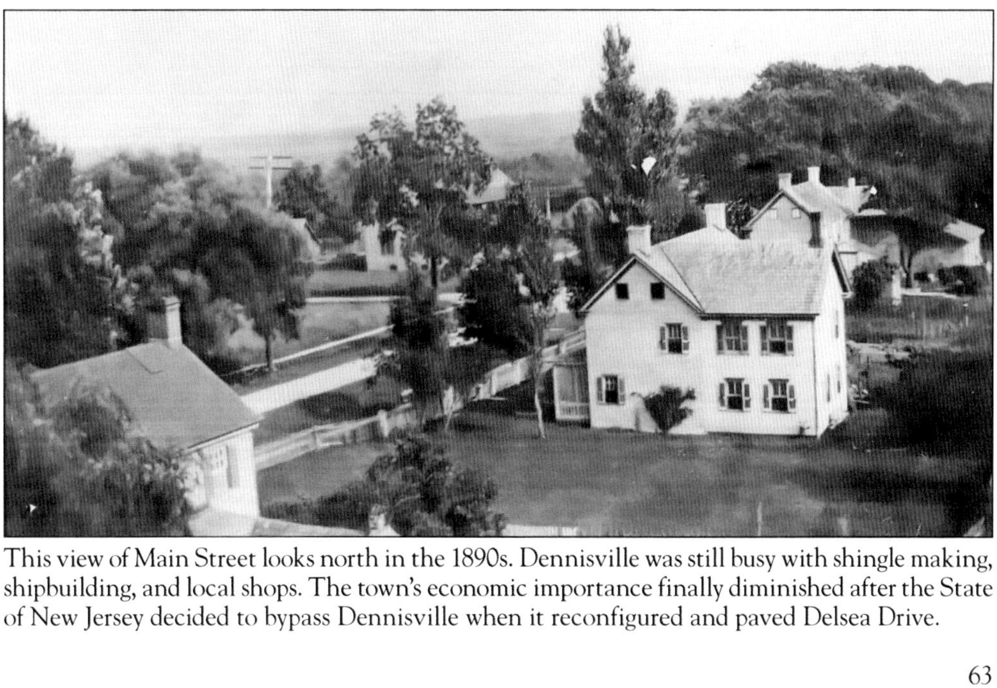

This view of Main Street looks north in the 1890s. Dennisville was still busy with shingle making, shipbuilding, and local shops. The town's economic importance finally diminished after the State of New Jersey decided to bypass Dennisville when it reconfigured and paved Delsea Drive.

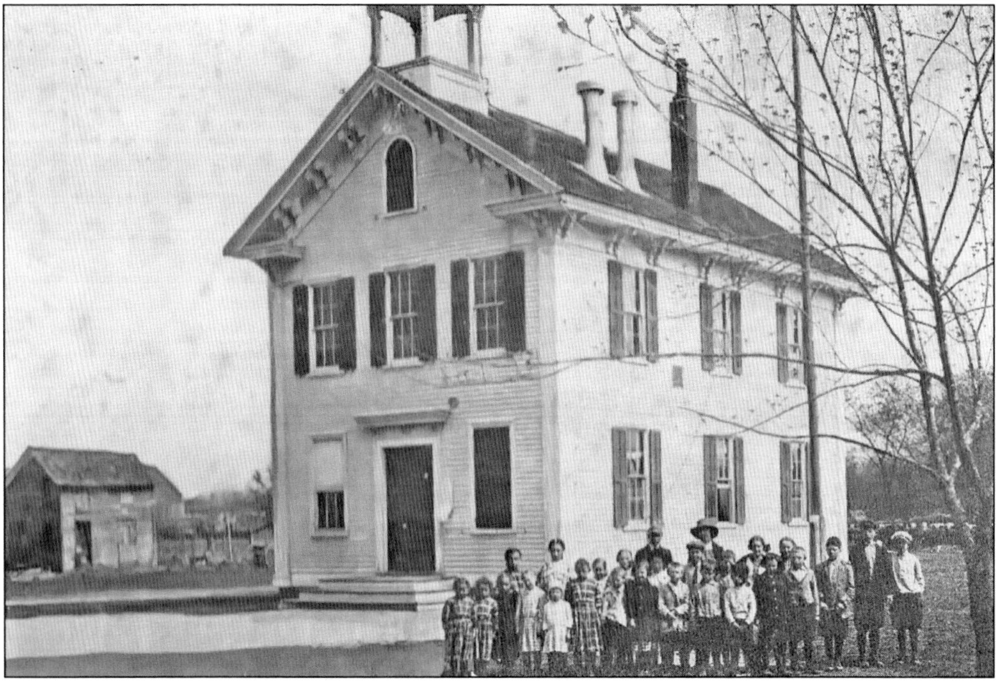

The one-acre site for Dennisville School was purchased from Charles Ludlam in 1872. The two-story schoolhouse opened in 1874. Lower grades were taught on the first floor, while higher grades moved upstairs. The school served the children of Dennisville for 74 years until a chimney fire in 1948.

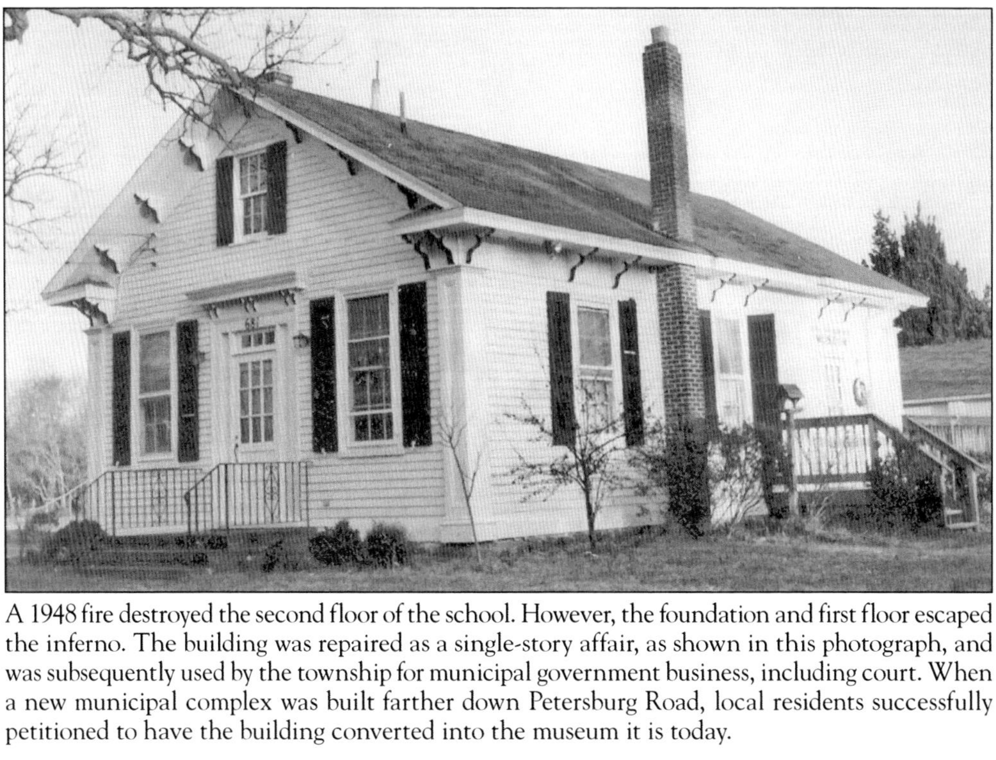

A 1948 fire destroyed the second floor of the school. However, the foundation and first floor escaped the inferno. The building was repaired as a single-story affair, as shown in this photograph, and was subsequently used by the township for municipal government business, including court. When a new municipal complex was built farther down Petersburg Road, local residents successfully petitioned to have the building converted into the museum it is today.

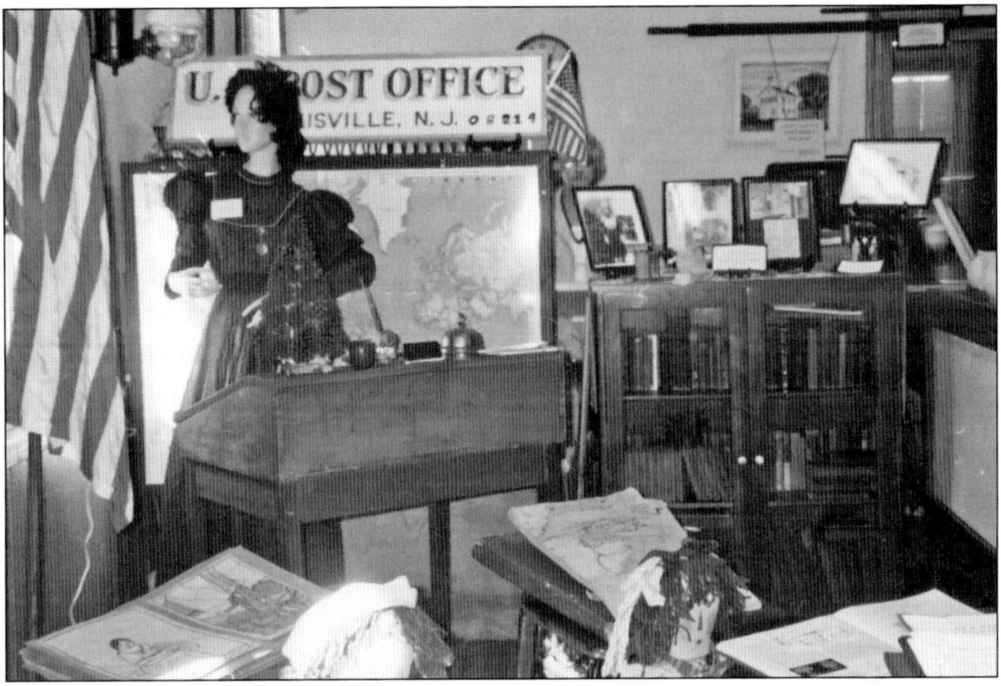

The "teacher" poses while waiting for students to occupy their desks in this museum display. Volunteers periodically rearrange the displays at the museum to emphasize a particular aspect of the township's varied history and, through it all, the teacher oversees their efforts. Many of the desks and the blackboard were salvaged from the old school.

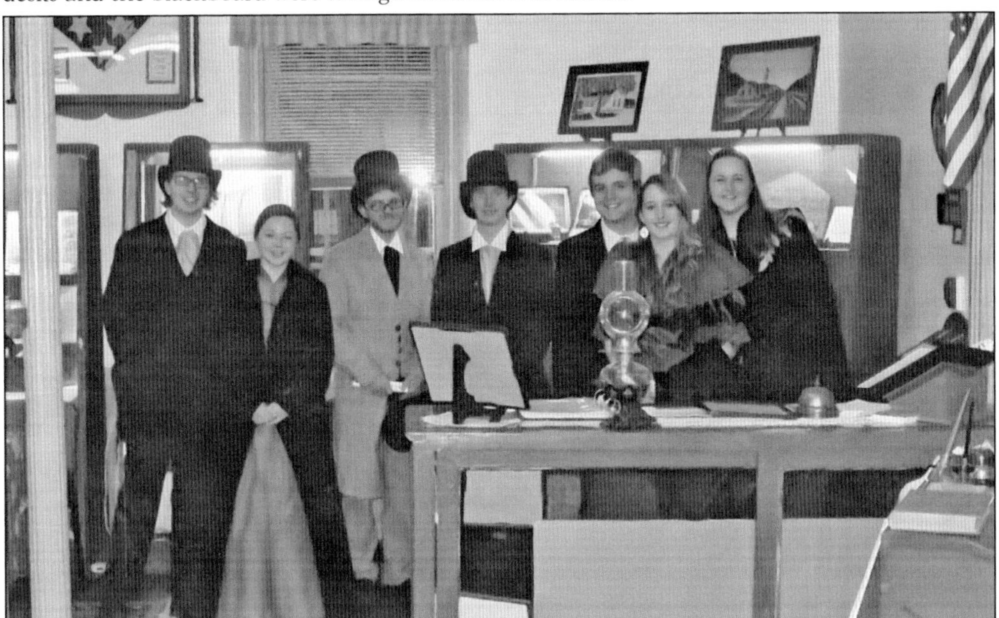

Middle Township High School carolers ring in the Christmas season during a Dennisville Historic Homeowners Association annual house tour, a hugely successful event that showcases the hamlet's many historically significant old homes and brings hundreds of visitors to the usually quiet streets of Dennisville.

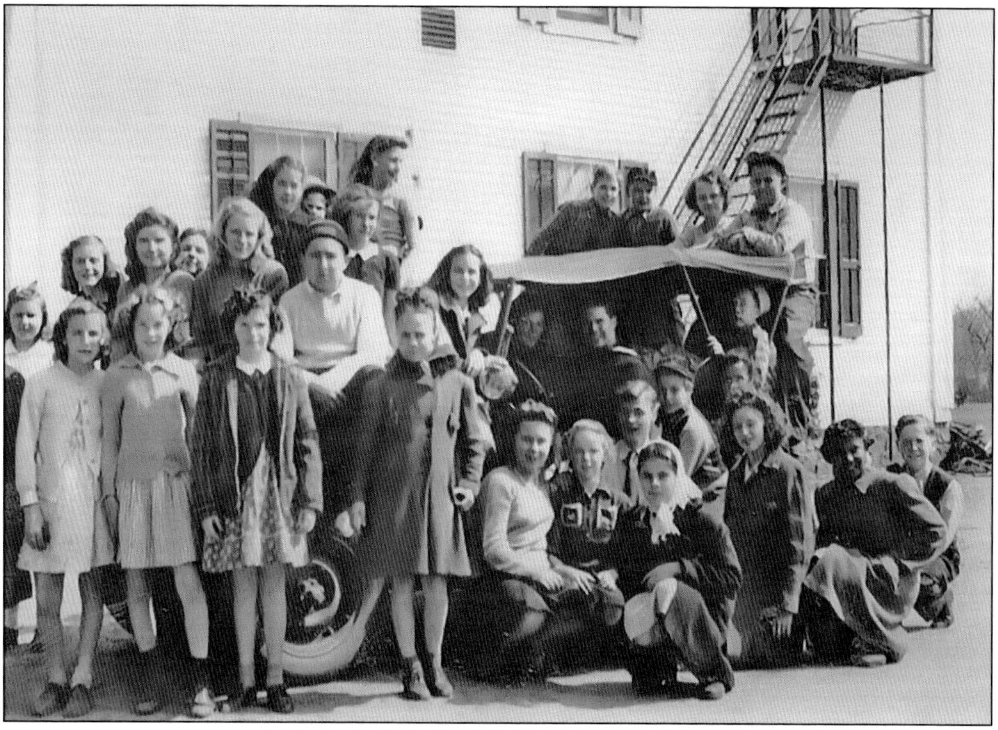

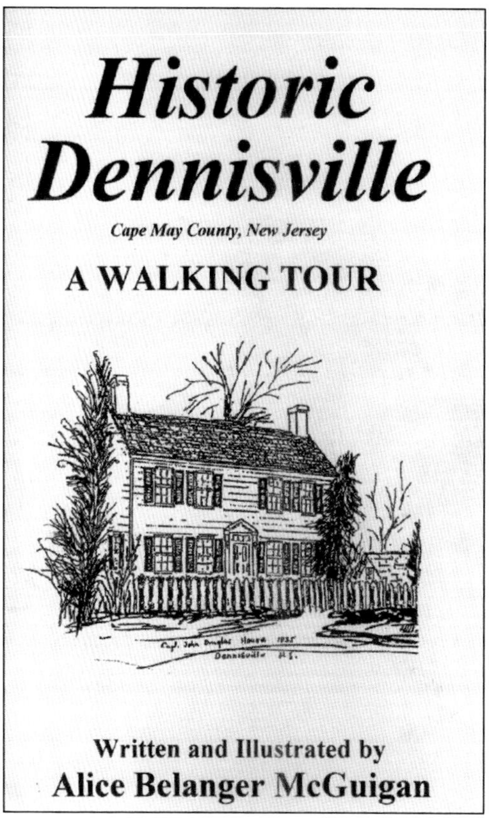

Students from Dennisville School pose with a jeep purchased for the World War II effort with savings stamps they accumulated during 1942. Note the fire escape leading up to the second story of the schoolhouse, which was destroyed in the 1948 fire.

Shown here is the cover of Alice McGuigan's illustrated book about the historic houses of Dennisville. McGuigan wrote and illustrated the book, which she has signed for many years at annual Dennisville Historic Homeowner's Christmas House Tours. As of publication, she is in her 90s and lives in her historic home on Main Street.

Volunteer history buffs apply last-minute touches in the Old School House Museum prior to engaging with the crowd at Old Dennisville Day, a community celebration of food, music, and crafts, all centered around nostalgia for the "good old days" along Dennis Creek.

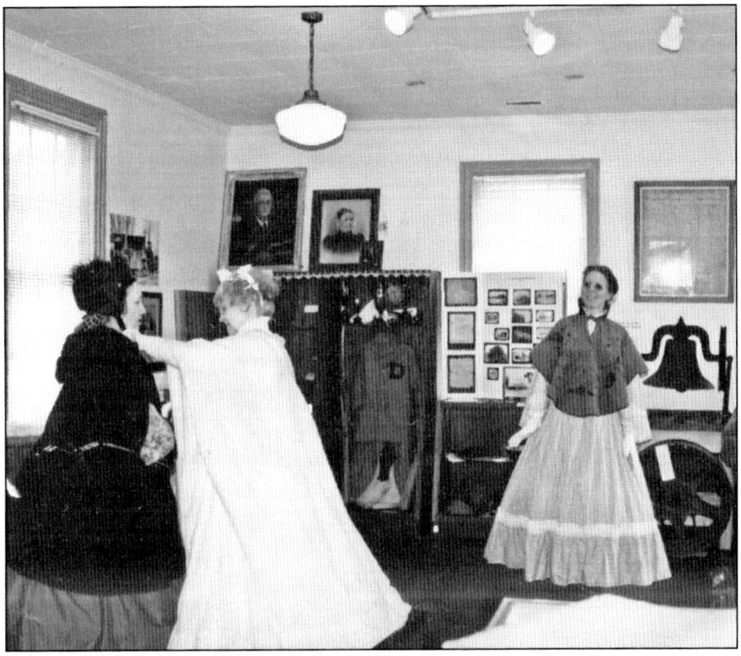

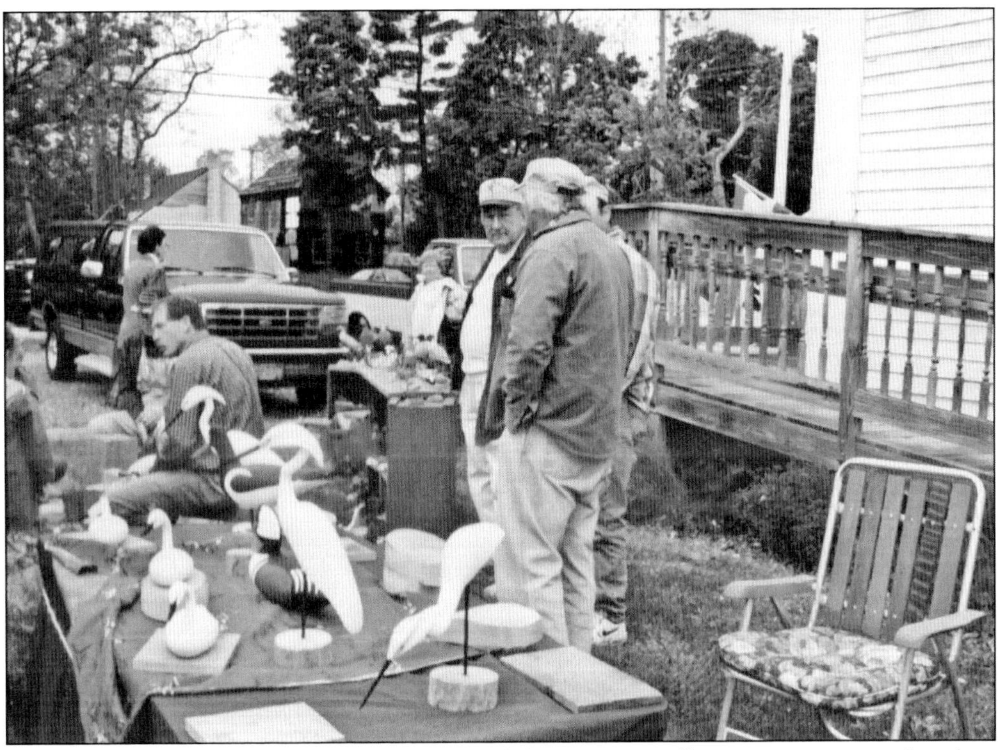

Woodcarvers swap stories outside the museum while waiting to talk to anyone interested in their craft. Bird carving is an art form that is held in high regard in Dennis Township, the home to, or at least frequently visited by, some of the best in the world, such as Harry Shourds, Anthony Hillman, and Jim Siebert. At one time, the local museum boasted an extensive collection of duck carvings.

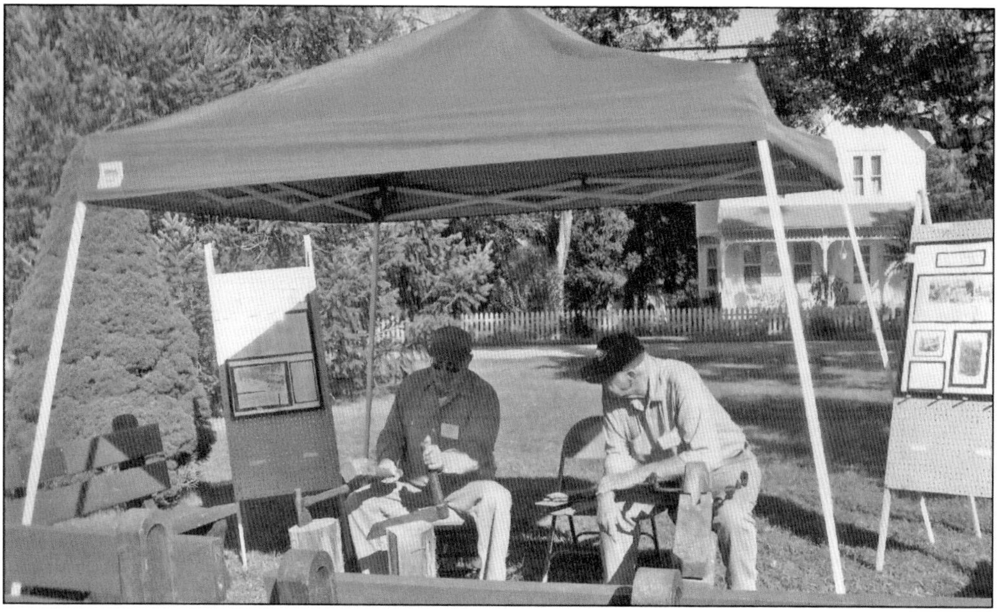

Pete Babbitt (right) and George Brewer demonstrate the art of shingle making during a Dennisville Days community event. A major 19th-century industry in the area, shingles are made from locally plentiful white cedar, using tools seldom mentioned these days with names such as froe, jointer, and schnitzelbank, which is a four-legged workbench on which shingles are shaped. The latter is pictured and is on display at Old School House Museum.

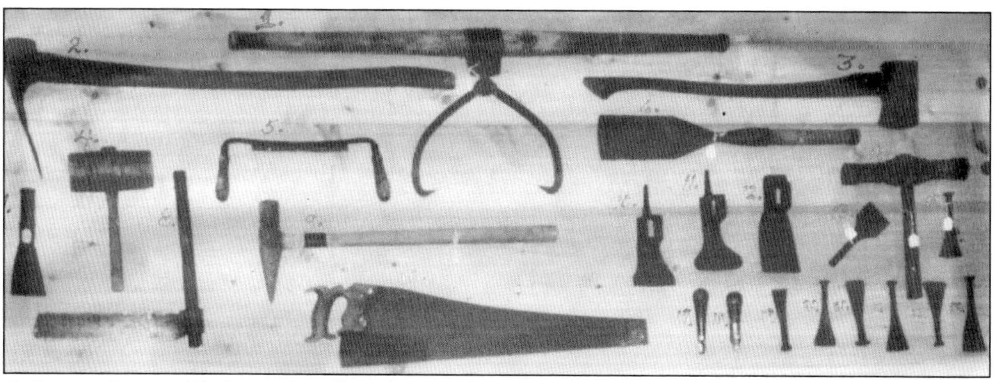

A fast worker could shave 600 shingles per day. A typical price per thousand was $16. As the supply of cedar diminished, enterprising locals developed the unique science of shingle mining. Logs buried for centuries in nearby swamps were resurrected and salvaged using tools such as the progue (an eight-foot pole used to probe swamp bottoms for candidate logs). Experienced miners could tell by the smell of a log if it was worth salvaging. There is a display of all the tools used in shingle mining and making at the Old School House Museum.

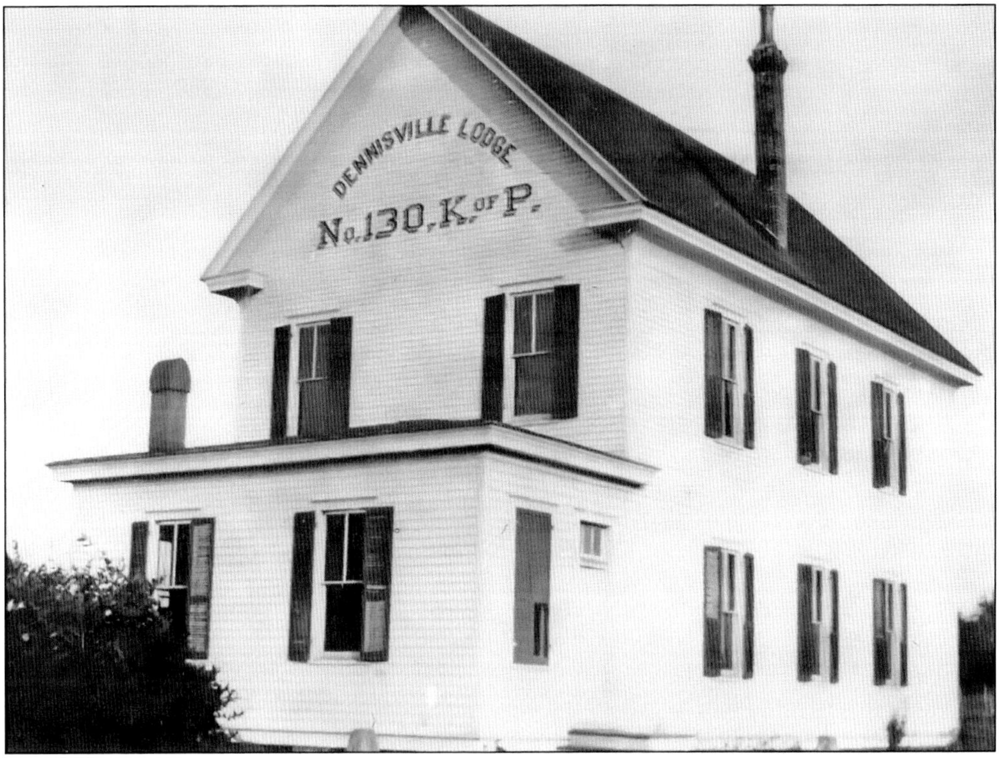

This photograph shows the Dennisville Knights of Pythias Lodge. The hall served temporarily as a local school after the 1948 schoolhouse fire. It was also a meeting place for the Red Cross during World War II. The building still stands and is a private residence today.

This office and drugstore of Dr. Maurice Bixby (1804–1882) was built in 1873. Dr. Bixby served the community for 53 years. He was also Cape May County's first county school superintendent. In addition, he served in the New Jersey Legislature and was a historian, authoring the book *Sketch of Early History of Cape May County*, published in 1857.

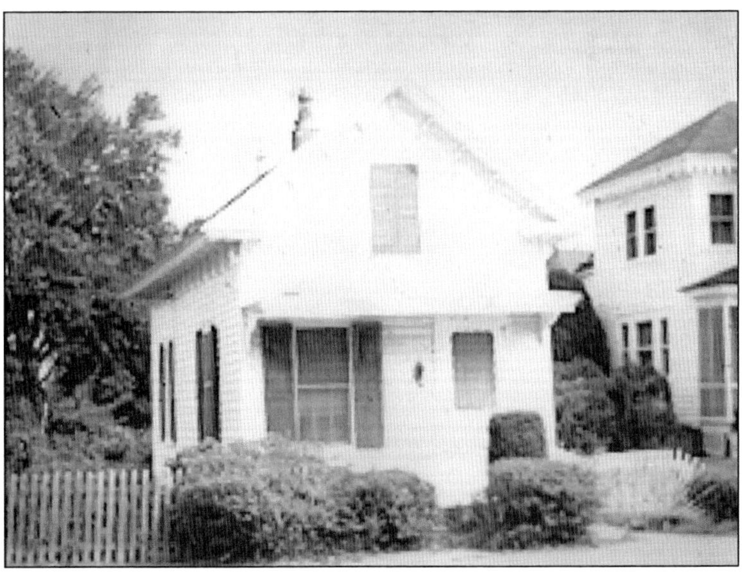

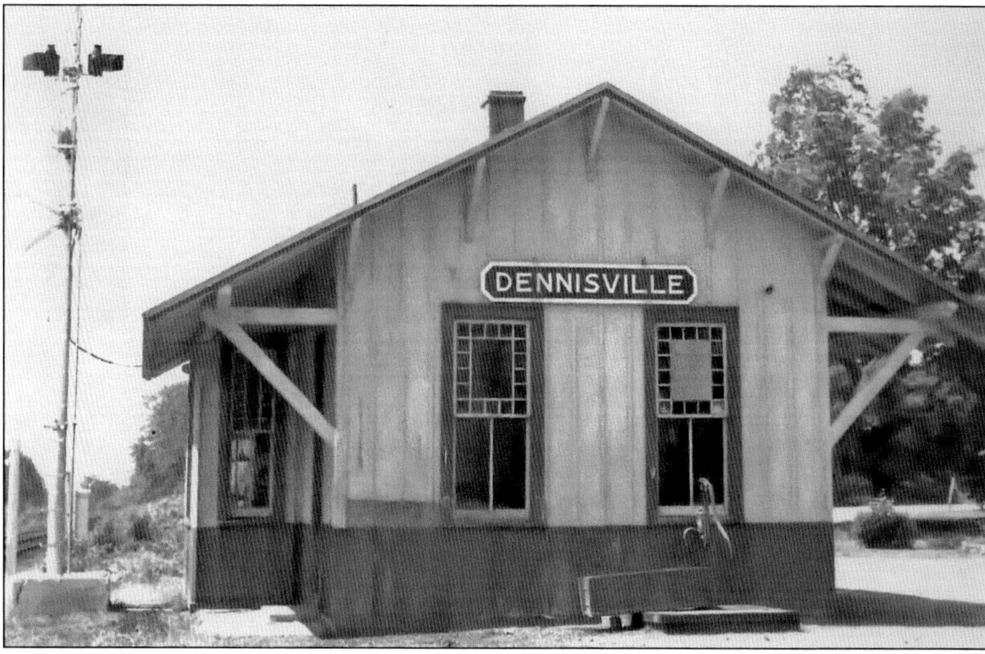

Dennisville Train Station was located at the edge of town. The station is gone, but the tracks are still there and cross Petersburg Road before leading south toward Dennis Creek. Because of its central location in Cape May County and importance as a commercial center, Dennisville certainly rated its own station in the 19th century. The town was so essential to the area that it was once considered for the county seat. An 1848 referendum pitted it against Cape May Court House. With all eligible males voting, Dennisville lost by 48 votes.

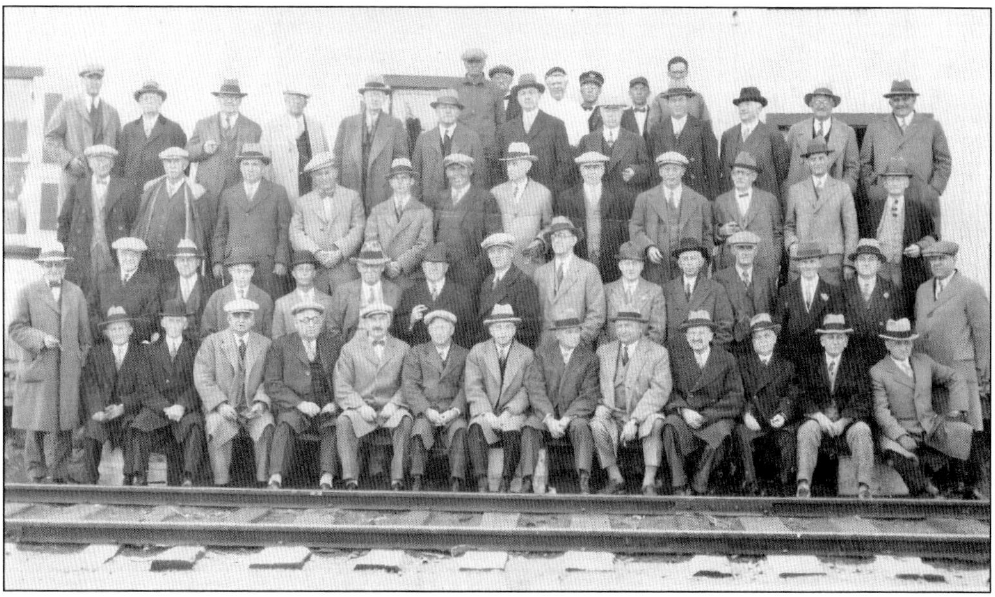

Capt. Sam Westcott of the New Jersey State Guard boat (pictured in the center background) was one of 91 sea captains to call Dennis Township home and one of three Captain Westcotts to hail from Dennisville. The guard boat worked daily to protect nearby Delaware Bay's flourishing oyster industry.

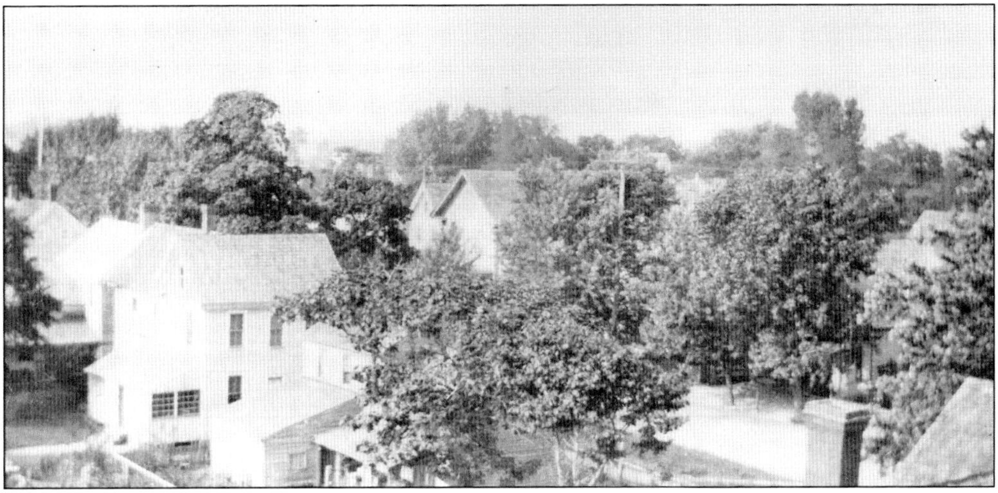

This view of Dennisville was taken near the center of town. In the 19th century, Dennisville was a major marketplace for the area. Farmers traveled into town to shop after delivering their goods to the docks at Dennis Creek. Main Street, today a residential area, was home to a number of shops and inns.

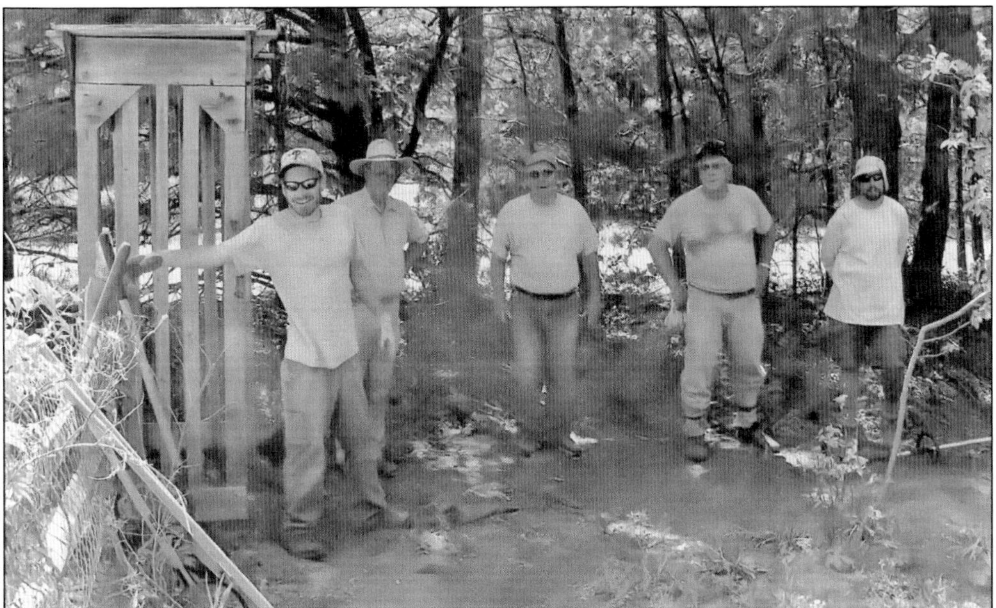

Members of Dennis Township Environmental Commission pause during a work session at the township's "natural garden" in Dennisville. Shown from left to right are Chris Castor, Bob Penrose (commission chairman), Gerry McManus, Frank Hoff, and Brad Rosenthal. The garden includes varieties of native plant species and is designed to attract birds and butterflies, which migrate through the Jersey Cape. Members chose a hot day during the summer to dig a pond for the garden.

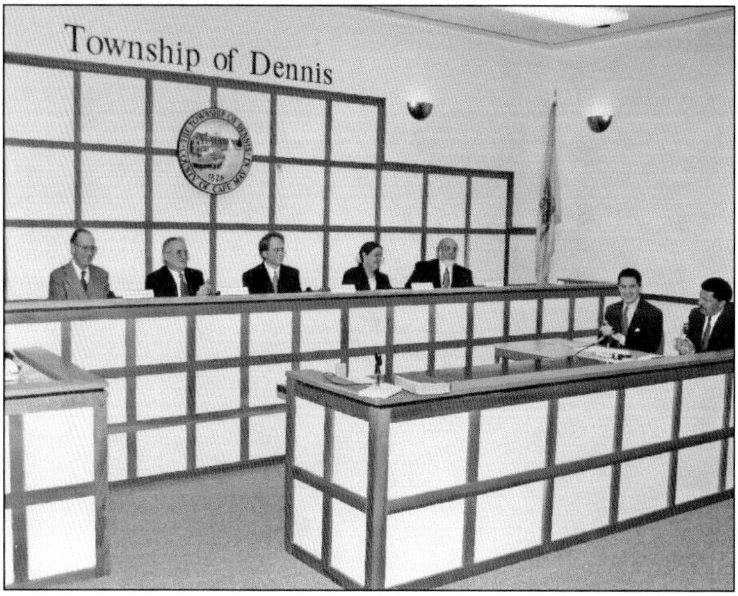

The Dennis Township Committee meets at the municipal building in Dennisville in the 1990s. The five individuals seated across the top of the dais are the township committee. They are, from left to right, Howard Halsey, Robert Blessing, then-mayor Jefferson Van Drew (currently a New Jersey state senator), and cousins Georgeanne and James Pettit, both from Belleplain.

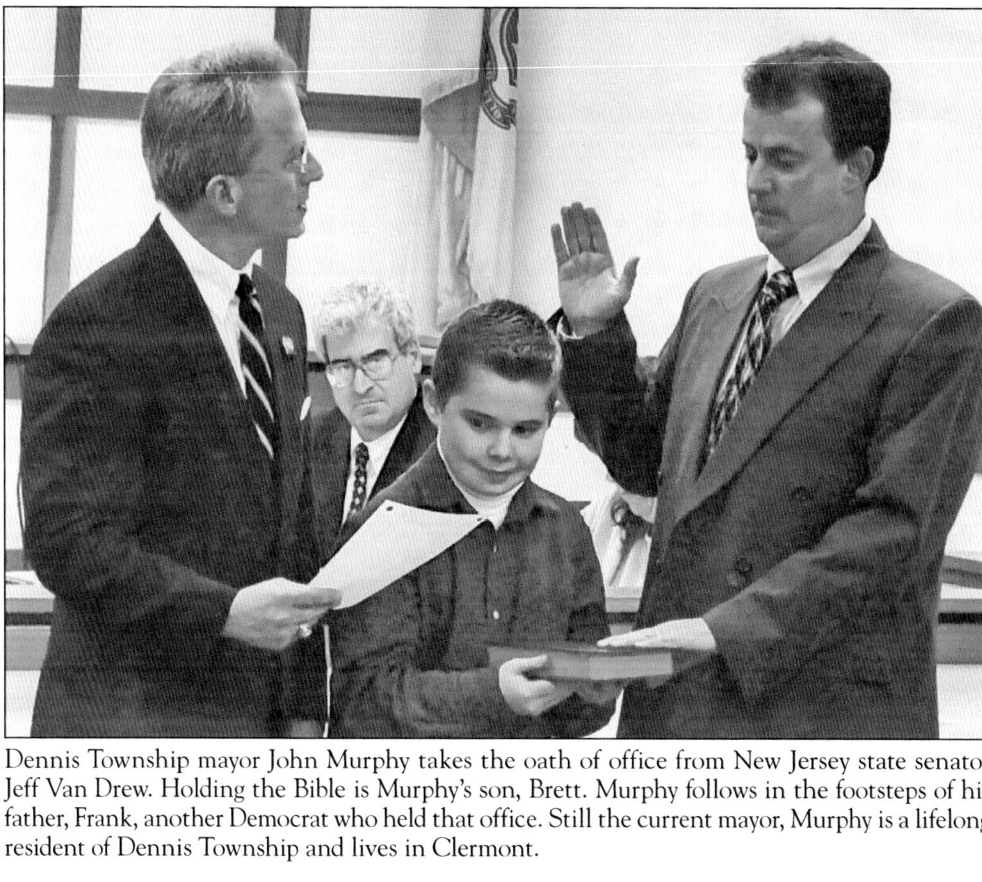

Dennis Township mayor John Murphy takes the oath of office from New Jersey state senator Jeff Van Drew. Holding the Bible is Murphy's son, Brett. Murphy follows in the footsteps of his father, Frank, another Democrat who held that office. Still the current mayor, Murphy is a lifelong resident of Dennis Township and lives in Clermont.

Five

Musical Interlude
Crossing Dennis Creek, Memories of School Days

According to *A History of Education in Dennis Township, 1664–1964* by William Garrison Hunter, free public education was a luxury communities could not afford in Colonial times. There was more work for uneducated people than educated ones in rural places like Dennis Township. The wealthy provided tutors or other private education for their children. Education was a family responsibility, and while youngsters were often taught how to read and write, it was more important for them to begin learning a trade.

In the late 18th century, thinking began to change, and in Dennis Township, local residents recognized the value of investing, perhaps modestly, in public education.

In 1793, thirty-one residents paid five shillings for land on the north side of what is now Schoolhouse Lane in South Dennis to be used as site of a school "for as long as time shall last." That did not happen, but it was a start for public education in Dennis.

In 1801, residents on the north side of the creek bought an acre for a $1 to build another schoolhouse. This group of community activists proved more prescient. That building, which housed the Ludlam School, operated for over 150 years.

Eventually, each village in the township supported its own one- or two-room schoolhouse where local boys and girls would matriculate faithfully—until they were needed to work on the family farm.

Notions about public education changed, especially as the numbers of family farms in the township diminished and new industries, requiring new skills, became more important in the lives of local residents. Student populations grew, as did the costs associated with providing a basic education. The first Dennis Township Board of Education was created by election in 1894 to address the growing complexity of education.

Those one-room schoolhouses proved inadequate to provide a growing student population with the basic skills they would need to function in a changing world. In 1952, the school board built the Academy Road School. It consisted of classrooms, clinic, a teacher's room, a principal's office, storage, and lavatories. Five years later, eight classrooms and a kitchen were added. All township schools were closed, and the children of Dennis Township attended school under one roof.

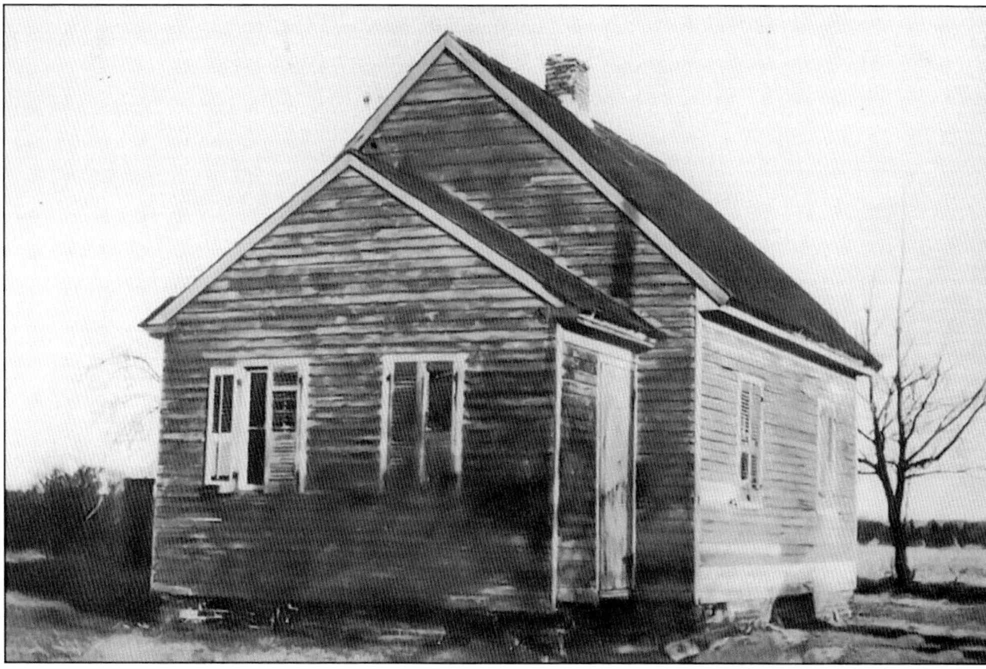

Belleplain School operated from 1884 to 1957. It was a two-room school, housing kindergarten and grades one through eight. A sliding door partitioned the classrooms, which opened into one large room that was used for various social and official functions, such as club meetings or weddings. Belleplain School was the last in the township to hold all eight grades under one roof.

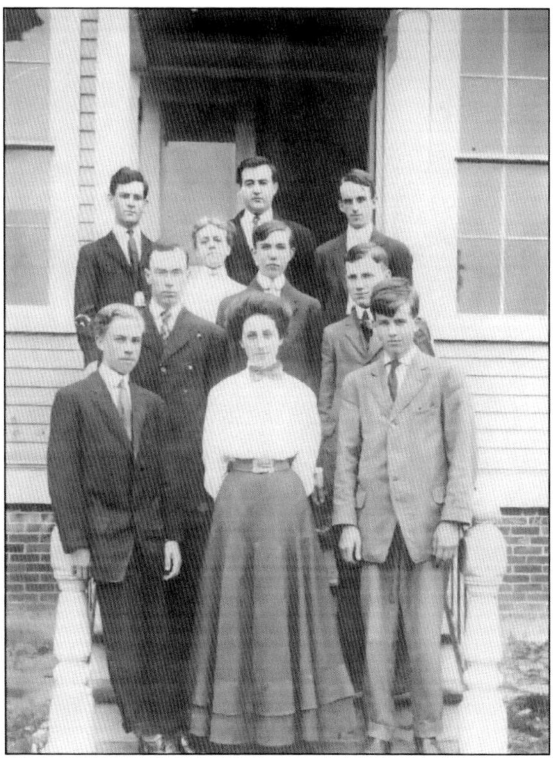

This 1909 photograph shows members of the first graduating class at Middle Township High School. Identified are six scholars from Dennis Township. They are, from left to right, (first row) Ralph Townsend, Nettie Anne Harris, and Jesse Diverty Ludlam; (second row) William S. Thompson and Howard Shaw Morton; (third row) Thomas Leaming.

Belleplain students visit Washington, DC, in 1950. Grades five through eight visited the Capitol, US Treasury, Washington Monument, Lincoln Memorial, and Arlington National Cemetery. Coauthor Tom Champion's mother, Elena, organized the visit. Later, as a school board member, Tom helped organize similar group trips to destinations like Orlando, Florida.

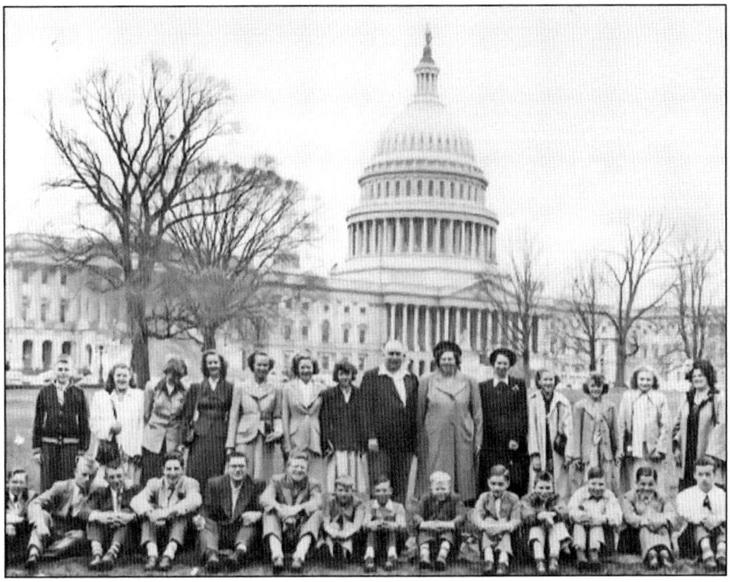

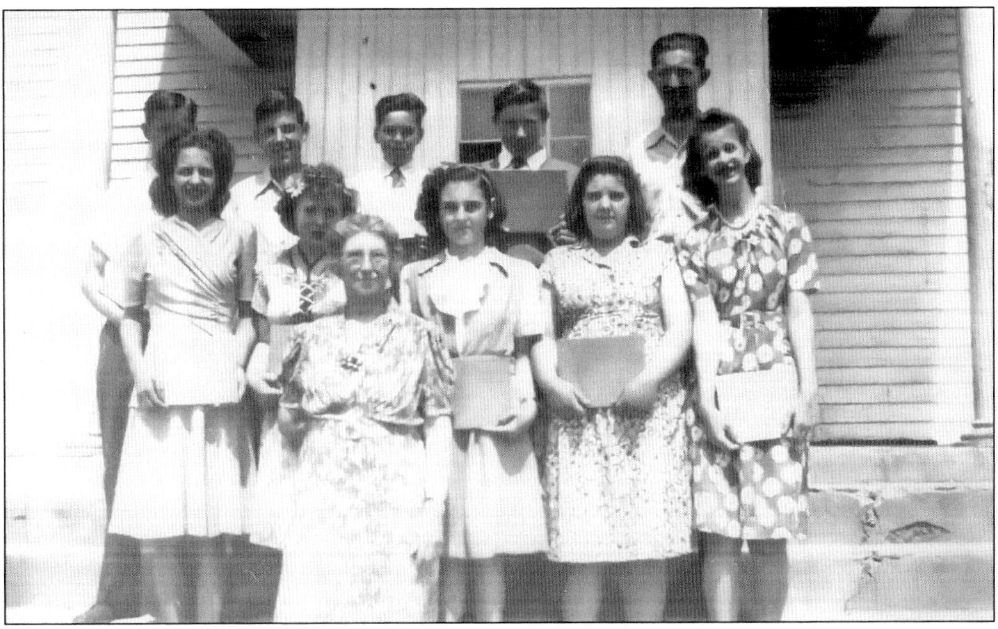

Belleplain School teacher Belle Miller, from South Dennis, poses with her eighth-grade class in this 1940s photograph. Coauthor Tom Champion stands in the rear, second from the left. Belleplain was the last community school in the township to hold classes for all eight grades. After the school closed in 1957, the building served as a warehouse for the R.B. Mason Basket Factory.

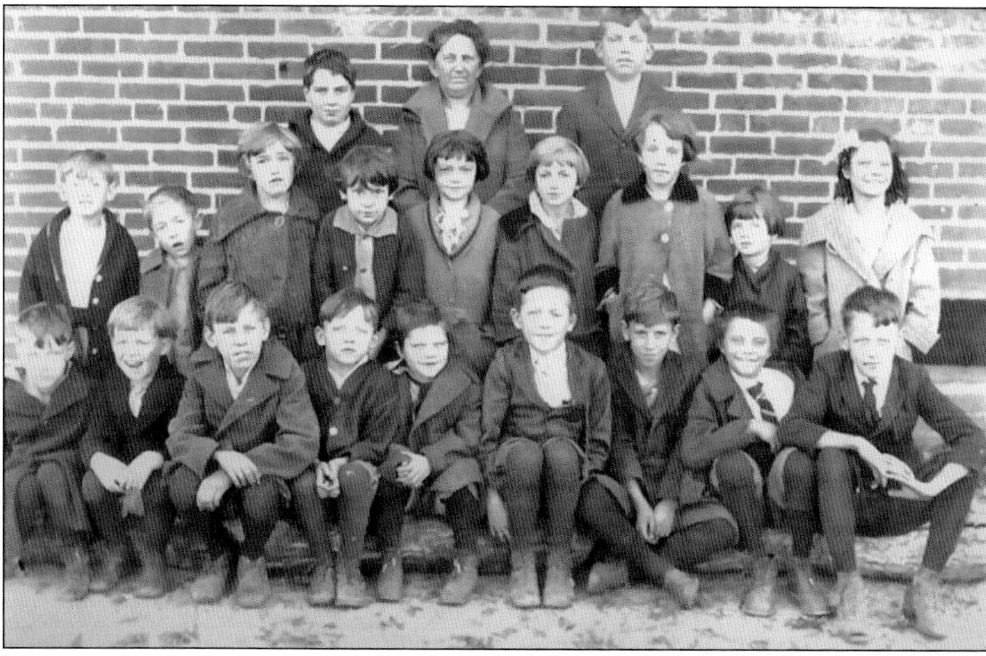

This is a 1925 photograph of the Eldora School student body posing with teacher Cora Chambers (center, rear). The school opened in 1913 and operated for 44 years. It was often referred to as the "Brick School."

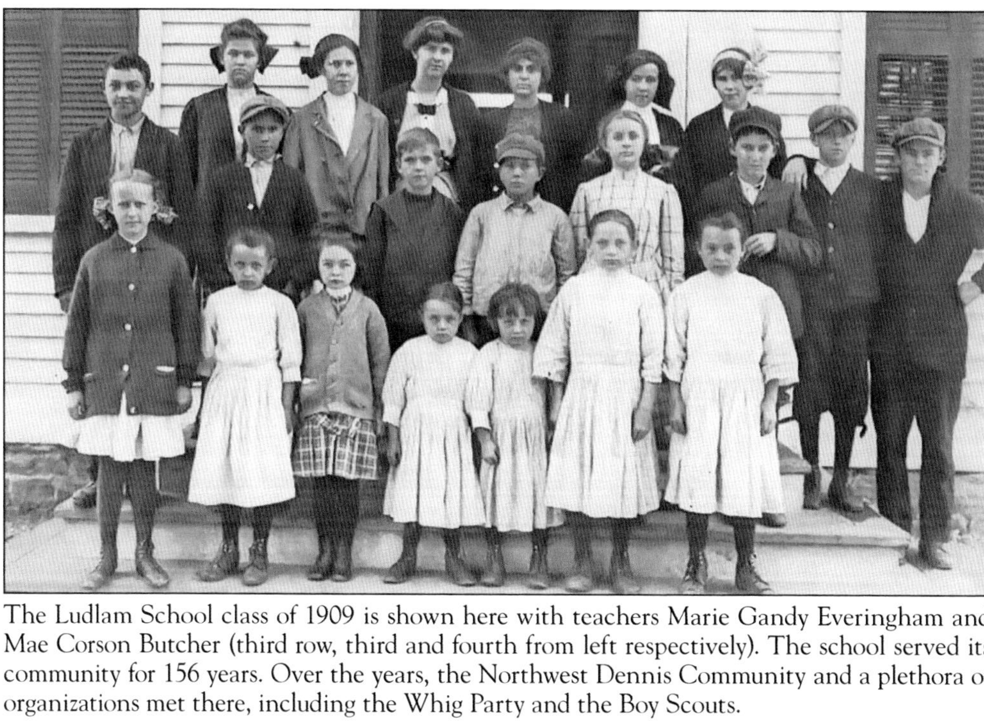

The Ludlam School class of 1909 is shown here with teachers Marie Gandy Everingham and Mae Corson Butcher (third row, third and fourth from left respectively). The school served its community for 156 years. Over the years, the Northwest Dennis Community and a plethora of organizations met there, including the Whig Party and the Boy Scouts.

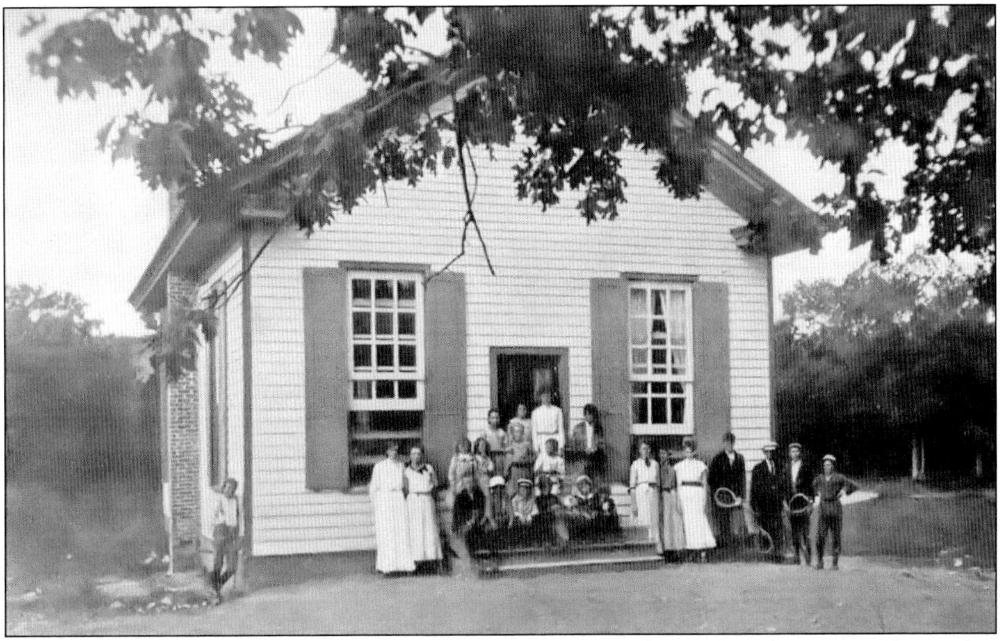

This is postcard photograph of the Atlantic School in 1903. The card sender writes, "Remember the good times we had." This school, located in Ocean View, operated from 1872 to 1915. The building was sold and relocated to the north shore of Magnolia Lake, where it was converted into a dwelling.

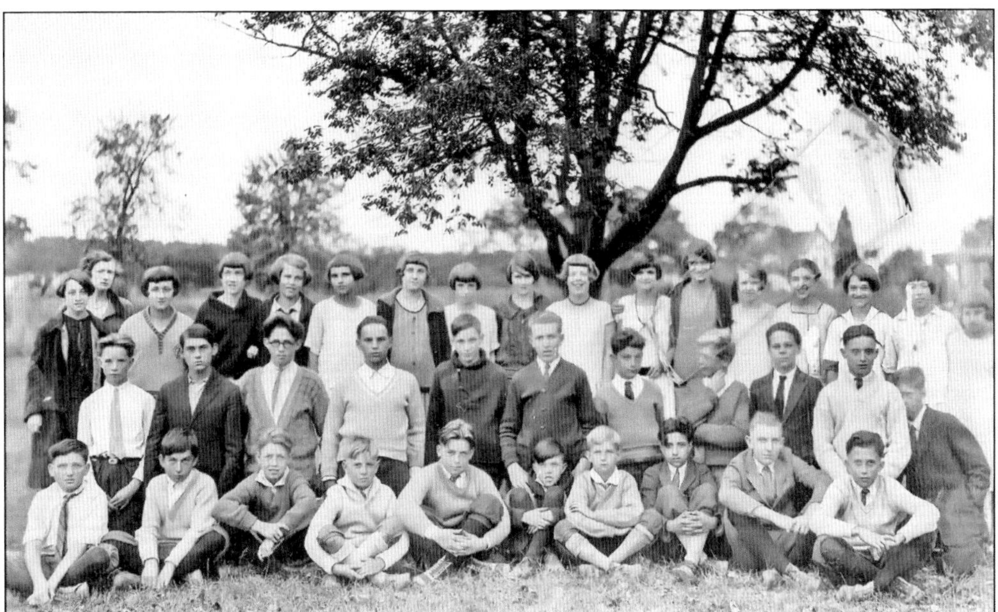

Students from the Blanton School pose in this 1925 photograph. The school was located on Kings Highway, south of the junction with the Dennisville Road. It served the South Seaville area for 59 years. In later years, it was converted into apartments.

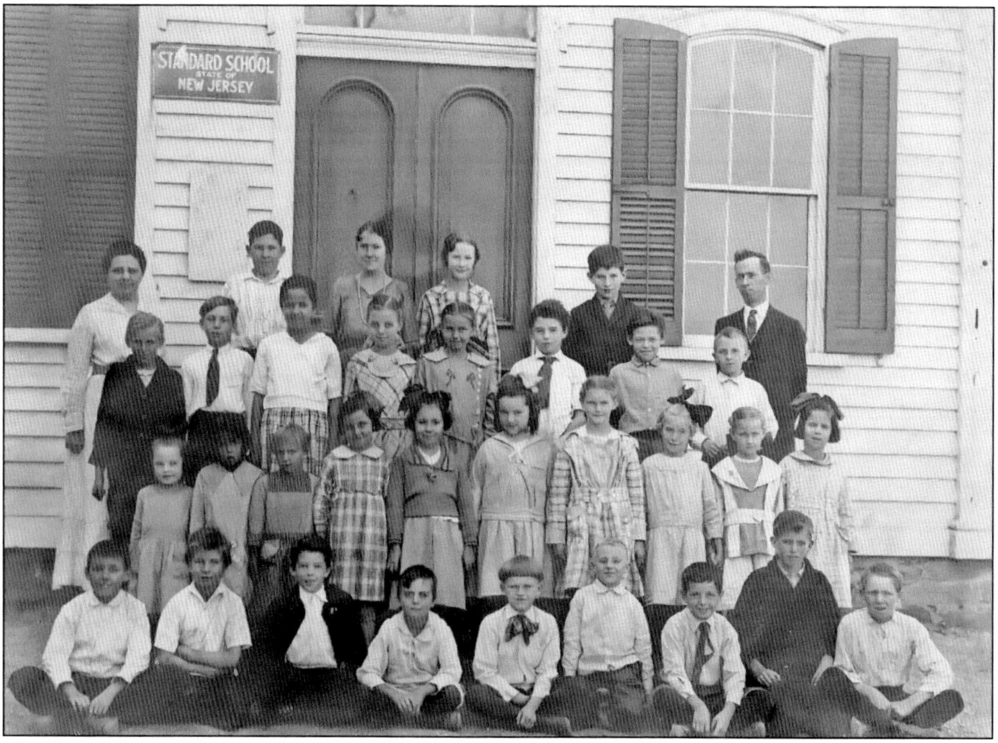

The South Dennisville School class of 1920 poses with principal Charles Meerwald. Built on land acquired from Christopher Ludlam for $10, this two-story school served South Dennis from 1839 to 1957. The building was subsequently converted into a private dwelling that was destroyed by fire in 1959.

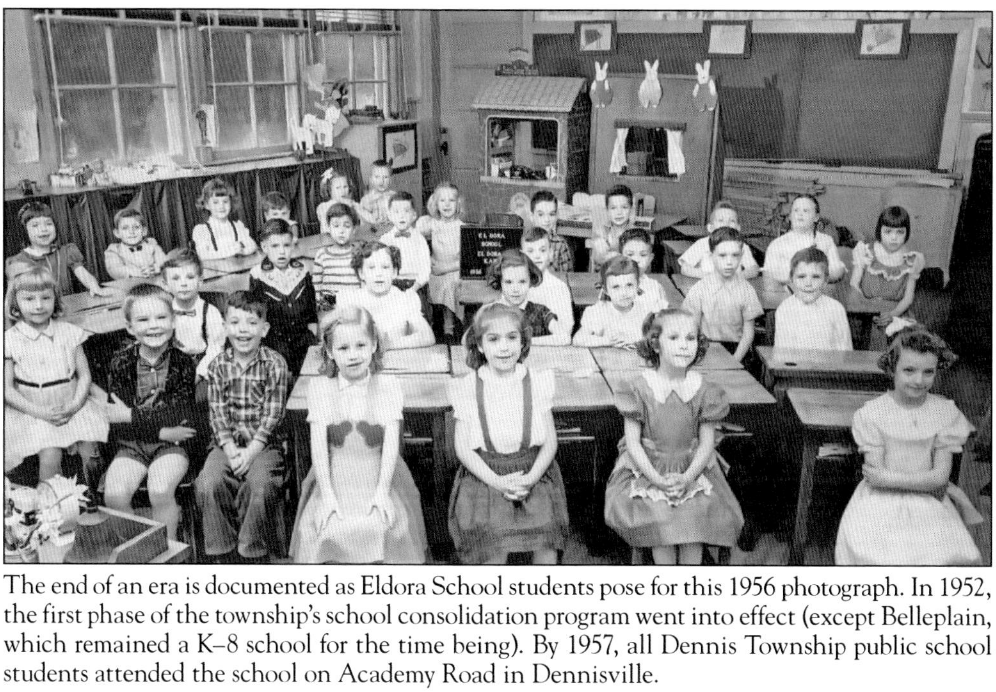

The end of an era is documented as Eldora School students pose for this 1956 photograph. In 1952, the first phase of the township's school consolidation program went into effect (except Belleplain, which remained a K–8 school for the time being). By 1957, all Dennis Township public school students attended the school on Academy Road in Dennisville.

Six

South Dennis Shipbuilding Center

The area was called Dennis Creek until 1873, when South Dennis was named. Before that, it was variously called Dennis Landing or Fostertown.

A deed was found that may be the earliest evidence of the name for Dennis Township. It covers a "transfer" of land from an Indian, Panktoe, to John Dennis in 1687. But that is the only mention of either of them; they recede from the pages of local history as abruptly as they appeared.

Names typically associated with early years of Dennisville are Ludlam, Spicer, and Leaming. In 1720, Jacob Spicer sold land to Joseph Ludlam, whose sons settled in 1726, with Anthony Ludlam to the north of the creek and Joseph Ludlam to the south. Other settlers followed, and development of the area commenced.

David Johnson built a sawmill, from which he transported lumber to Thomas Leaming's shipyard. Dennis Creek was centrally located, and a stagecoach stop was situated there. Ships plying the nearby Delaware Bay regularly sailed up the creek, bringing provisions and goods from other parts before carrying away local farm and wood products.

Industries flourished, including lumbering, shingle making, and shipbuilding, and all of which depended on the abundant convenient cedar and hardwood forests that were cut down to make masts, fence posts, and shingles. In 1850, over 600,000 shingles were sold at $13 to $15 per thousand. In the early 1800s, 25,000 shingles were shipped to Philadelphia to reroof Independence Hall.

A motorist driving along Delsea Drive today could easily miss Dennis Creek after he bypasses Dennisville to his left. At low tide, the creek looks hardly capable of serving as a launching pad for the sizable ships that were once built there. Between 1850 and 1900, more than 50 ships were constructed and launched at Dennis Creek. A list of the ships' names is displayed at the local museum. The shipbuilders were typically named Leaming, Gandy, Diverty, or Wentzell.

Shipbuilding on the creek faded toward the end of the 19th century. Locals unsuccessfully lobbied Congress to dredge the silting creek. Some blamed the railroads and freight-hauling competition for the dramatic change, while others cited the condition of the creek. Whatever the reason, the shipbuilding era came to an end.

Today, at low tide, Dennis Creek is a mudflat with a few idle boats and little activity but plenty of memories.

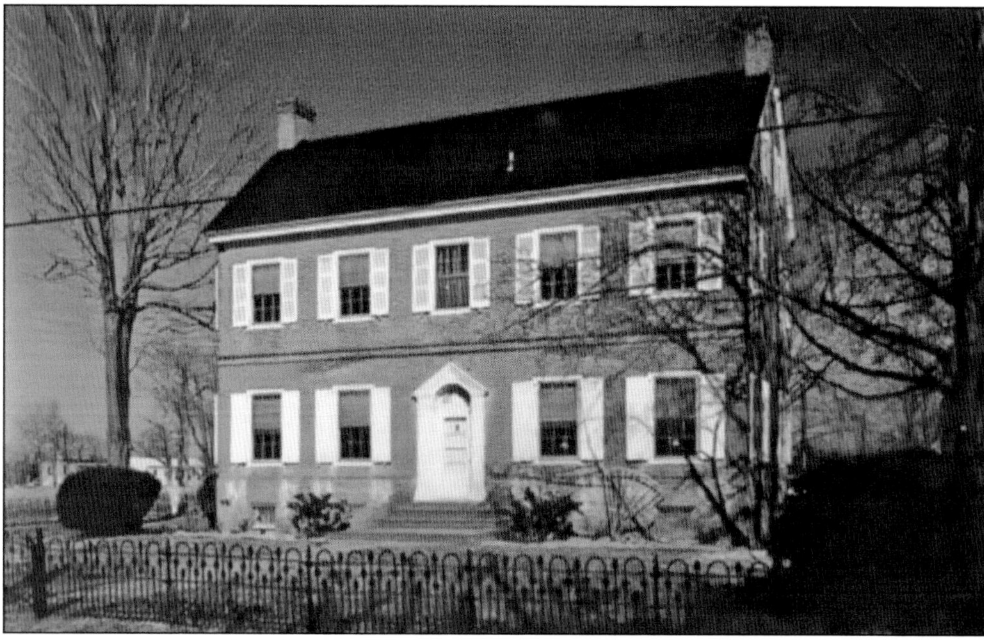

The Association for Retarded Citizens purchased the Falkinburg House in 1989 to house its administrative offices. Today, the property covers eight acres, including the two-story Federal house built in 1806, a frame barn, and other sheds. The property is also home to a number of oak trees that have been listed among the most "significant" in the county due to size and age.

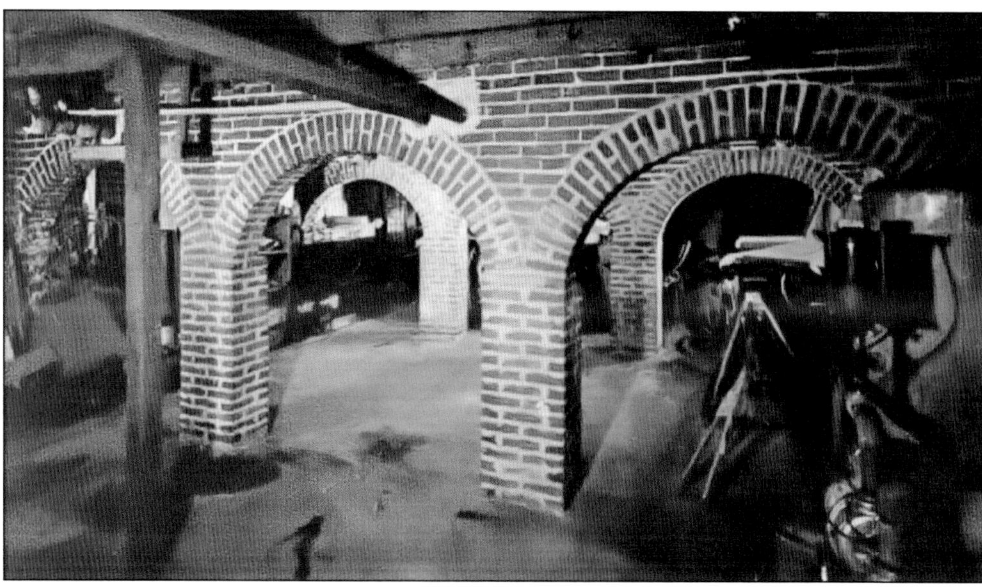

Joseph Falkinburg, builder of one of the few brick houses in the area, appeared in Cape May County in 1791. The basement of the house shown in this photograph is one of the few houses to have a basement and most likely the only one to have brick arches. One story has it that Falkinburg built his house with bricks brought here as ballast on a British ship. He married into the wealthy Ludlam family, served in the New Jersey Assembly, and was the richest man in the county when he died in 1846.

Richard S. Leaming, grandson of Joseph Falkinburg, became one of the prominent shipbuilders on Dennis Creek in the latter half of the 19th century. His largest schooner, the *Thomas F. Pollard*, was built in 1890. It was almost 160 feet long and engaged in hauling ice from Maine and coal to Philadelphia. In this photograph, the young Leaming enjoys a bike ride, but close at hand is a hint of his future calling.

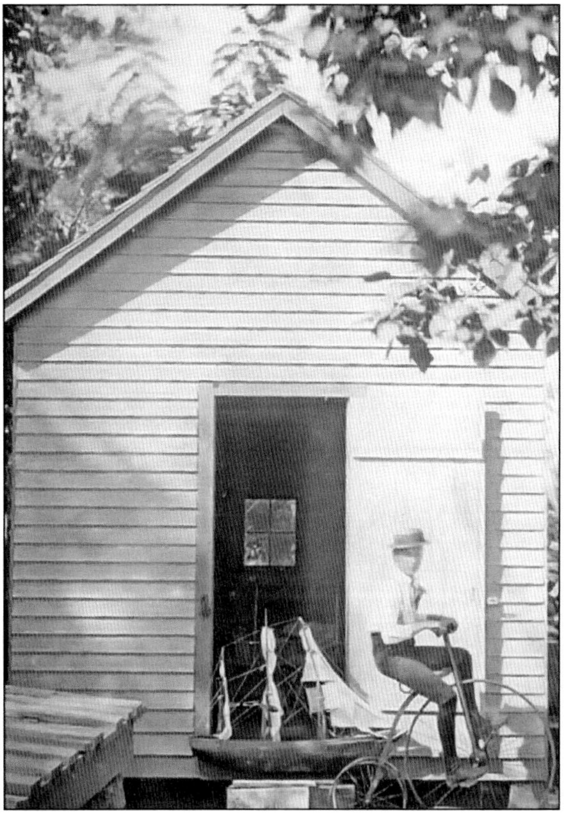

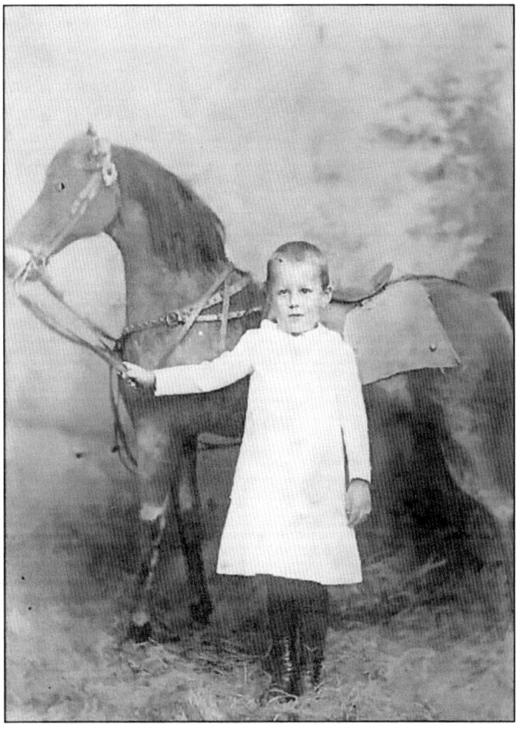

This photograph is a childhood portrait of Richard's brother Lewis Cresse Leaming, the future doctor. The Leaming family has deep roots in Cape May County, having arrived at Town Bank on Delaware Bay in 1670. A descendant of this family, Jeremiah Leaming, married Abigail Falkinburg, Joseph Falkinburg's daughter—thus the connection with the stately brick mansion.

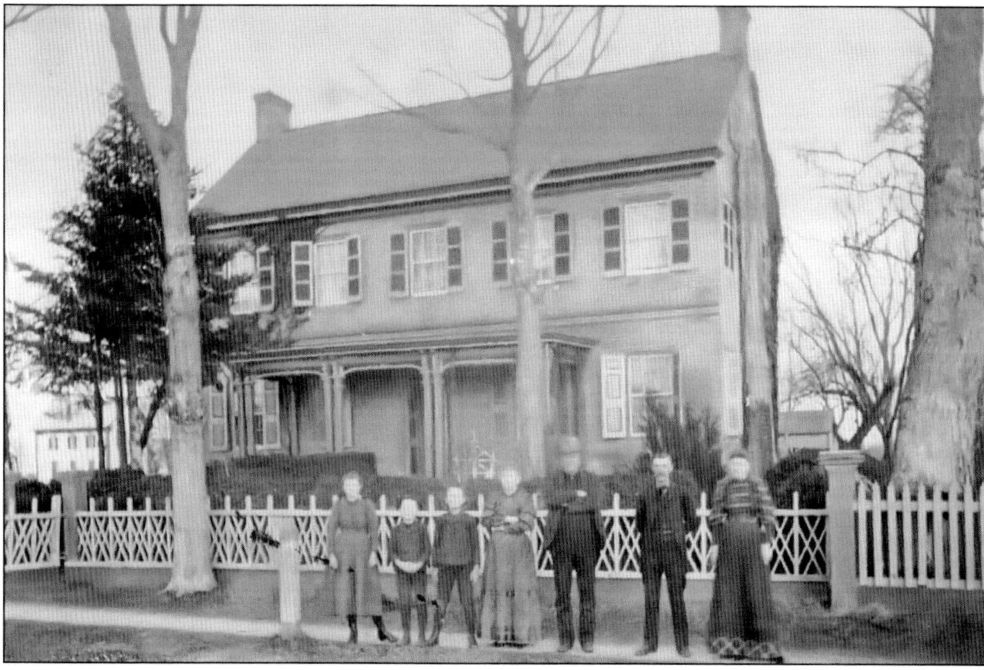

The Leaming family poses in front of their home. Lewis Cresse Leaming and Richard Smith Leaming are second and third from the left respectively. Young Richard (1828–1995) grew up to become not only a prominent shipbuilder and businessman on the landing, but to also serve as county freeholder and state senator.

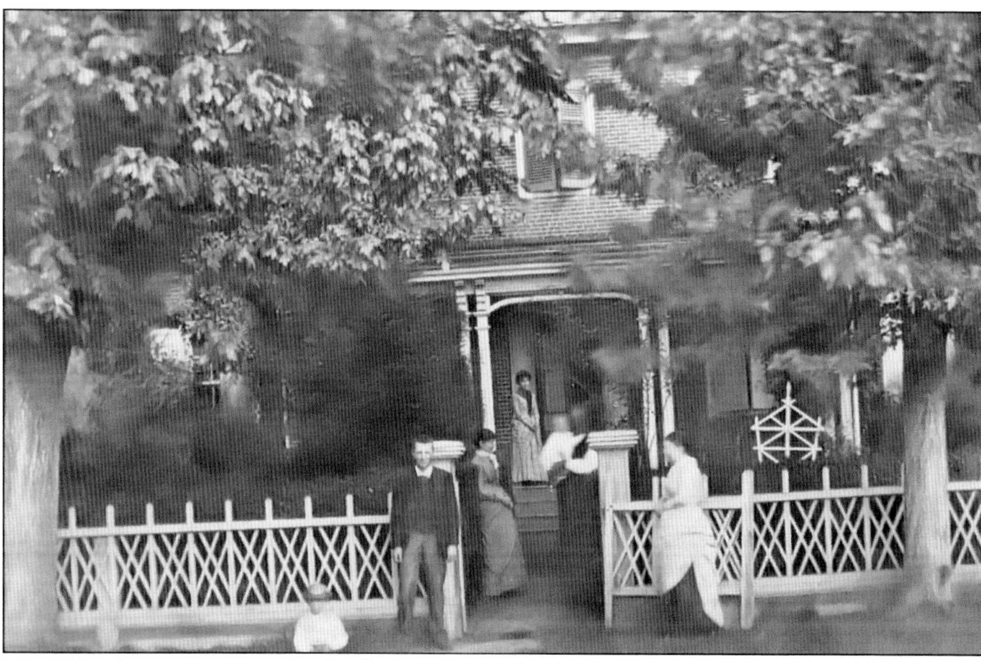

The Falkinburg House was the birthplace of Lewis Cresse Leaming Sr. Other Leaming children included Georgia Leaming (Wells), the youngest of three children. Her brothers Coleman Fisher Leaming and Rev. Lewis Cresse Leaming preceded her.

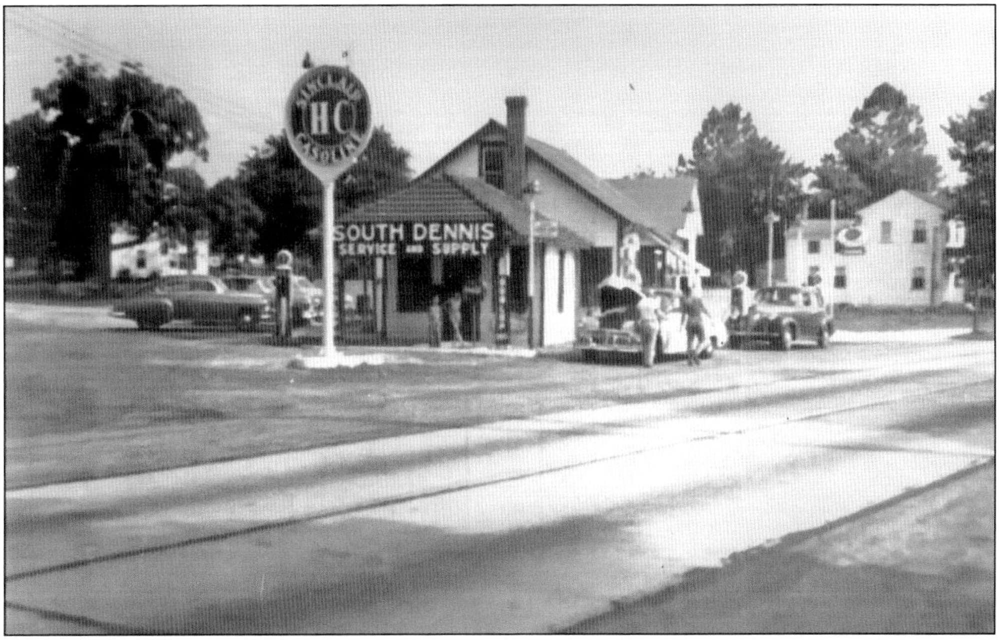

The photograph shows Otis McKaig's service station on Route 47, current site of the South Dennis Post Office. The McKaig family also owned one of the last large fields in Clermont. The Dennis Township Board of Education acquired the property and built a preschool-to-third-grade school on Hagen Road.

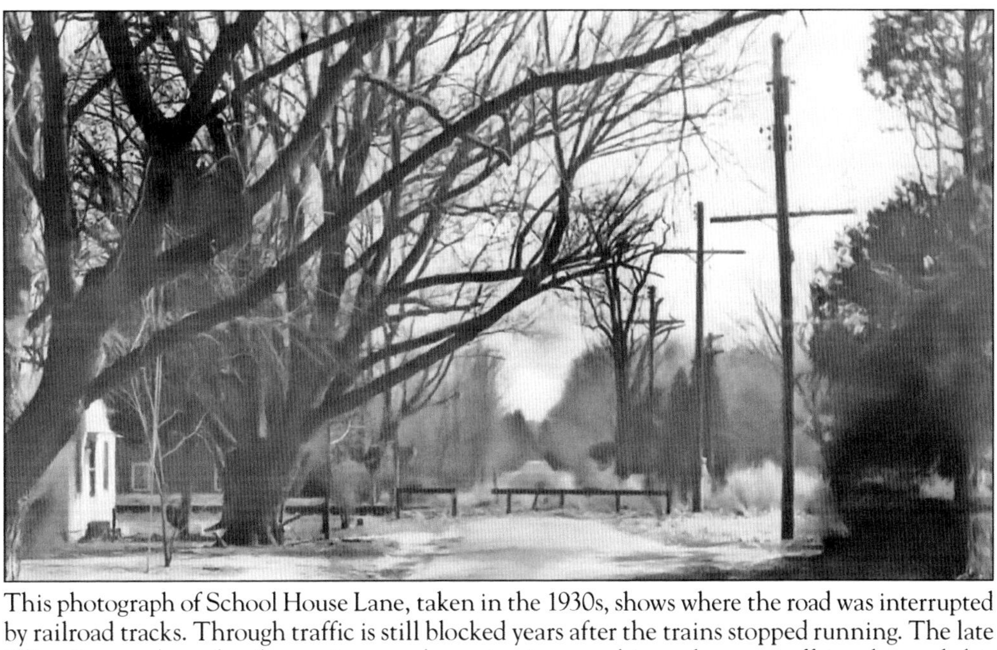

This photograph of School House Lane, taken in the 1930s, shows where the road was interrupted by railroad tracks. Through traffic is still blocked years after the trains stopped running. The late Olive Barry, whose family continues to be active in township and county affairs, donated this image to the Old School House Museum.

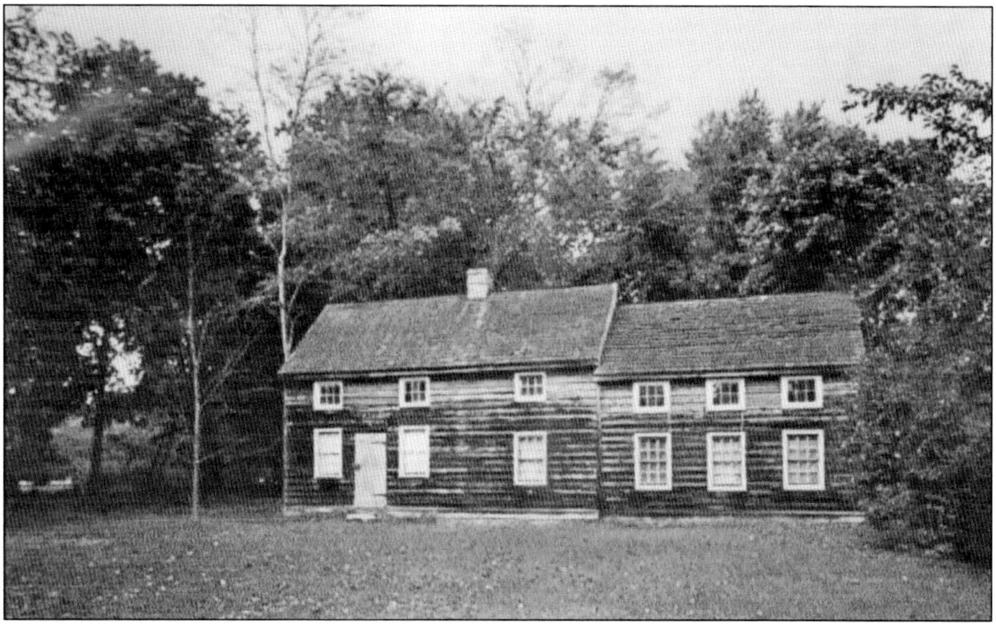

This is a photograph of the Thomas Ludlam House, taken in springtime from Route 47. Thomas's great-grandfather was Joseph Ludlam. The original house had been moved twice and several additions have been made, but it has been restored by its current owners, architectural historian Joan Berkey and her husband, Scott Smith. Both are skilled artisans whose work on the house earned them an award from the New Jersey Historic Preservation Office in 2010

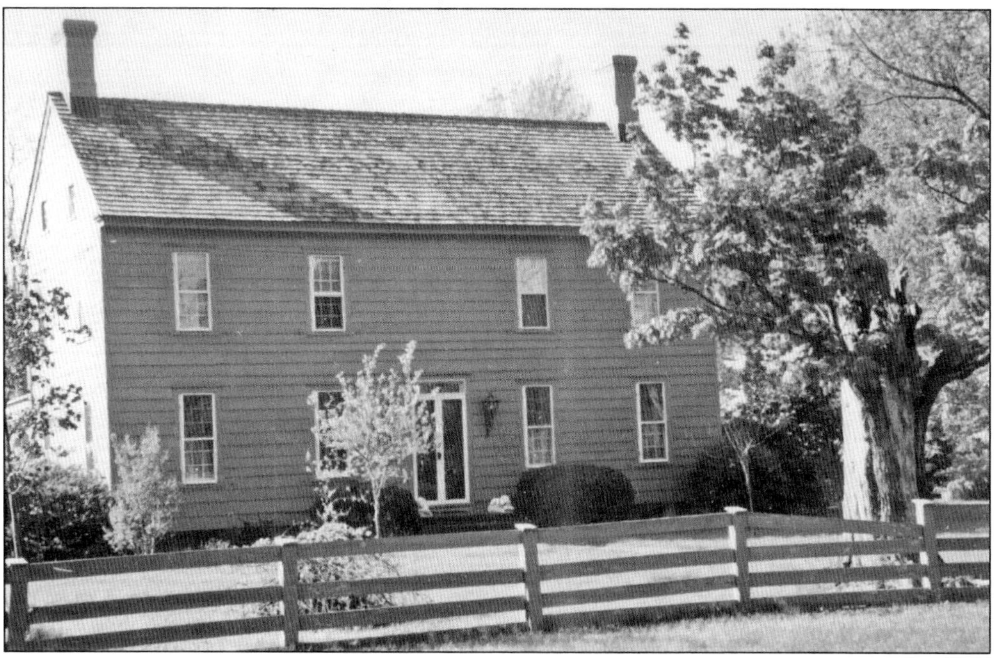

The Christopher Ludlam House was built on the original 500 acres purchased by Joseph Ludlam (1670–1761). Ludlam's two sons founded the original settlements on either side of the creek that eventually became South Dennis and Dennisville. Great-grandson Christopher Ludlam owned the house until he died in 1805. The house remained in the family until 1909.

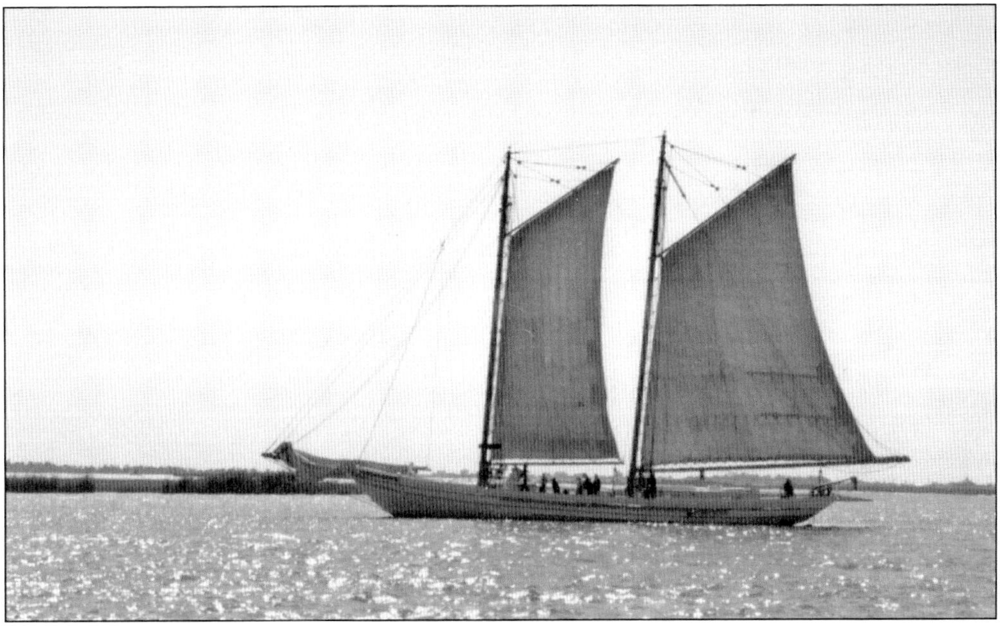

The restored A.J. *Meerwald* still sails area waters, these days as an interactive museum. Although not built at Dennis Creek, the solid oak vessel was commissioned by the Meerwald family of South Dennis to work as an oyster dredge. These days, the *Meerwald* is a New Jersey official tall ship and is listed in the National Register of Historic Places.

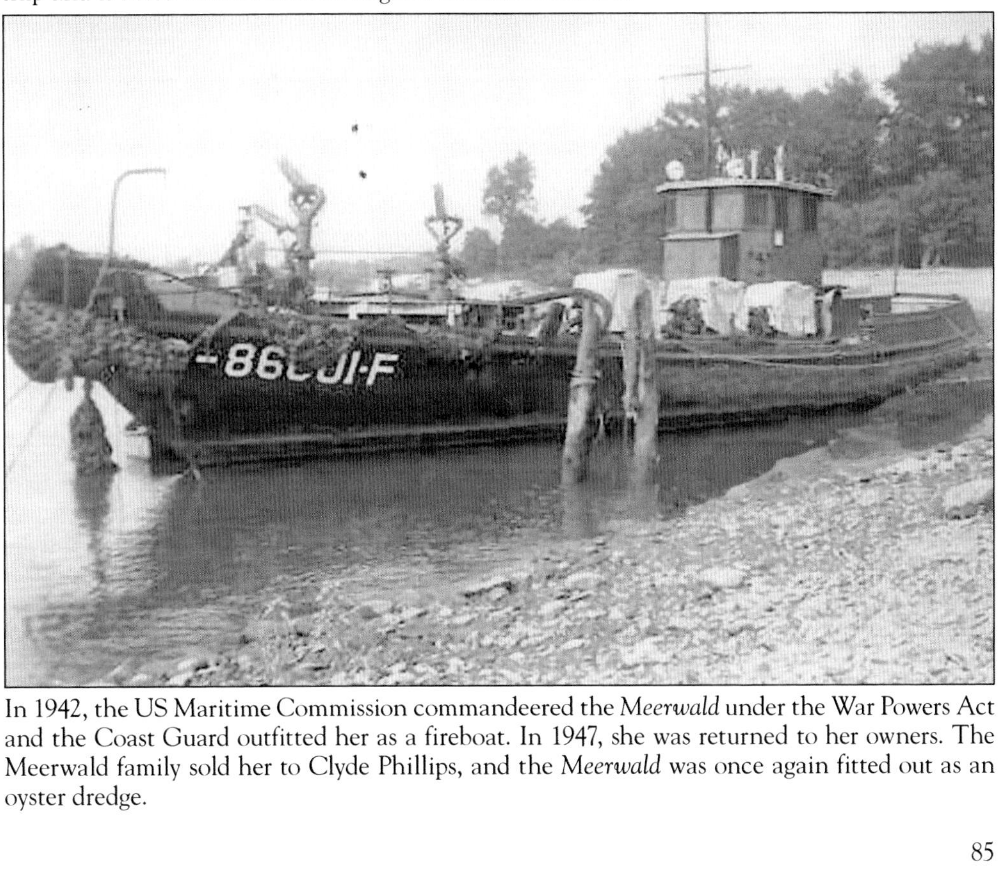

In 1942, the US Maritime Commission commandeered the *Meerwald* under the War Powers Act and the Coast Guard outfitted her as a fireboat. In 1947, she was returned to her owners. The Meerwald family sold her to Clyde Phillips, and the *Meerwald* was once again fitted out as an oyster dredge.

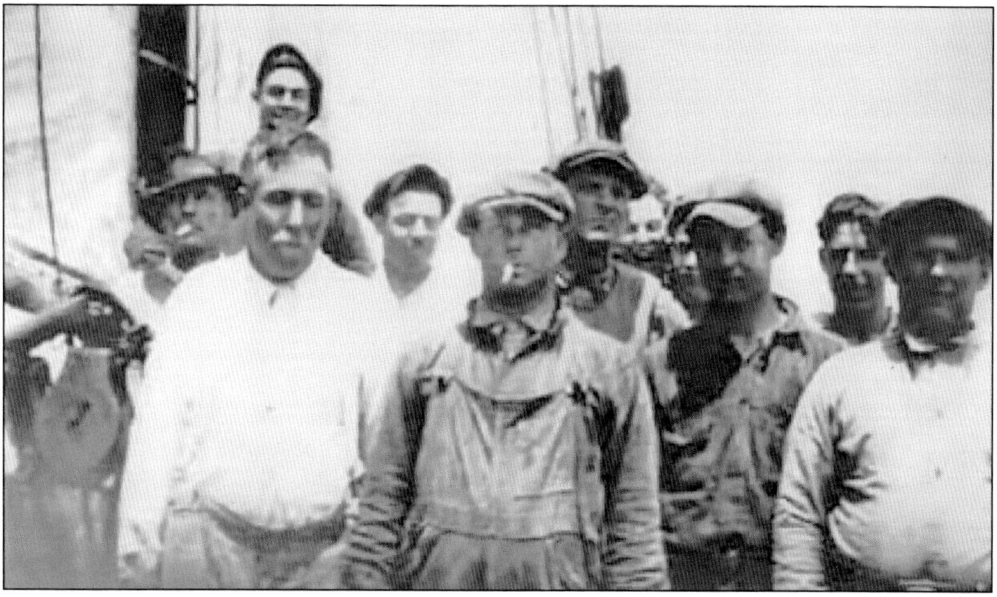

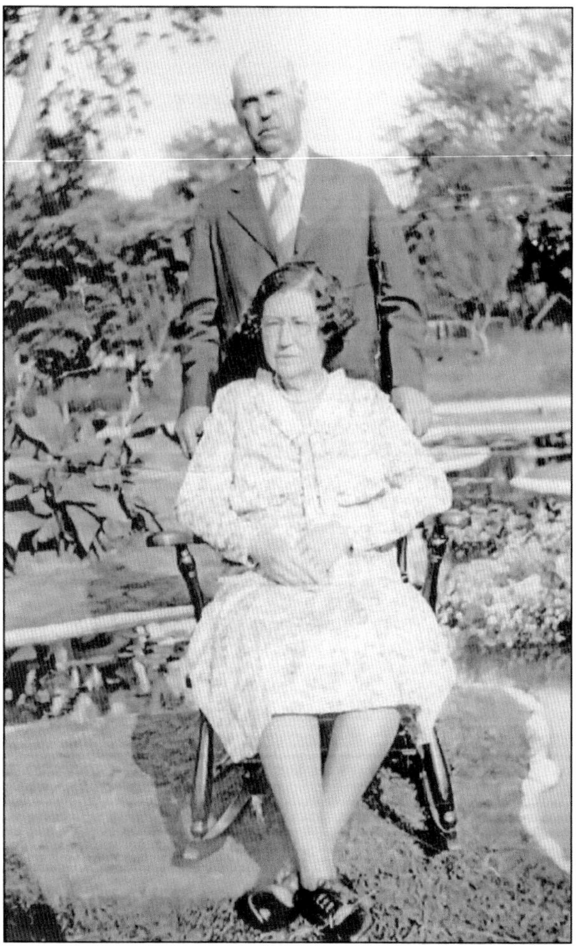

This photograph shows the original crew of *A.J. Meerwald*, made up of all local baymen and oystermen. Locally famous oysterman Nathan Gandy worked the boats into his mid-80s. He is credited with harvesting over a million oysters. The oyster industry on Delaware Bay finally succumbed to pollution; however, in recent years, major efforts have been underway to revive it.

This photograph shows Capt. and Mrs. Augustus Meerwald. The Meerwald family was also known locally for decorating their farm home each Christmas. The annual Meerwald light extravaganzas drew visitors from as far as Philadelphia. In recent years, the family sold the farm and houses were built on the property. Old-timers still recall their Christmas light displays.

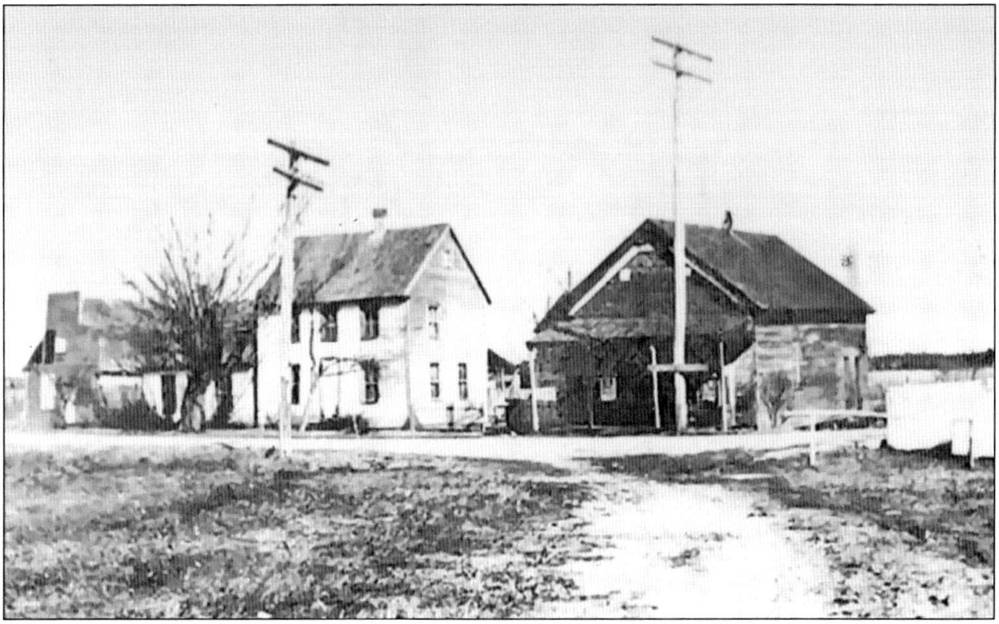

The stores at Dennis Creek Landing were a major commercial hub for the entire area. The creek was the only outlet for products from the upper reaches of the county in the 19th century. Prominent men like James Diverty, Nathaniel Holmes, and C.F. Leaming owned stores at the landing.

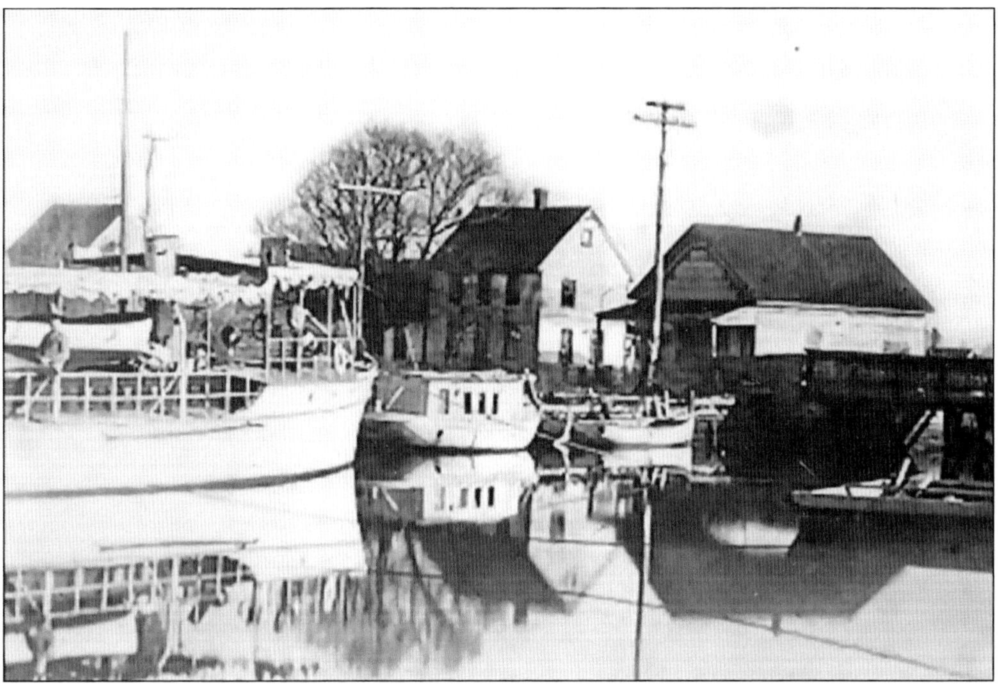

Though it hardly looks it from this photograph, Dennis Landing, Cape May County's major port up until the Civil War, remained a major shipbuilding center until the end of the 19th century. At one time, three shipyards on the creek employed more than 150 men. The three-masted schooner was the most typical type of ship built.

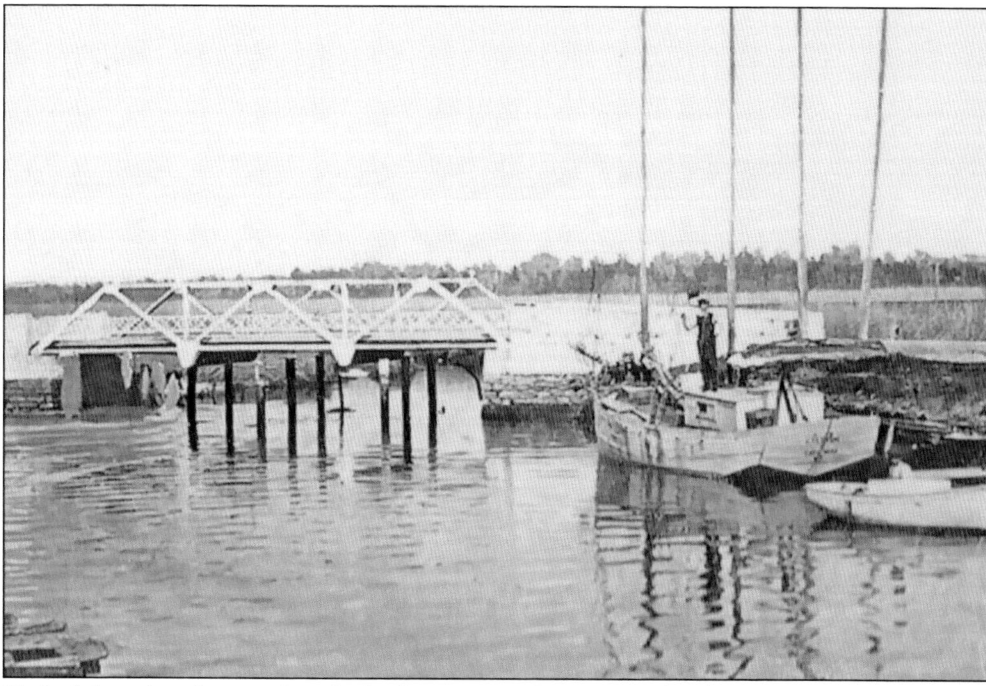

To the left in this photograph is the bridge spanning Dennis Creek. This bridge replaced a covered wooden bridge that had joined Dennisville to South Dennis in the days before hordes of tourists driving automobiles converged upon the Jersey Cape.

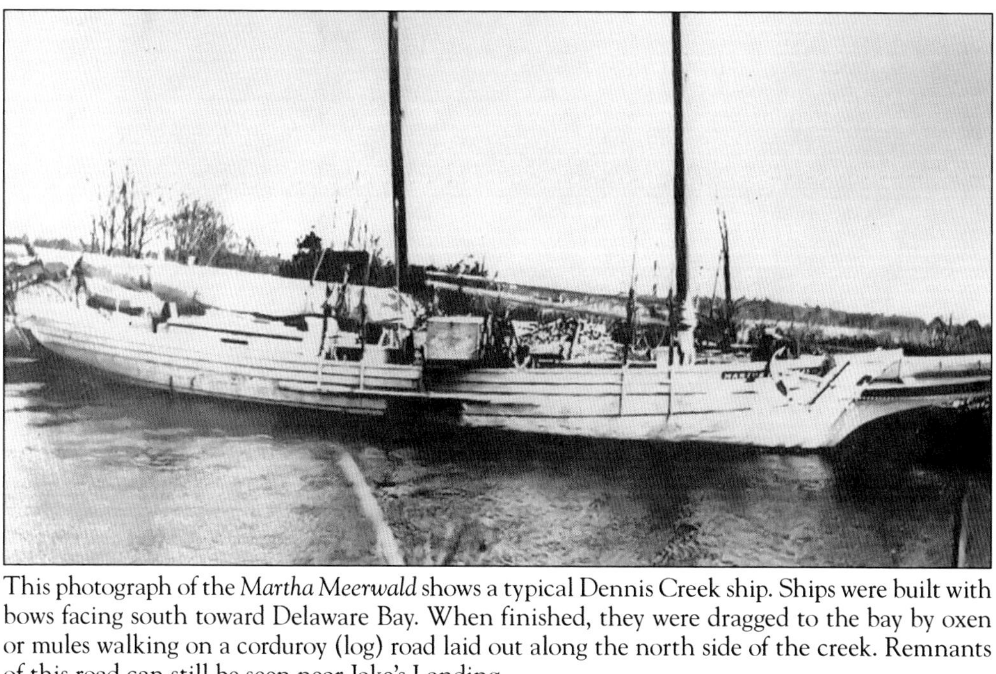

This photograph of the *Martha Meerwald* shows a typical Dennis Creek ship. Ships were built with bows facing south toward Delaware Bay. When finished, they were dragged to the bay by oxen or mules walking on a corduroy (log) road laid out along the north side of the creek. Remnants of this road can still be seen near Jake's Landing.

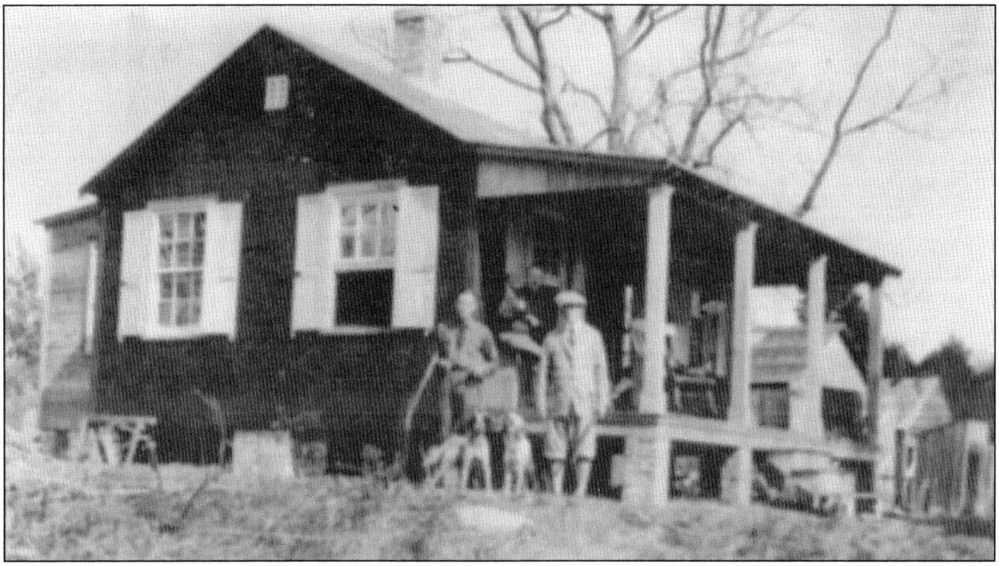

Sportsmen pose with their dogs in this 1922 photograph taken at the Beaver Dam Hunting Club. Pictured are Walter (left) and Robert Stevenson. The Stevenson Brothers Game and Fish Protective Association of New Jersey operated the club.

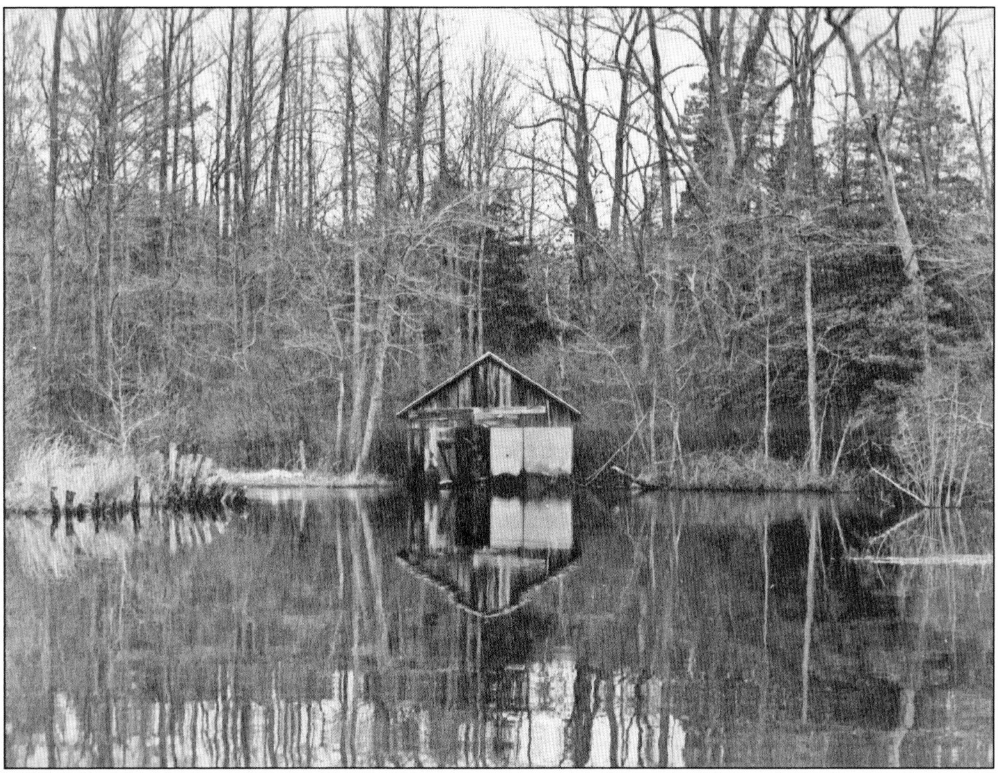

This photograph shows Clint's Mill, owned and operated by Christopher Ludlam. The swamp is actually bordering Sluice Creek, a five-mile tributary of Dennis Creek in Cumberland County, and was also the site of Clint Mill Pond Sawmill, where lumber was produced for housing and shipbuilding.

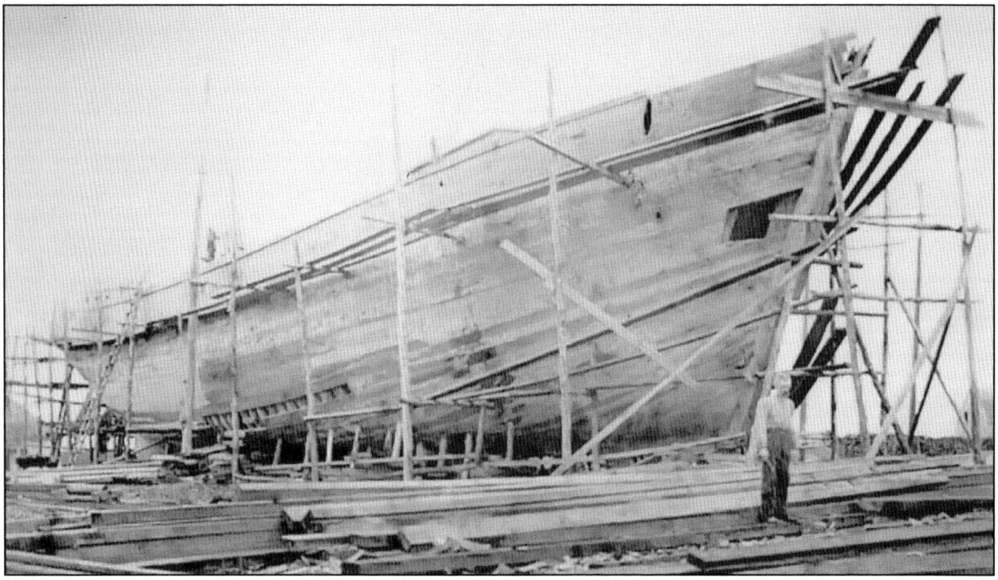

The last big ship built and launched at Dennis Creek was the *Gertrude Abbott* by R.S. Leaming. Three-masted at 900 tons, it was built by Amos Wentzell. On the day of the launch, outsiders coming to view the event lined the south, or opposite, side of the creek. When the ship hit the water, its massive wake soaked them head to toe. The locals, lining the north side of the creek, were greatly amused.

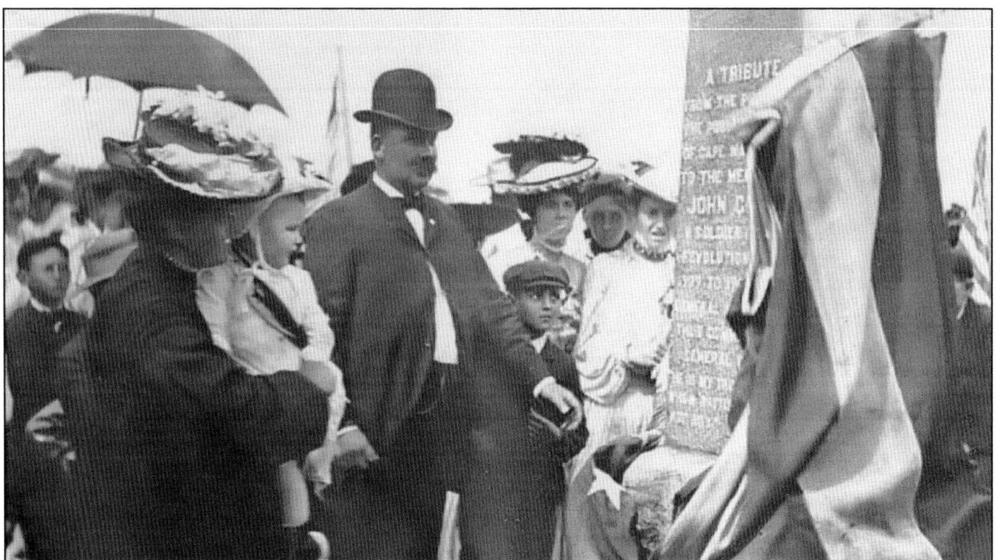

This photograph, taken at Union Cemetery, shows the memorial to Revolutionary War veteran John Grace from North Dennisville. Grace served in a number of campaigns, including General Sullivan's effort against the Six Nations in upstate Pennsylvania. He was with New Jersey troops at the Battle of Yorktown. He died in 1835. In 1904, area schoolchildren collected pennies in order to erect this monument in his honor. The entire community turned out for the marker placement ceremony, despite a pouring rain. Words on the monument come from a comment made about Grace by George Washington, who called Grace his "trusted scout whom British gold can't buy."

Seven

South Seaville
New Jersey's Original Methodist Camp

Tucked away in the heart of the township is the village of South Seaville. As settlers spread across the Cape May peninsula in the early 18th century, a road was built in 1707 to connect settlements. People built homes and established businesses about halfway on the King's Highway between Dennisville, near Delaware Bay, and Beeseley's Point, which is located in the upper part of the county.

One of the first settlers in South Seaville was John Voss. He was married in the Townsend House, the Quaker meetinghouse at the time, in 1829. Grandchildren of Voss would one day develop a process that led to the creation of asbestos shingles, while another would create a steam turbine engine for General Electric.

The center of Dennis Township consisted of lumbering camps, farms, and swamps when the Cape May and Millville Railroad laid tracks in the mid-19th century. South Seaville became an important stop, especially since it already offered stagecoach transportation to surrounding population centers like Beeseley's Point to the north and Cape May to the south.

The railroad helped establish South Seaville as a commercial hub, particularly for local seafood, which was shipped to Philadelphia and other metropolises. Especially popular were Cape May Salts, oysters transplanted from Chesapeake Bay and raised in local beds.

The establishment of a Methodist camp near South Seaville added to the hamlet's significance, making the area a destination point for religious pilgrims every summer. The camp was one of the first of its kind in New Jersey, being incorporated in 1875 by the South Seaville Camp Meeting Association. The camp still meets every summer.

Camp planners envisioned a grid design, with individual lots situated in rectangular blocks. Lot purchasers were expected to build in compliance with a concept of a basic two-story cottage, neatly trimmed in gingerbread. The cottages were illuminated with oil lamps and candles. Water was provided from a community well.

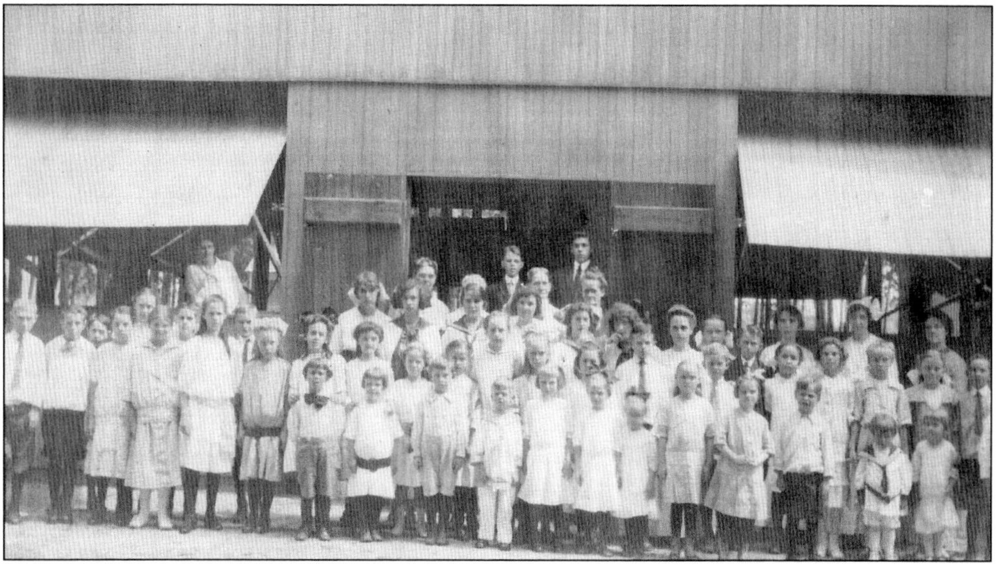

Children gather for Sunday school. Organizers worked to keep children gainfully occupied during camp meetings, so special programs were initiated in 1879. This particular activity was conducted by Mrs. Ludlam Hand at the pavilion. Bible messages were taught using blackboard messages known as "chalk talks." In 1903, a young people's temple was built, and every afternoon included a children's hour.

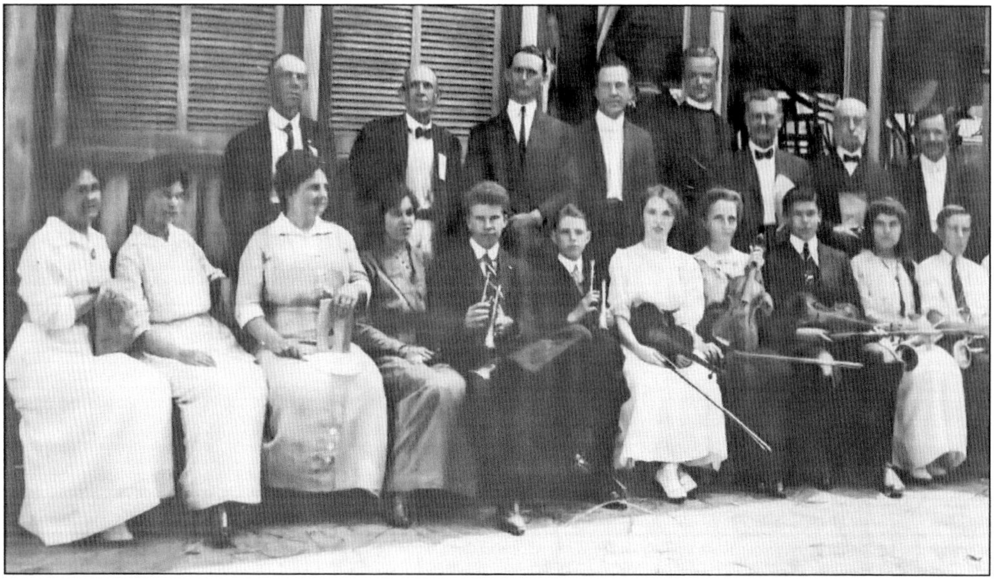

The camp choir is shown here poised before a performance. Music was a major component of camp meetings, and each camp meeting had a song "leader." One of these was prominent Dennis Township resident Rev. James Diverty. Music created for these events became known worldwide. Cape May County native Edgar Page Stites (1836–1920) composed a number of pieces, including "Beulah Land."

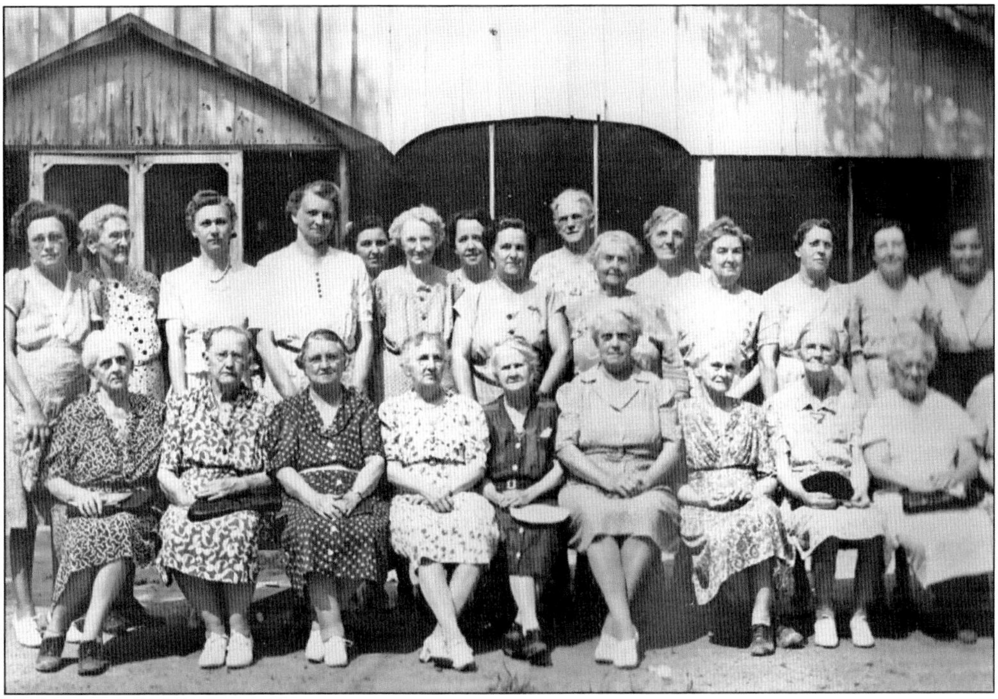

The Ladies Auxiliary poses for this 1947 photograph. While the men managed general camp business, the ladies made all the day-to-day activities function smoothly. The first reference to the auxiliary at South Seaville was in 1928. That year, the auxiliary raised money sufficient to pay off the camp's debt.

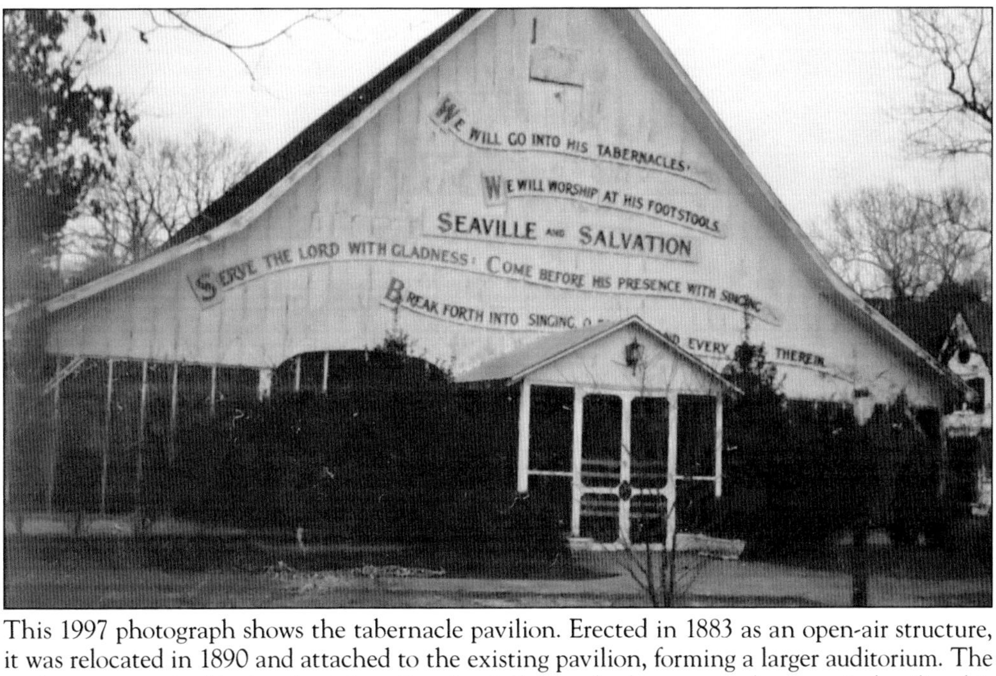

This 1997 photograph shows the tabernacle pavilion. Erected in 1883 as an open-air structure, it was relocated in 1890 and attached to the existing pavilion, forming a larger auditorium. The work was supervised by local minister Rev. Jacob Price, who later penned a memoir detailing his experiences at camp meetings.

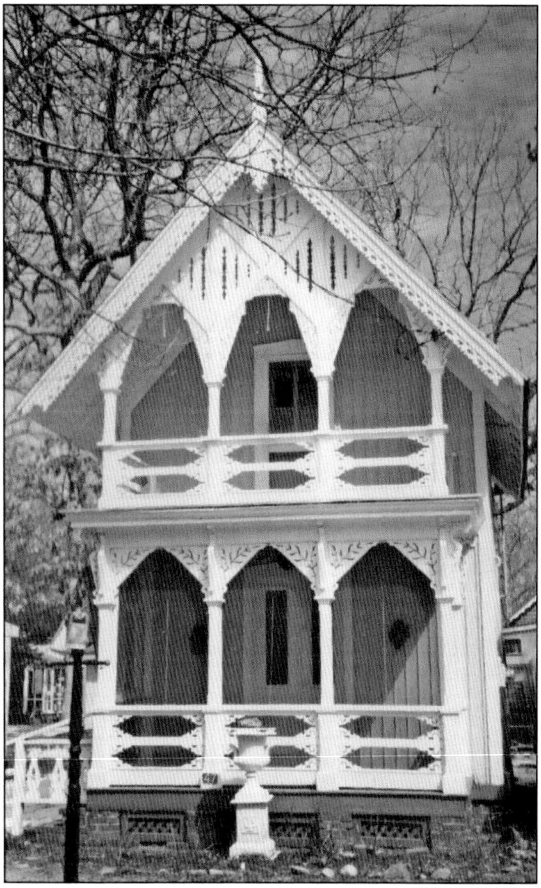

Built in 1882, this steep-gabled American Gothic–style cottage is one of many similar cottages still in use at the camp. This one was constructed for Capt. Charles Bowser from nearby Townsend's Inlet. Land on which it was built was purchased from Charles Ludlam of South Dennis. Many of the original cottages are still occupied today.

The 1999 photograph below shows the boardinghouse. It was built in 1881 at a cost of $1,250 to accommodate visiting ministers. A sitting room and porch were added 11 years later. Until 1895, when rooms were more comfortably furnished, boarders slept on bunk beds with straw mattresses. The main room continues to be used as a dining facility.

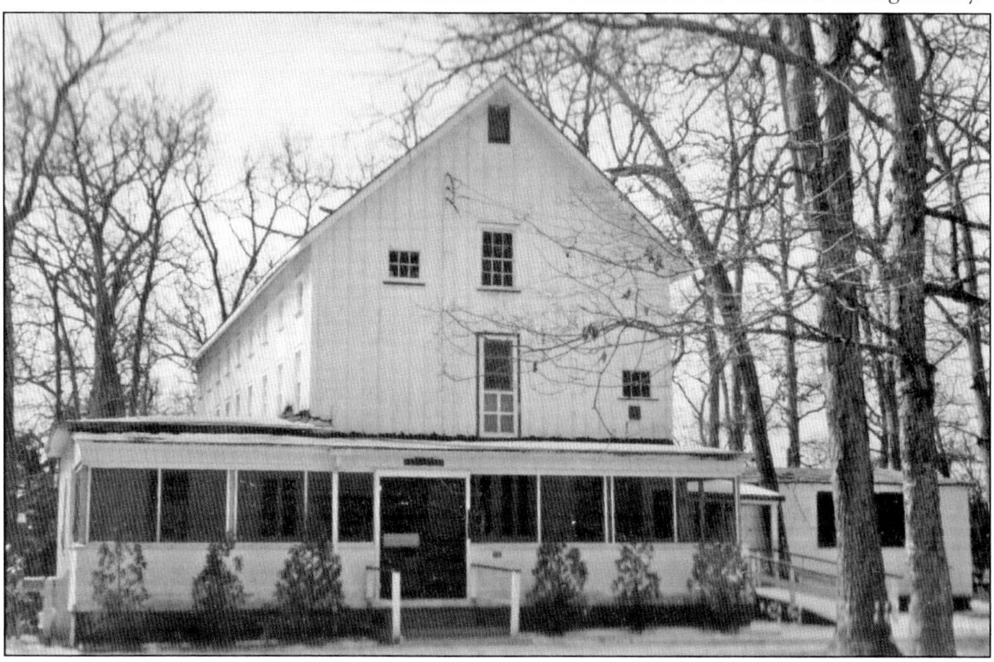

The South Seaville Methodist Church is shown here as it originally looked in the 19th century. Henry Cheeseman was the first pastor. Initial Sunday school classes were conducted at the nearby train station until an addition to the church permitted classes to be held there.

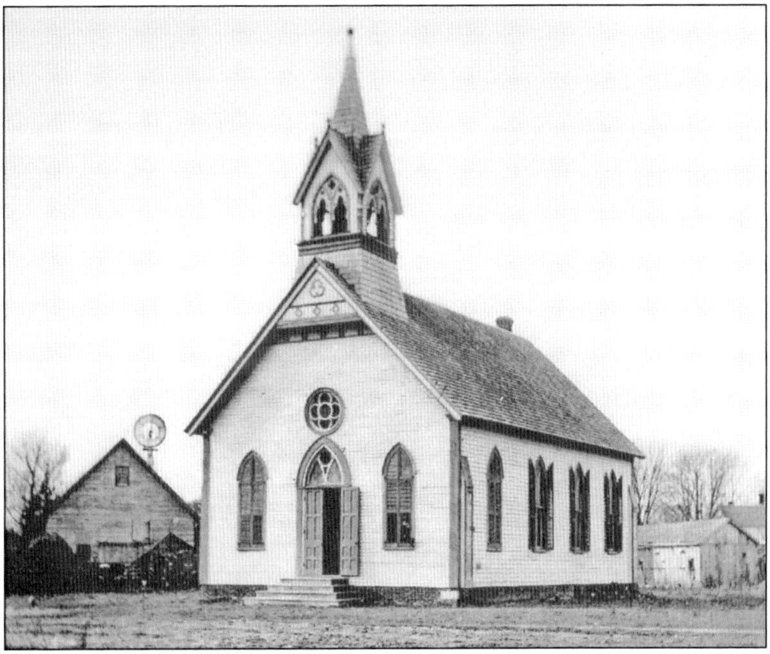

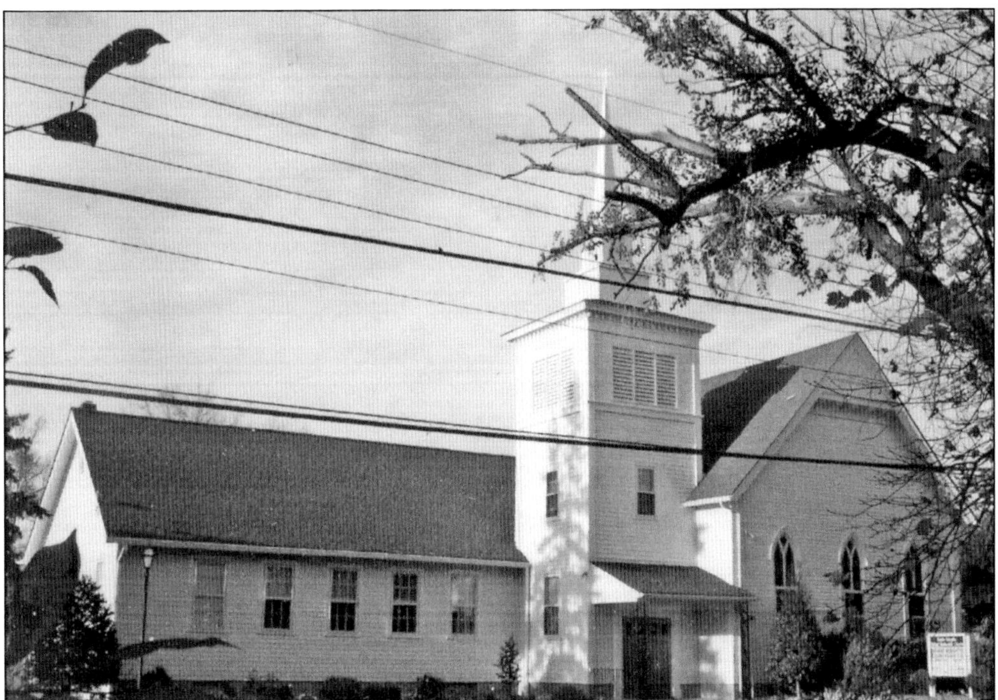

South Seaville Methodist Church is pictured as it looked prior to a lightning-ignited fire in 2011 that burned the structure to the ground. The 127-year-old church has been rebuilt bigger and better than ever not far from its former location.

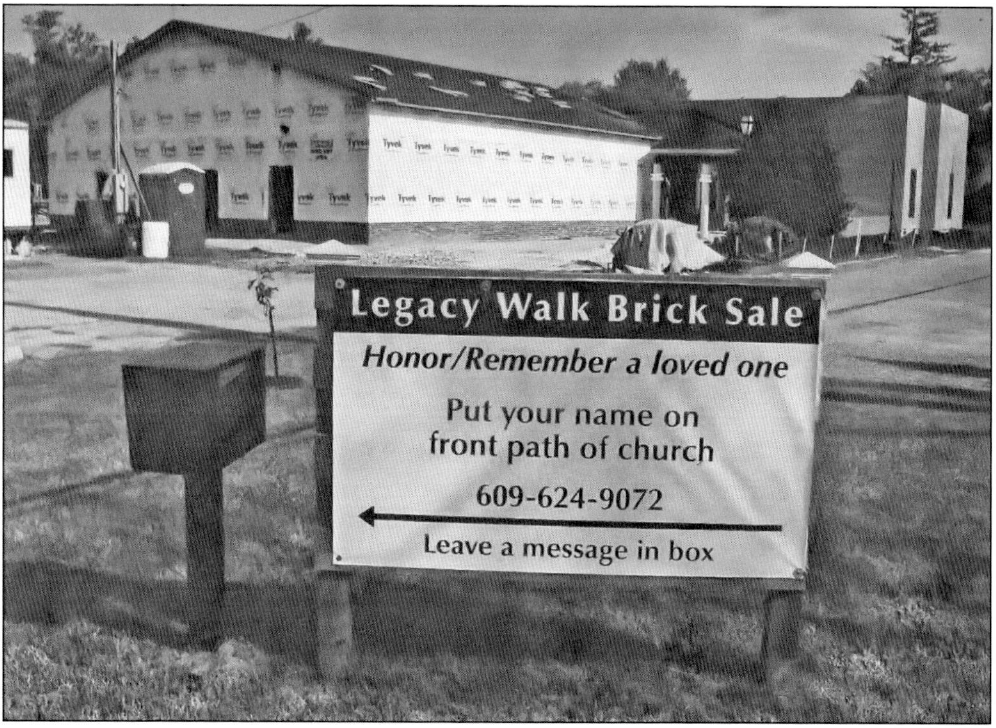

South Seaville Methodist Church is pictured in 2012 as it appeared during the rebuilding process. While the church was being rebuilt, services were held at the old Grange Hall on the corner of King's Highway.

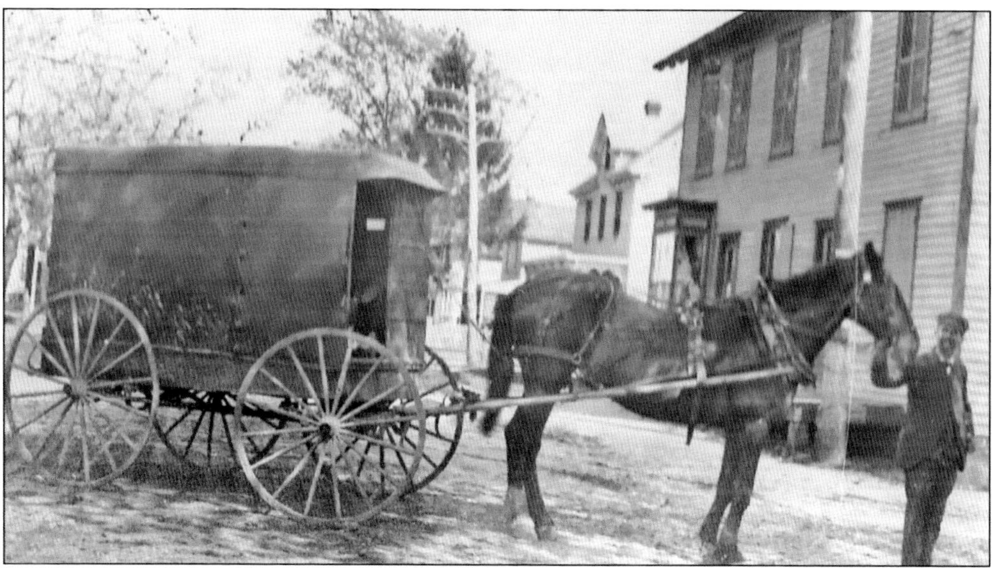

Pictured here is Charles Lloyd, first chairman of the board when South Seaville Methodist Church was incorporated in 1884. Lloyd leads his delivery wagon through the crossroads at South Seaville. He lived on Main Street.

This 1996 photograph shows the old Grange Hall empty, but only temporarily. Better known as Alpha Hall, it has served the residents of South Seaville in many ways over the years, including as a meeting site for several denominations in need of temporary quarters. These days, the hall, owned by local attorney James Pickering, is bustling with activity again, serving as a community thrift store.

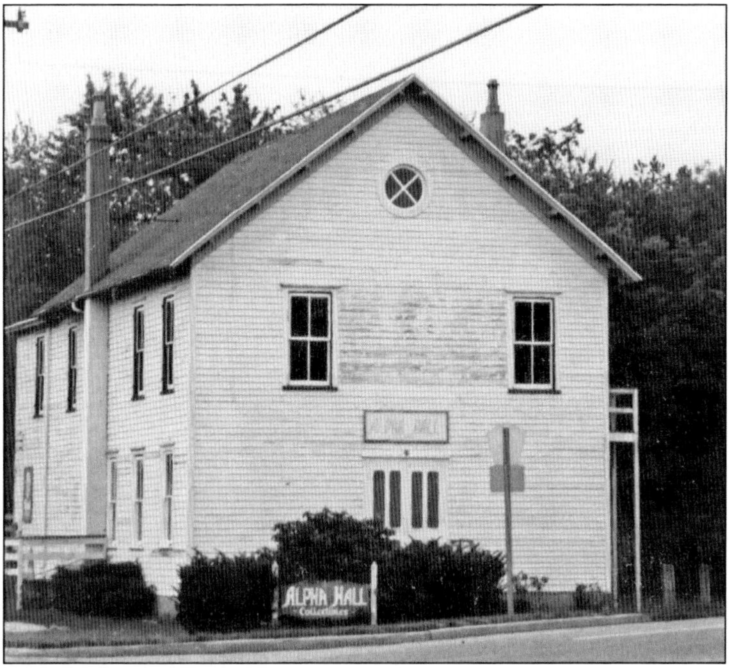

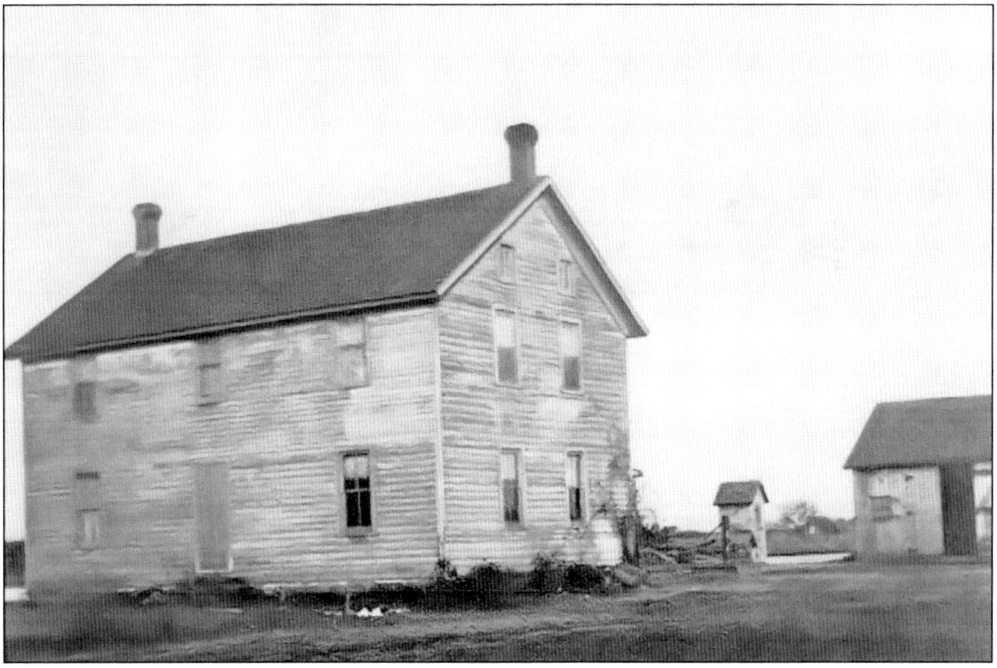

Handcock House on King's Highway was a boardinghouse back in the days when South Seaville was a major area train stop. The story goes that Cora Temple, a widow, married John Handcock, a traveling salesman who always stopped at Cora's boardinghouse. She bore him three children. Incidentally, Temple's father and late husband are credited with building Alpha Hall.

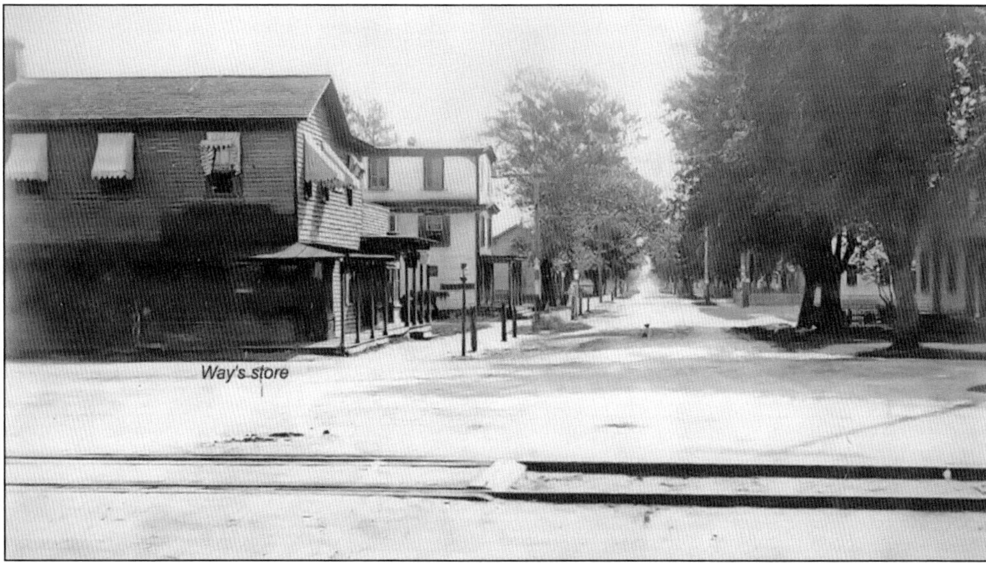

Downtown South Seaville is pictured in its heyday. The foreground shows the tracks of the West Jersey Railroad. That line ran 81 miles from Camden to Cape May; in Cape May County, it stopped at Belleplain and South Seaville. The building closest to the tracks on the left side of Main Street is Way's Store.

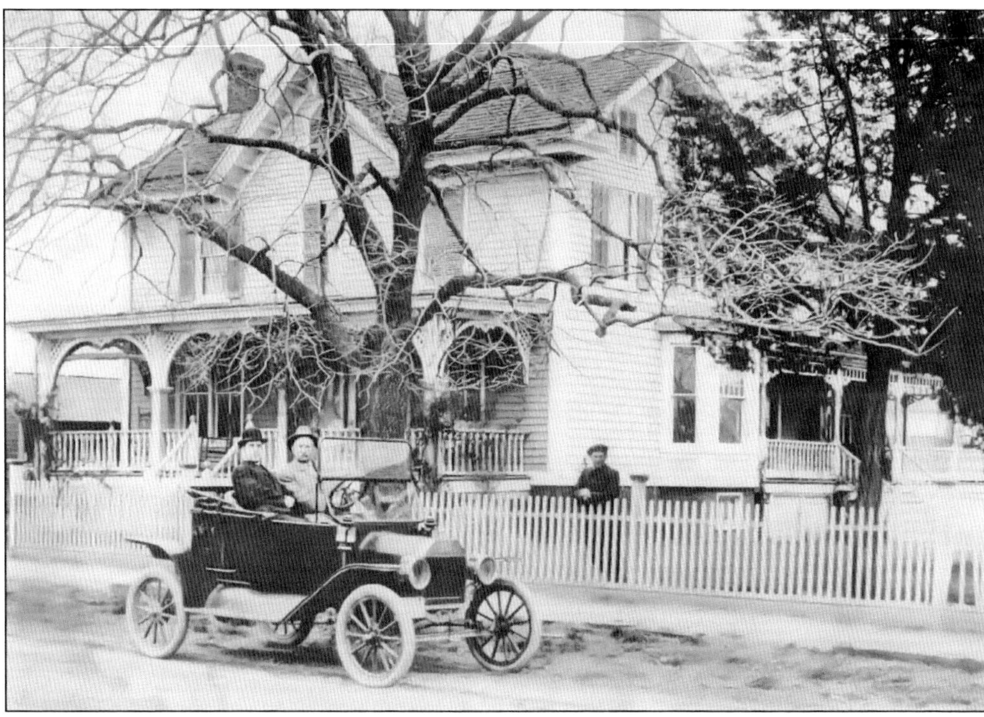

Pictured is the Bonham House on Main Street in the center of town. John Bonham is in the driver's seat, and Warren Willis stands next to the picket fence. Many of the old houses on Main Street still stand and are occupied as private residences. With the coming of the railroad, South Seaville grew out, including construction of a fairground complete with racetrack.

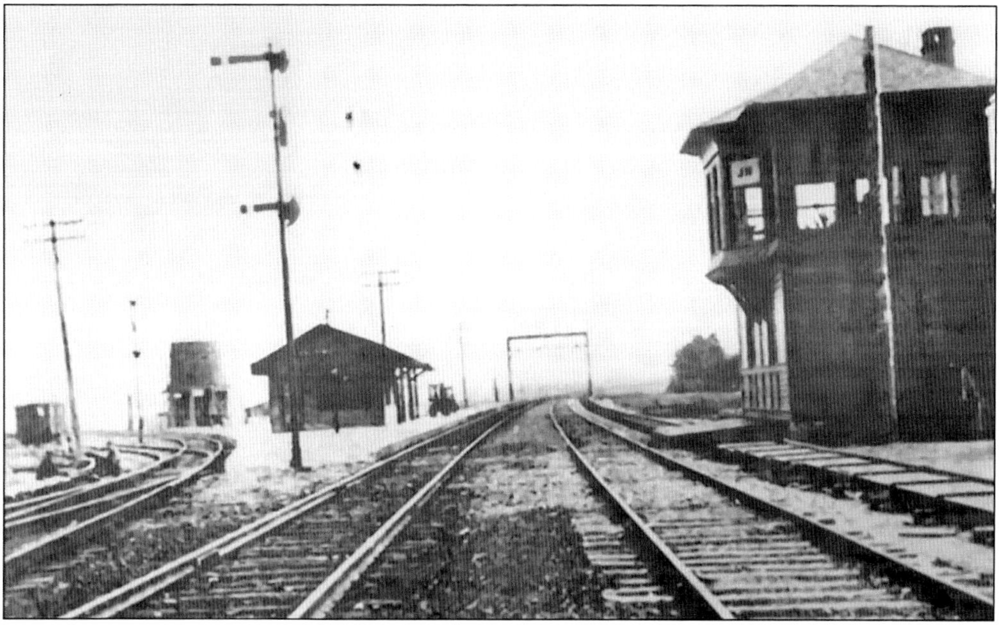

This photograph of the West Jersey Railroad's junction near South Seaville shows tracks running straight ahead to Cape May, while those turning left lead to Sea Isle. At the height of its railroad involvement, South Seaville not only handled passenger traffic, but was also a shipping center for seafood harvested nearby and sent from South Seaville for Philadelphia.

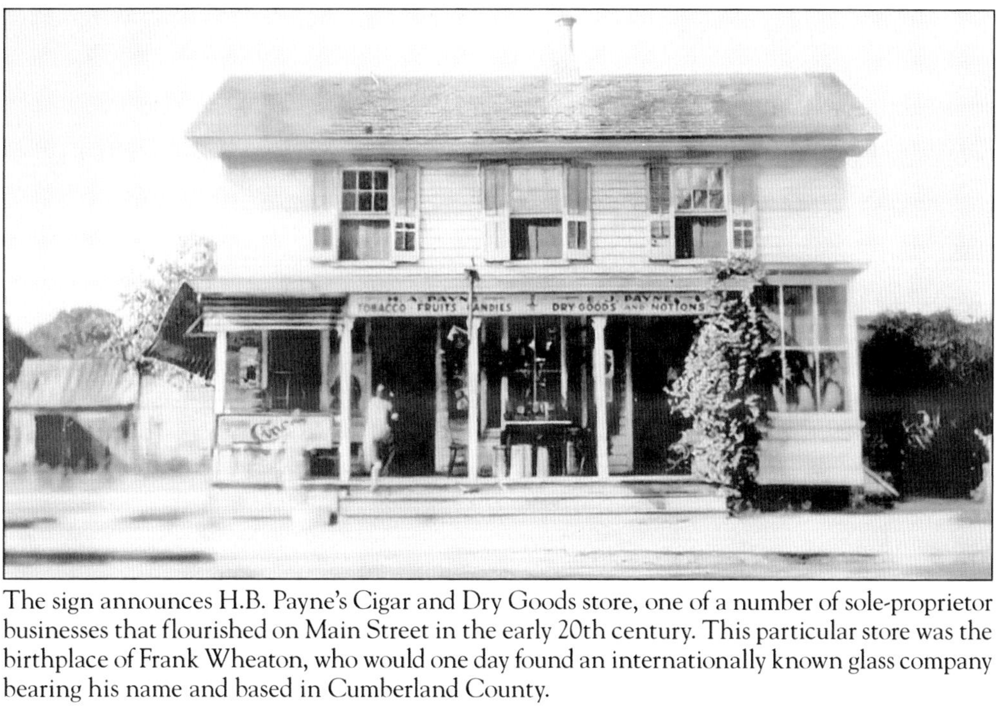

The sign announces H.B. Payne's Cigar and Dry Goods store, one of a number of sole-proprietor businesses that flourished on Main Street in the early 20th century. This particular store was the birthplace of Frank Wheaton, who would one day found an internationally known glass company bearing his name and based in Cumberland County.

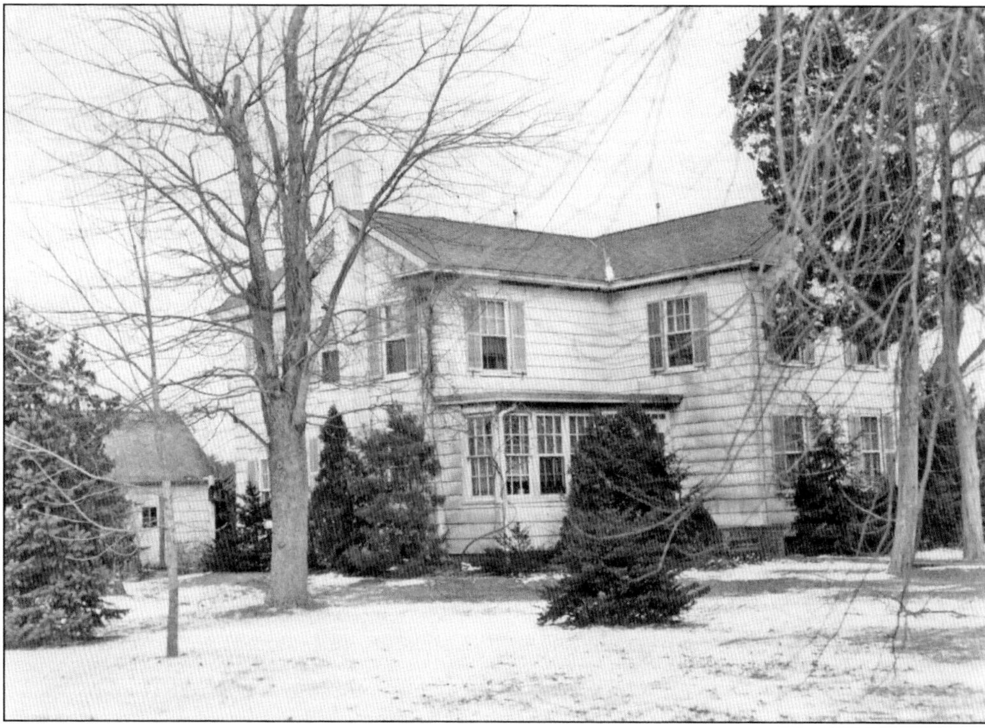

The photograph shows the home of David Collins, third generation of the family that owned Collins Lumber Yard. David assumed control of the business in 1947 when his father Harold Collins died. David operated it for half a century and died in 2006. His son Roger Collins, who had become active in the business in 1976, was the fourth-generation Collins to take the helm.

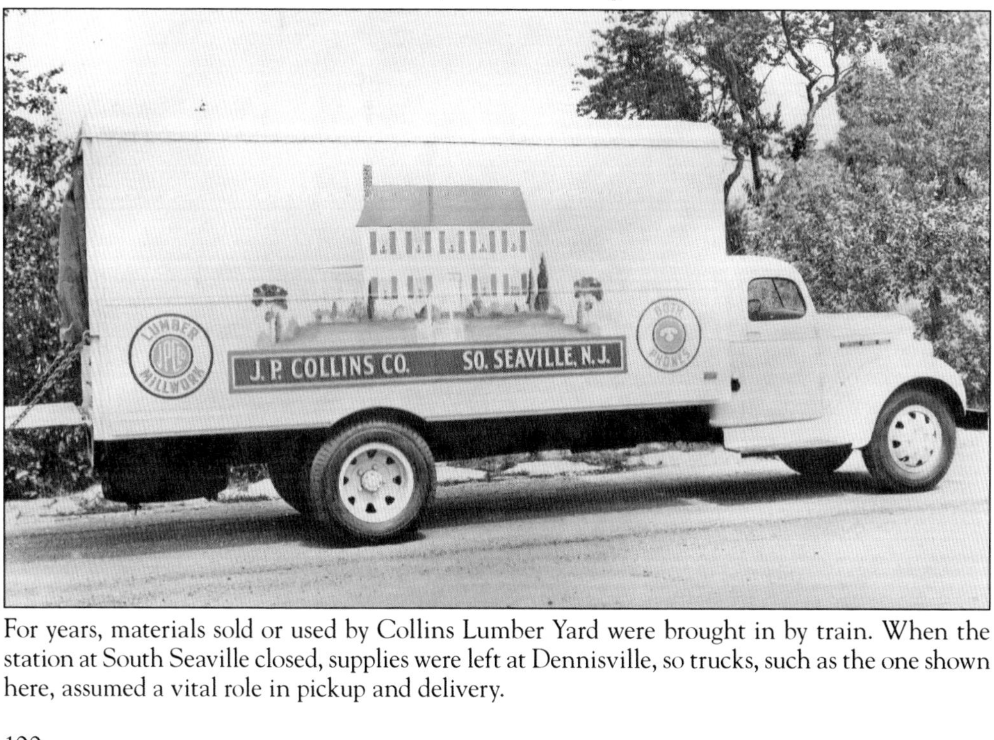

For years, materials sold or used by Collins Lumber Yard were brought in by train. When the station at South Seaville closed, supplies were left at Dennisville, so trucks, such as the one shown here, assumed a vital role in pickup and delivery.

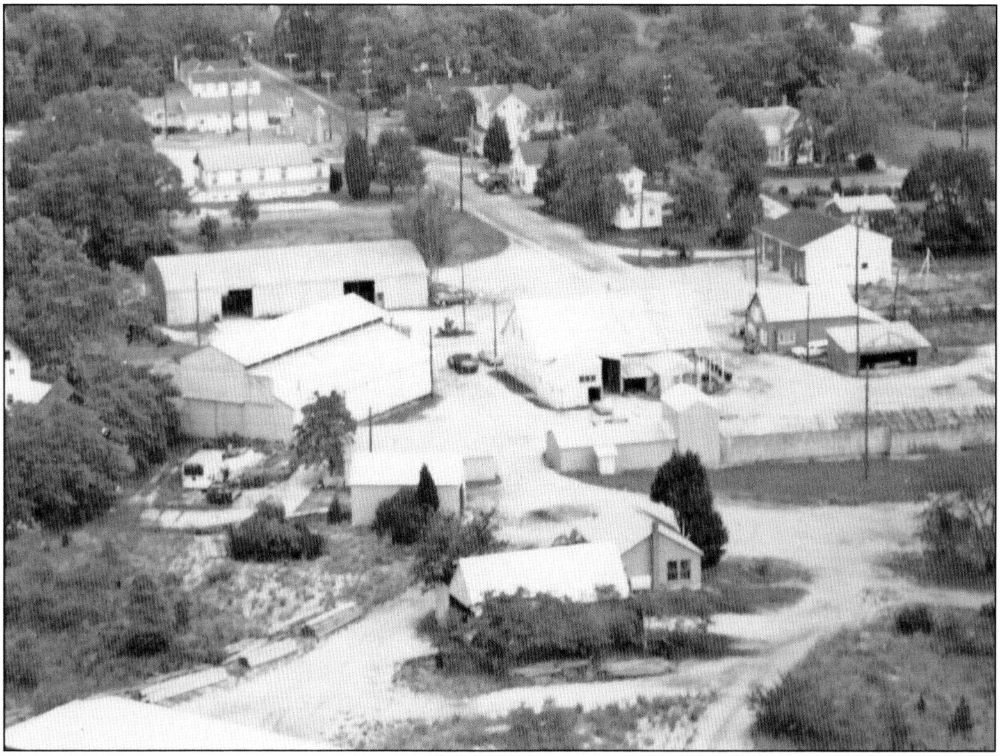

This aerial photograph shows the spread of Collins Lumber Yard in the foreground. Main Street South Seaville leads away to top of the photograph. Founder Jacob Collins relocated his enterprise to this location from the corner of King's Highway and Dennisville Road (later the site of Alpha Hall).

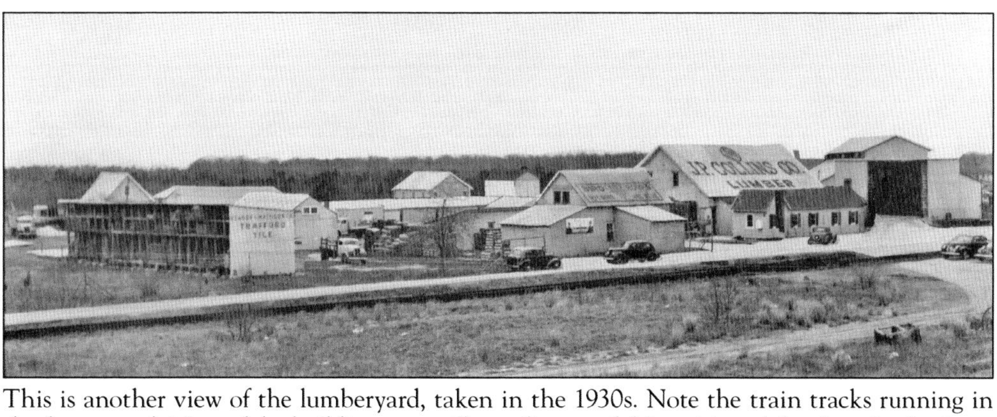

This is another view of the lumberyard, taken in the 1930s. Note the train tracks running in the foreground. Most of the buildings are still standing as of this writing. A landscaping business is currently utilizing a portion of the property. Future plans include additional small businesses moving to the site.

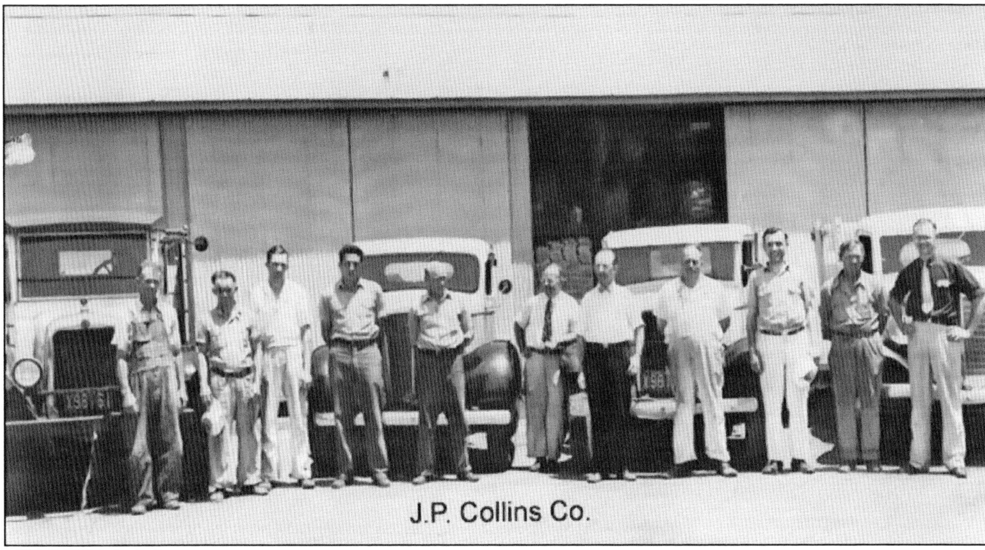

J.P. Collins employed a significant workforce. In this 1940s photograph, from left to right, are Roger Whittington, Frank Frye, Morris Reeves, Elmer Ellenburger, Harry Heinskel, Harold Collins, Les Foster, Ben Swing, Leo Carr, Ed Meher, and Ed Carr.

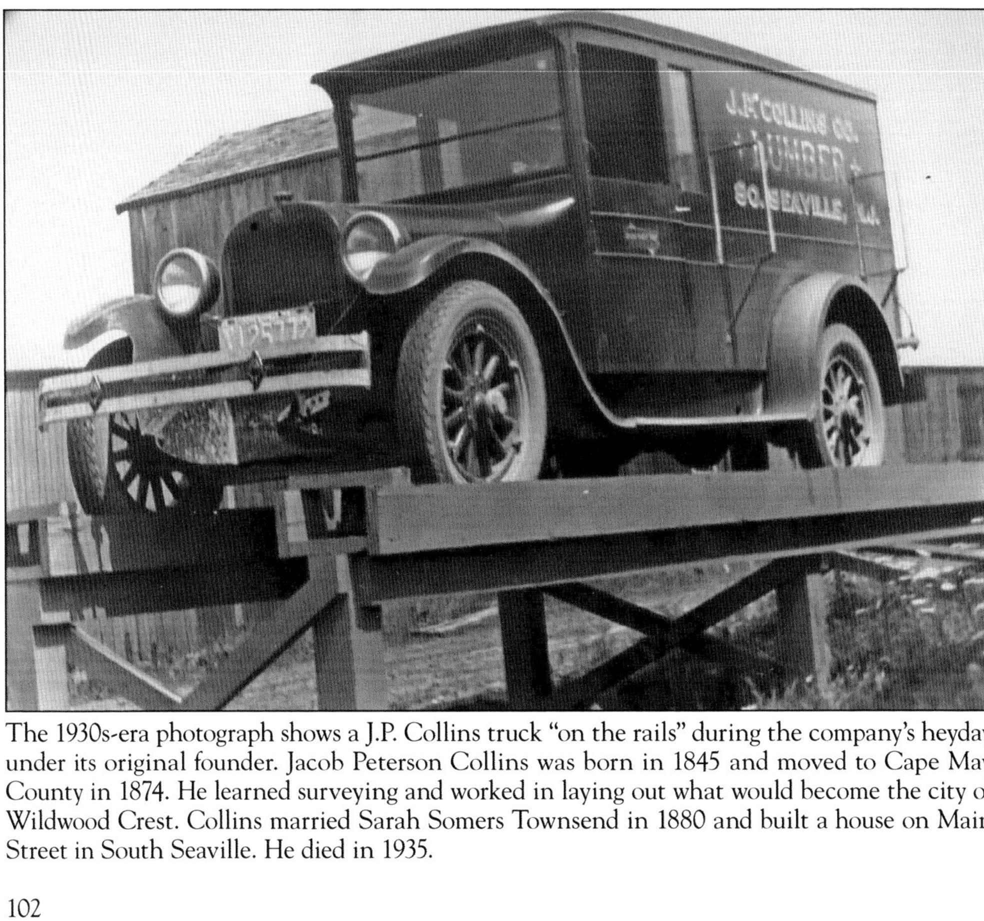

The 1930s-era photograph shows a J.P. Collins truck "on the rails" during the company's heyday under its original founder. Jacob Peterson Collins was born in 1845 and moved to Cape May County in 1874. He learned surveying and worked in laying out what would become the city of Wildwood Crest. Collins married Sarah Somers Townsend in 1880 and built a house on Main Street in South Seaville. He died in 1935.

Eight

Mill Hill
Generations Maintaining a Sense of Place

John Townsend was banished from Long Island for defying a government ban on harboring Quakers. Already imprisoned several times for this, he decided to move. In 1690, he traveled south along Indian paths, crossed the Great Egg Harbor, and continued until he reached a stream. He decided the place would make a good site for a mill. He cleared land and built the mill and a cabin.

There is a story about building that cabin: Townsend needed help cutting and hauling logs for the cabin. Joseph Ludlam and Christopher Leaming from Dennisville helped, as did local Indians. According to Lewis Townsend Stevens's *The History of Cape May County*, the Indians began wrestling among themselves and then communicated that they wanted to wrestle a white man. Ludlam lifted his Indian opponent and lodged him in the limb of a tree. The Indians believed the white men possessed a magic power that gave them strength. Afterward, there was no trouble between them and the newcomers, and Mill Hill went on to be one of the longest-operating family farms in the county, and it still is today, with a female farmer named Alma Van Gilder Waltz George.

She is the fourth "Alma" to till the soil that has been in her family since the 1800s. Her roots in Cape May County are deep; she is the eighth generation to live in either Upper Township or Dennis Township since before the Revolutionary War, and her family's tenure on the farm extends back five generations. Through the centuries, various crops have been grown on the farm, which has been under one family's ownership since Alma's great-great-grandfather, Thompson Van Gilder, purchased the property in 1836. Salt hay, watermelons, bush lima beans, pumpkins, soybeans, and even Christmas trees have been grown on the land.

The current Alma, no. 4, started tending the farm in 2010. She has concentrated on native beach plum and aronia (chokecherry) production, tending to 2,000 beach plum trees and 500 aronia berry bushes. Aronia is gaining recognition as a superfruit packed with cancer-fighting anthocyanins and antioxidants. She would like to see the farm preserved as open space.

All photographs in this chapter appear courtesy of Alma Van Gilder Waltz George.

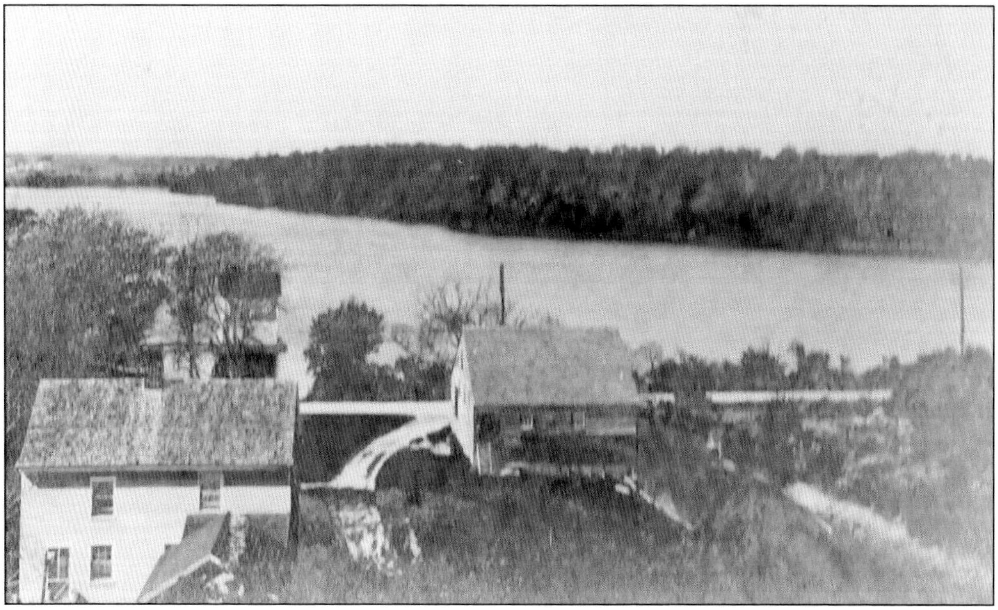

This photograph of Magnolia Lake was taken from Mill Hill in the early 1900s. The old millhouse was once used as a tomato-processing factory. Prior to that, it served as a gristmill and before that, a sawmill. The dirt road runs parallel to the lakefront. The dirt road was designated as Route 4. Early in the 20th century, the path was widened and paved to accommodate automobile traffic. This photograph shows a boathouse; boating was (and still is) a popular pastime for both residents of Mill Hill and locals who were (and are) permitted to use the lake. The bunkhouse in the foreground was eventually moved and connected to the main house, at which time it was converted into a kitchen.

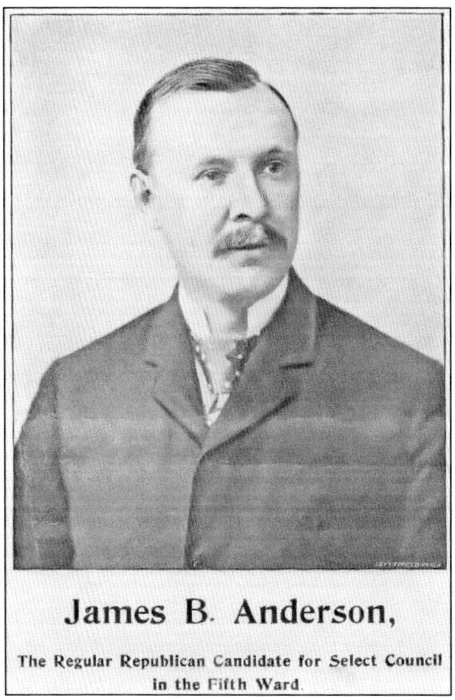

James B. Anderson, a prominent Philadelphia attorney, visited in the summers and stayed in the bunkhouse. One summer, he met Alma Van Gilder and fell in love. His great-granddaughter Alma Van Gilder Waltz George currently lives at Mill Hill with her husband, John. This appears to be a political photograph for Anderson. Also a developer, he was a summer visitor at Mill Hill. He ran for Philadelphia City Council, Fifth Ward, as a Republican.

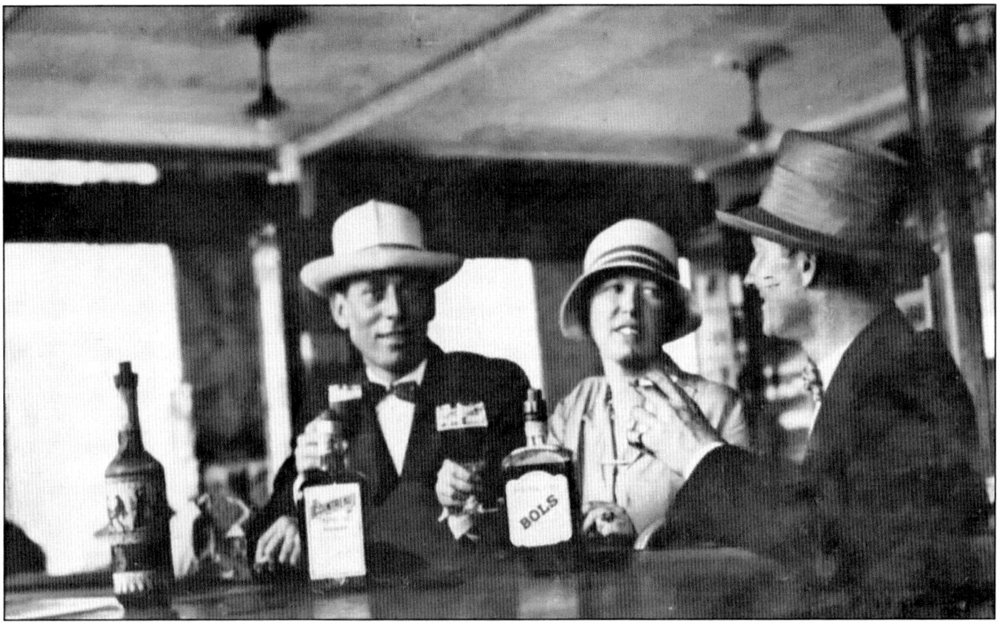

The photograph postcard shows Alma Van Gilder Waltz George's grandparents Arthur Cecil Patterson and Alma Van Gilder Anderson Patterson at Sloppy Joe's Bar on their honeymoon in Cuba in 1927. Cecil died in 1942, and his wife passed in 1959. Cuba was once a fashionable honeymoon destination, and a stop at the watering hole made famous (or infamous) by Ernest Hemingway was a must for the savvy traveler.

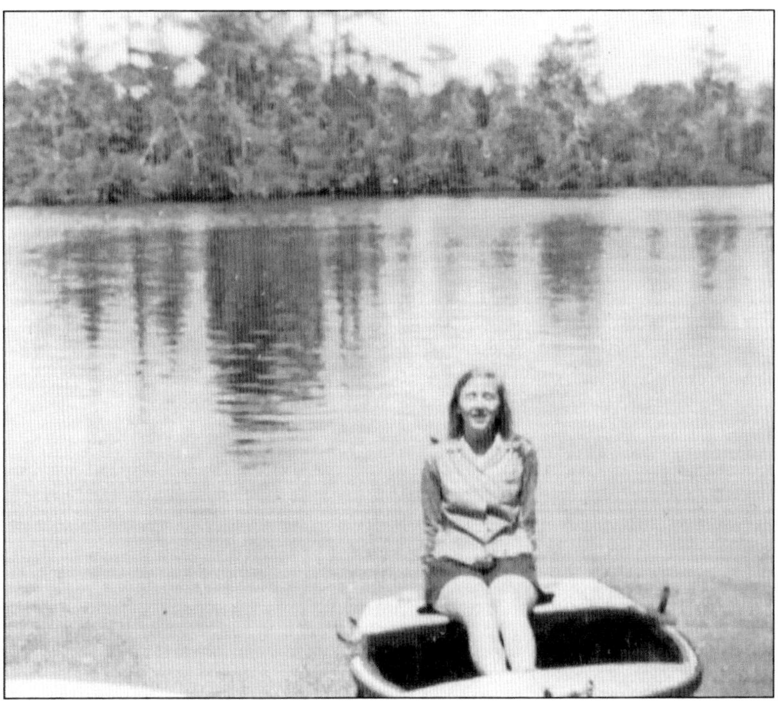

This photograph of Alma Patterson was taken in the summer of 1945 at Magnolia Lake. Mother of the current resident at Mill Hill, she lived at the family homestead until her death in 2012.

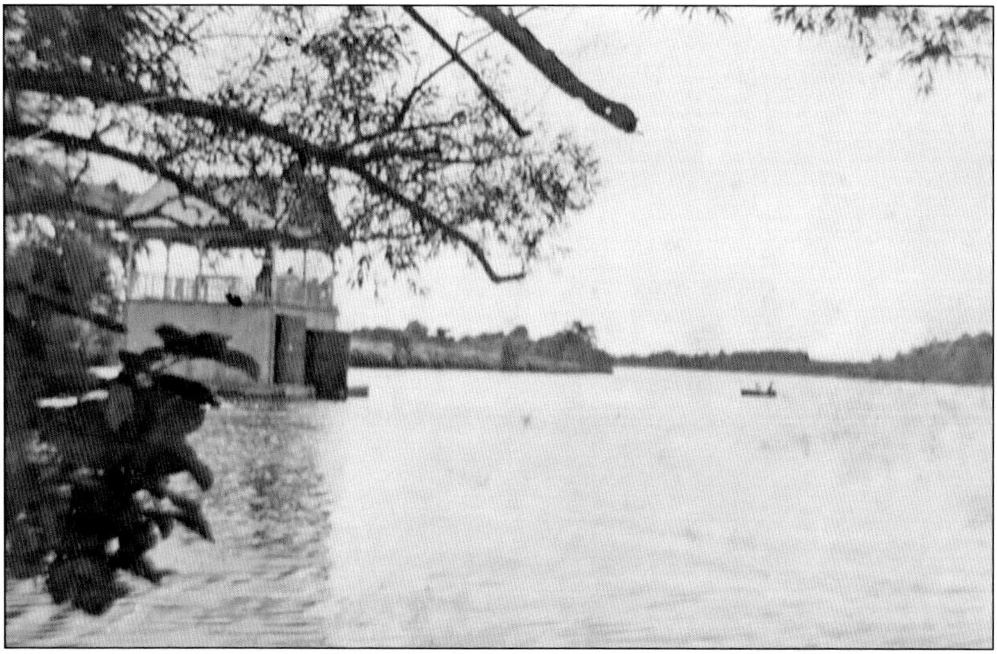

This photograph, taken in July 1899, shows the boathouse at Magnolia Lake. The lake was a popular recreational spot for locals and visitors alike and continues today as a landmark along one of the routes to the Jersey Shore.

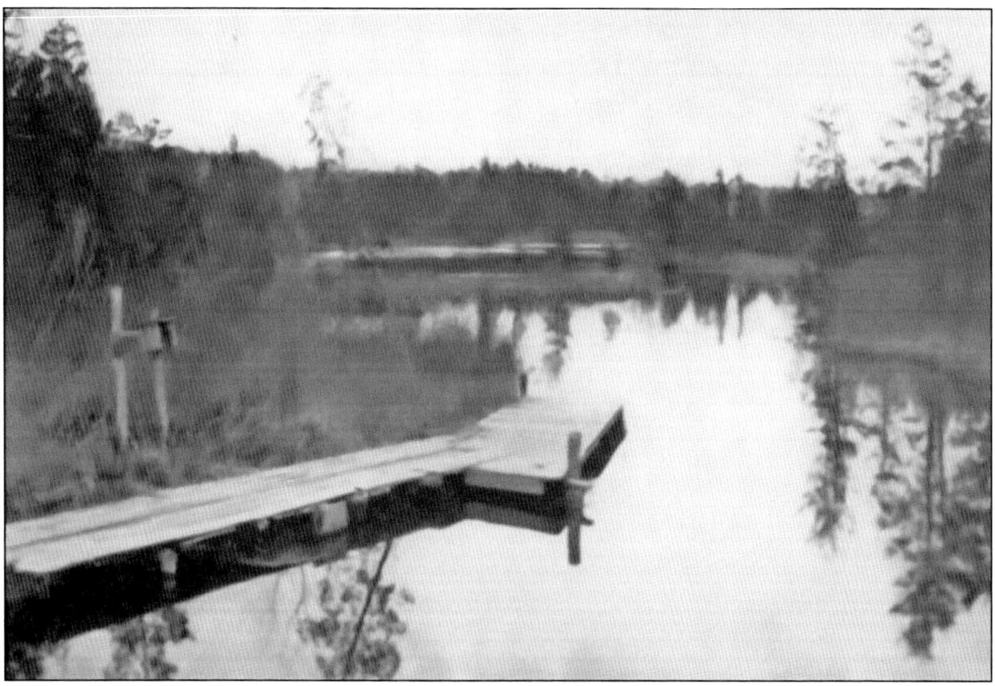

The photograph shows the south fork of Magnolia Lake. A bridge passed over Mill Creek on what is today's Main Street, leading from Route 9 to South Seaville. A bridge is still there; however, it now looks like a culvert. To the right is Magnolia Lake. John Townsend, the original settler to the area, dammed Mill Creek for a mill over 300 years ago.

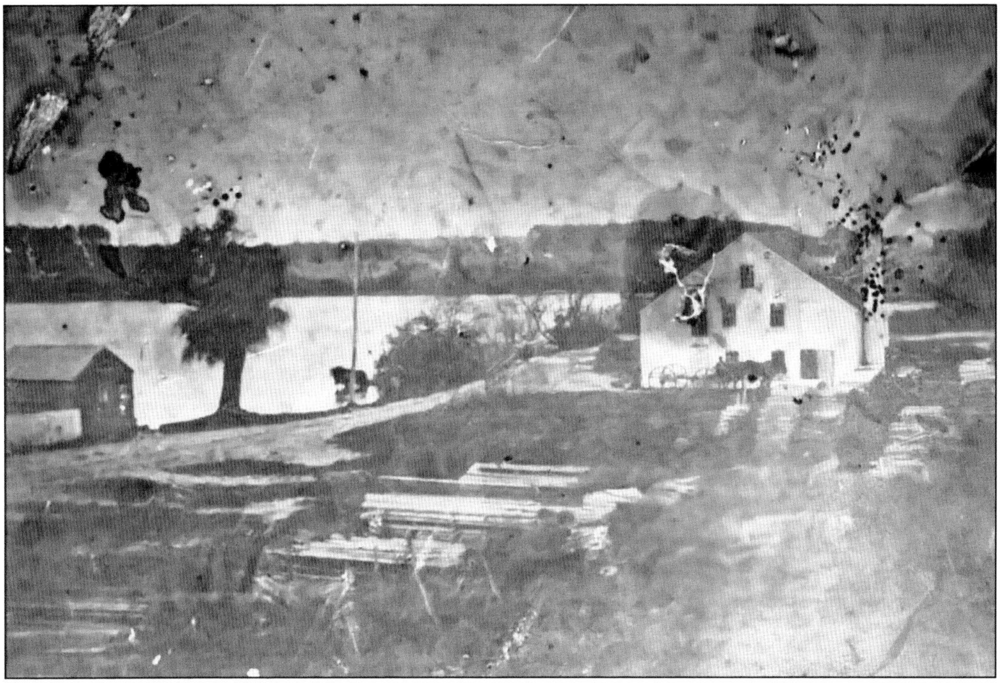

In the 19th century, a wintergreen still operated at the lake at this time, as seen in the left side of photo; it was later replaced by the boathouse. Note the cart and buggy and the dirt road running along the front of the lake. Typically, the lumber milled in the area was white cedar. Wintergreen oil, steam distilled from the leaves, was used to flavor food and candies. Natives also used it for a number of medicinal treatments, including back pain, headache, and sore throat.

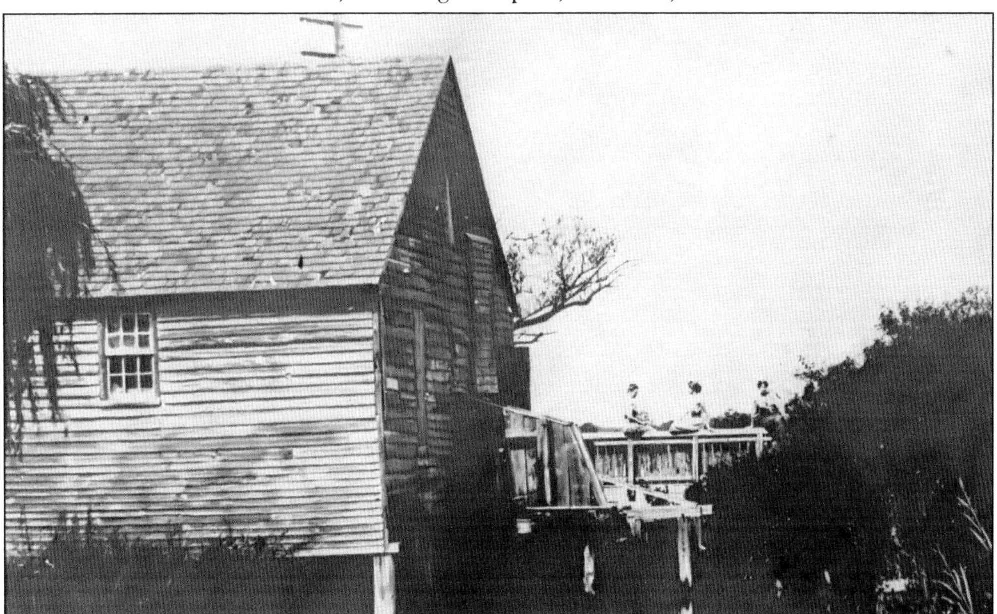

Local residents relax on the deck at the old mill on Magnolia Lake in this postcard photograph. While the lake was private property, visitors were permitted to enjoy the scenery and sporting opportunities the body of water offered.

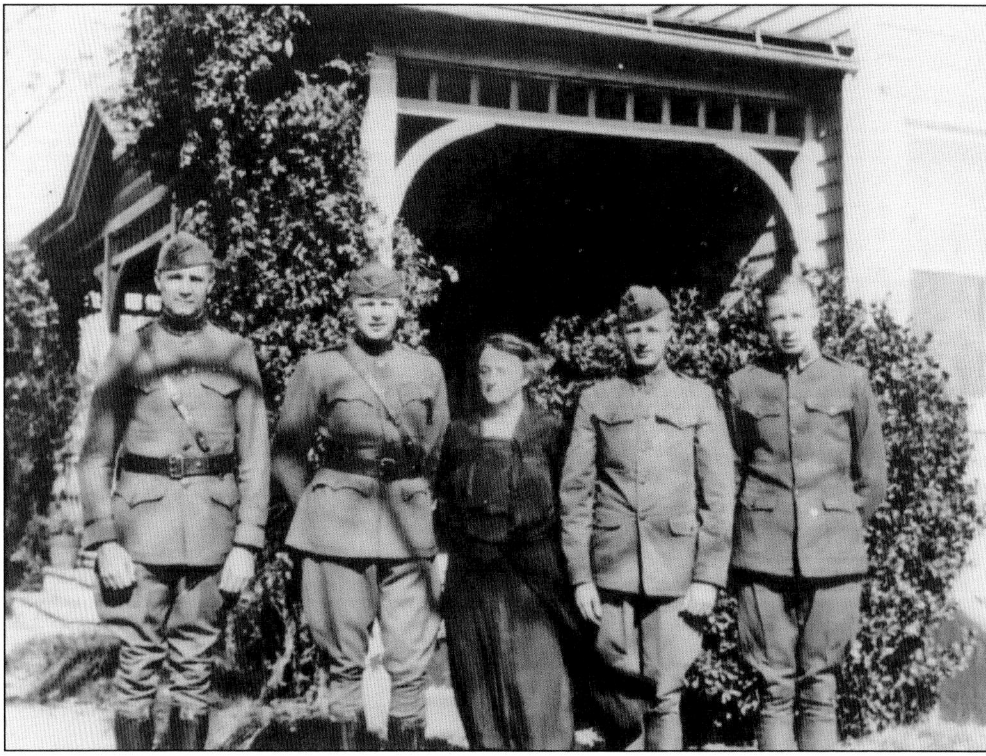

The Anderson family sent four sons off from Mill Hill to fight in World War I. They served their country proudly. Posing with their mother, Alma, in front of the front porch are, from left to right, James (or Jim), Charlie, Fred, and Dick.

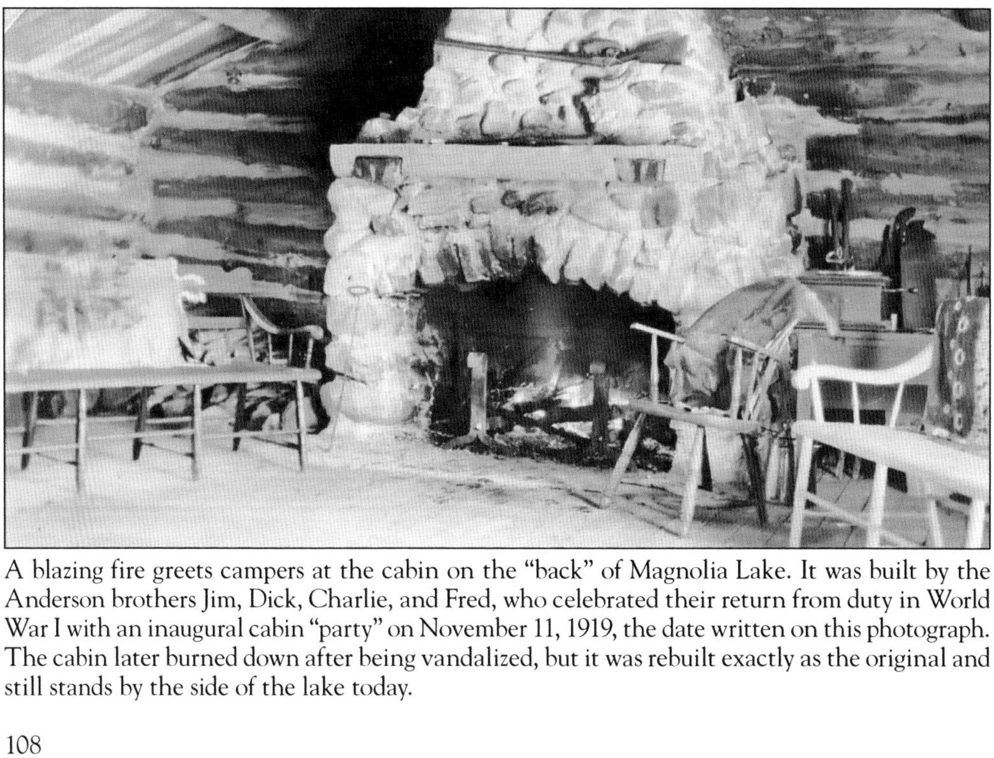

A blazing fire greets campers at the cabin on the "back" of Magnolia Lake. It was built by the Anderson brothers Jim, Dick, Charlie, and Fred, who celebrated their return from duty in World War I with an inaugural cabin "party" on November 11, 1919, the date written on this photograph. The cabin later burned down after being vandalized, but it was rebuilt exactly as the original and still stands by the side of the lake today.

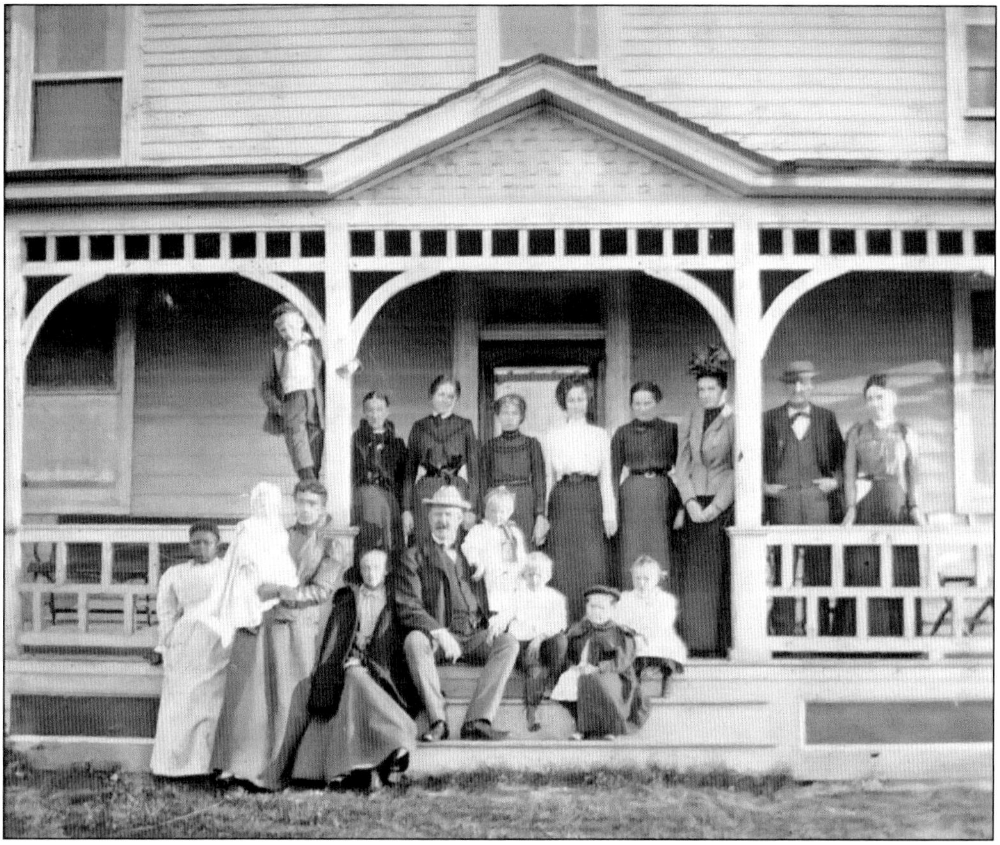

In this image taken in 1899 on the front porch, Capt. Thompson Van Gilder, the patriarch, poses with his family. Captain Van Gilder changed professions and became a farmer during the Civil War when he left the shipping business due to rebel predations upon Northern ships doing business in the South. He later was a founding member and first secretary of the Cape May County Board of Agriculture. The captain married three times and, according to records, left quite a few Van Gilders in the Cape May County area.

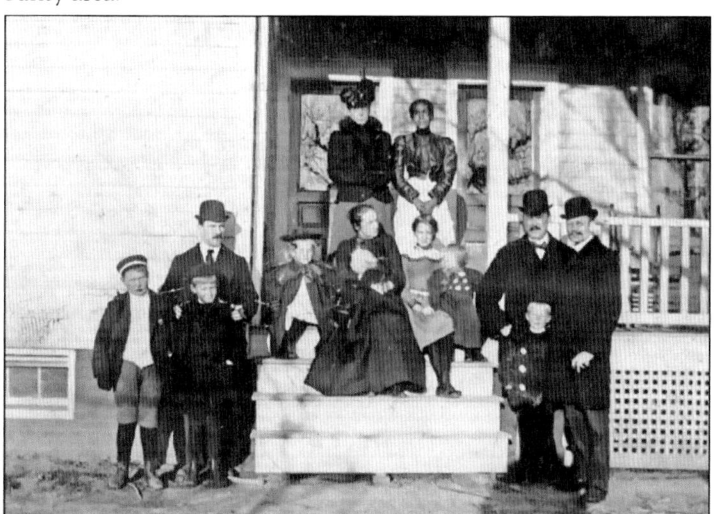

The early 1900s photograph shows Van Gilder/Anderson family members posing on the south porch on the side of the "Big House." The woman seated center is Alma Van Gilder (great-grandmother of the current Alma in residence).

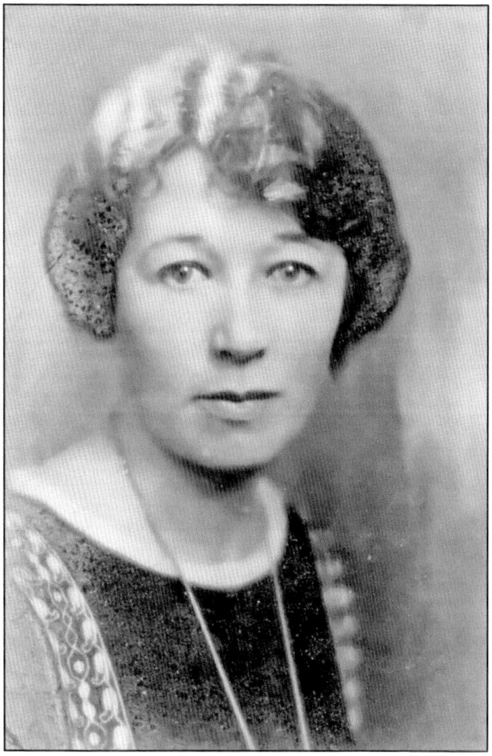

Alma Patterson Anderson, Alma Van Gilder Waltz George's grandmother, is pictured here. She was born on May 3, 1887, and died on February 12, 1959.

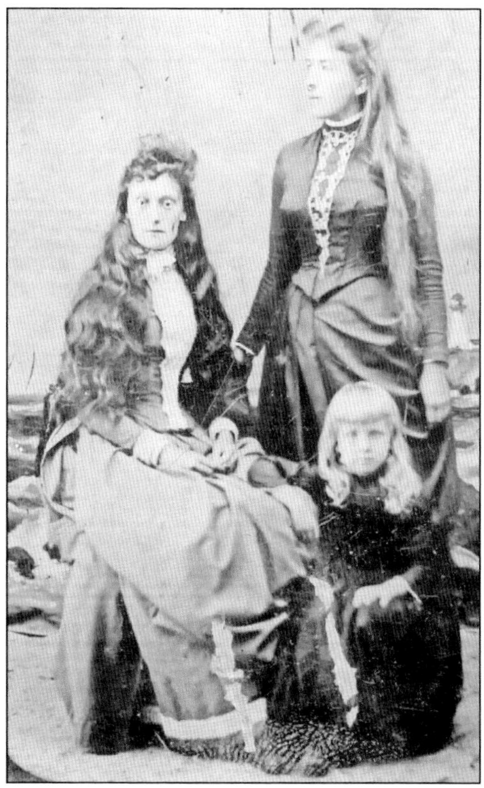

Aunt Polly (left), sister to James B. Anderson (1868–1917), poses with Elizabeth Van Gilder Way (center) and Rachel Gray Anderson (July 7, 1883–July 9, 1976). All three women attended college. Rachel wrote music and played ragtime piano as well as teaching fashion design in Philadelphia.

This is an official photograph of Richard Van Gilder Anderson when he served as the Cape May County clerk.

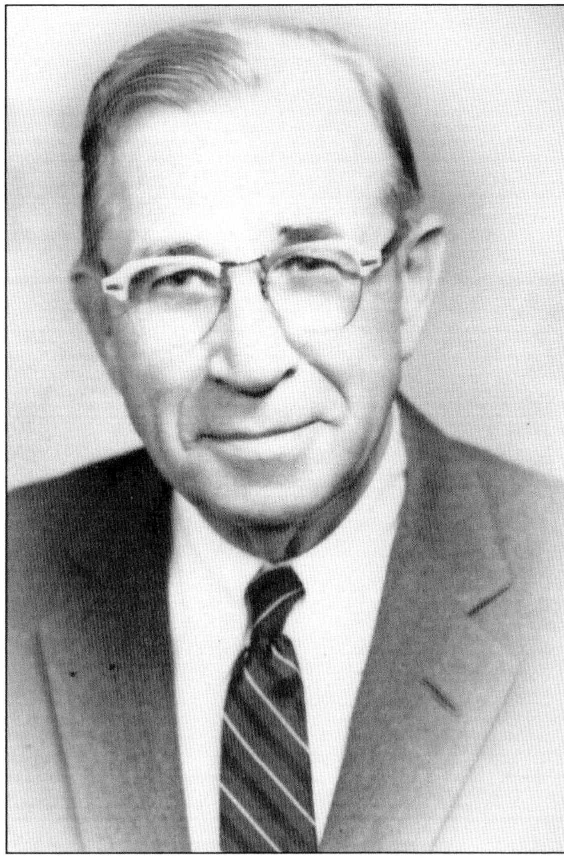

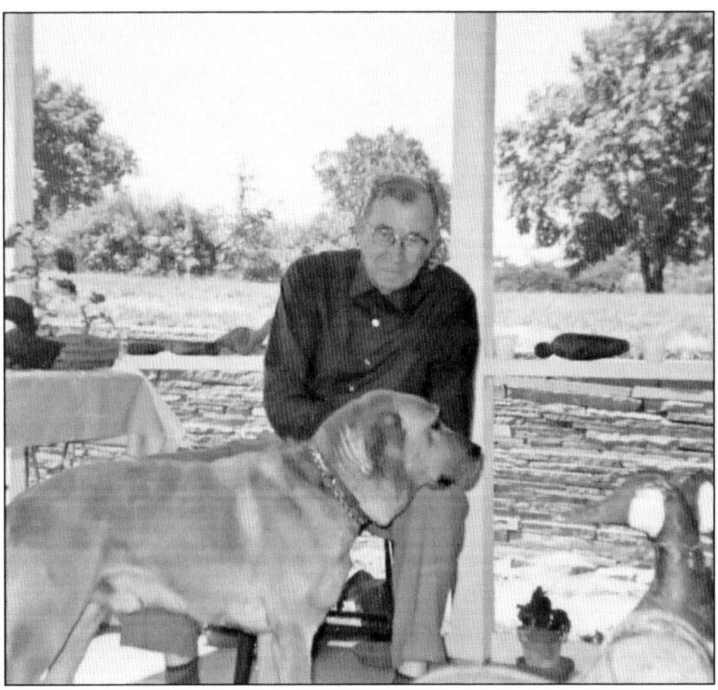

Dick Anderson poses with Bajo on the porch of the old house in 1969. Partly visible in the background is Dick's collection of duck decoys from local carvers. Cape May County is home to a number of world-renowned decoy carvers like J.P. Hand, and a few great carvers call Dennis Township home, including James Siebert from South Dennis and Joe Walton from Clermont. Dick donated his collection to the Cape May County Museum on Route 9 in the Cape May Court House.

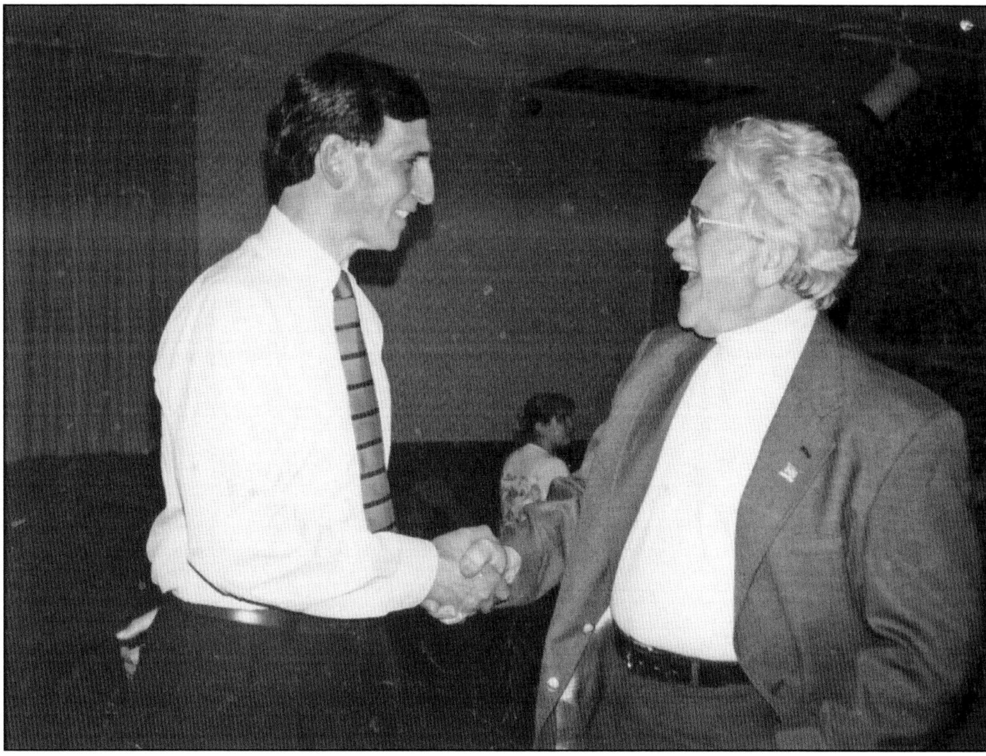

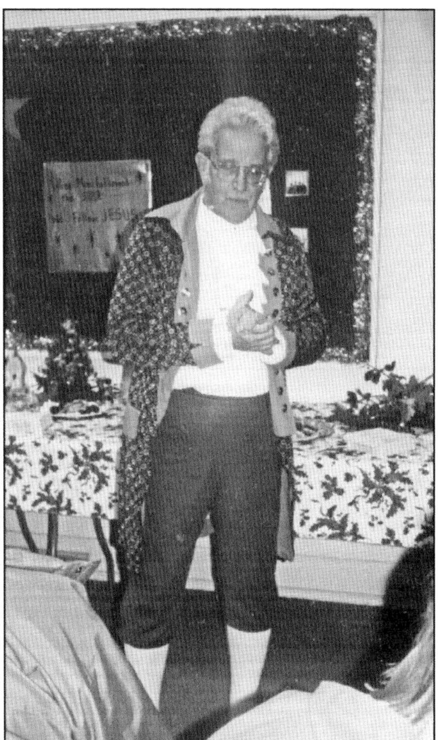

Jim Waltz (right), Alma Waltz George's father, greets New Jersey First District congressman Frank LoBiondo on August 6, 1999. Jim was active in the Cape May County Republican Party. In addition to serving as party committeeman for his district, he was an unsuccessful candidate for Dennis Township Committee. Jim also served on the township zoning board and cowrote Dennis Township's first master plan.

Jim combined his loves of local history and performance in public programs, such as this 2001 appearance in Dennisville. He regularly donned his Benjamin Franklin costume to tell groups of all ages about the area's history. His particular area of interest was Dennis Township land ownership throughout its 300-plus-year existence.

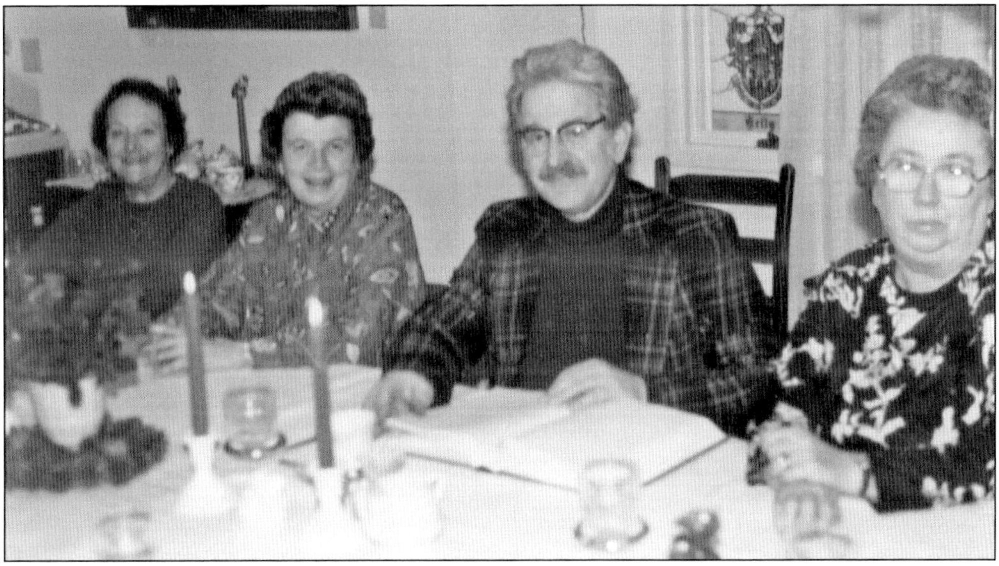

In this 1987 photograph are, from left to right, Evelyn Way, Marian Anderson, Jim Waltz, and Alma Waltz. A professional engineer with a degree from Drexel University in Philadelphia, Jim was active in the Dennisville Historic Homeowners Association, and both he and Alma were active in both the county and the local Old School House Museum. He also served 12 years as president of the Cape May County Museum. Evelyn, married to architect Albert Way, was postmistress in Ocean View. Albert served for many years on the Dennis Township Planning and Zoning Boards.

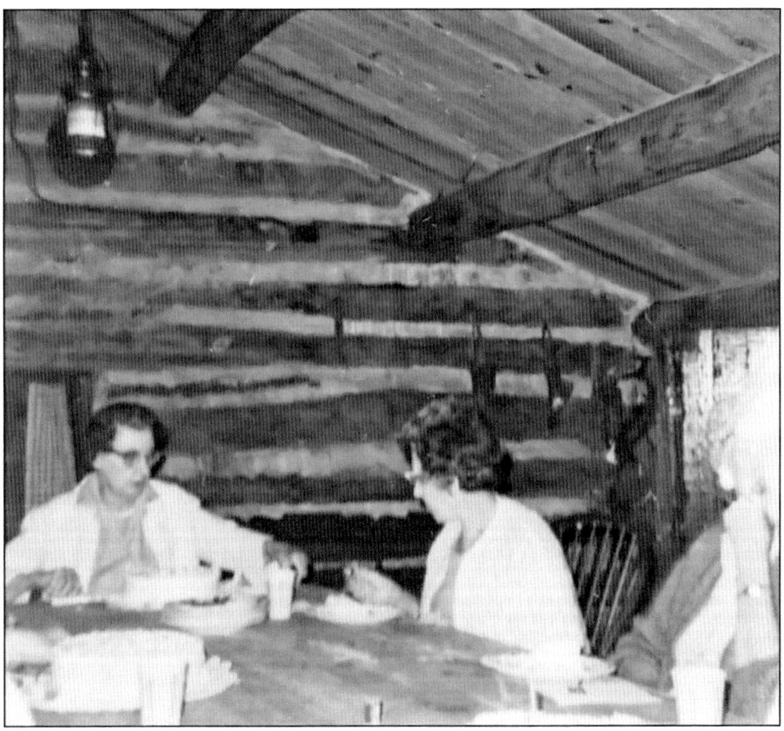

Louisa Van Gilder (left) visits the cabin with "Keet" Anderson in this photograph taken in the mid-1960s. Louisa immortalizes her childhood days spent in Ocean View in the early 20th century in her book *The Story of Mill Hill.*

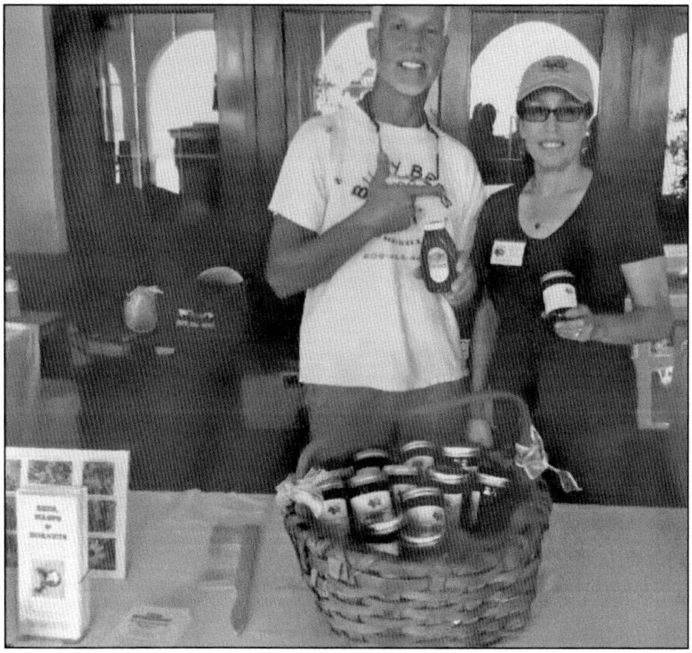

Alma Waltz George regularly sells the products of Jalma Farms at area farmers' markets. Alma is shown here with friend Gary Schempp. Jalma Farms, named for Alma George and her husband, John, has been handed down through four generations of women, starting with Alma Van Gilder Anderson (1861–1939).

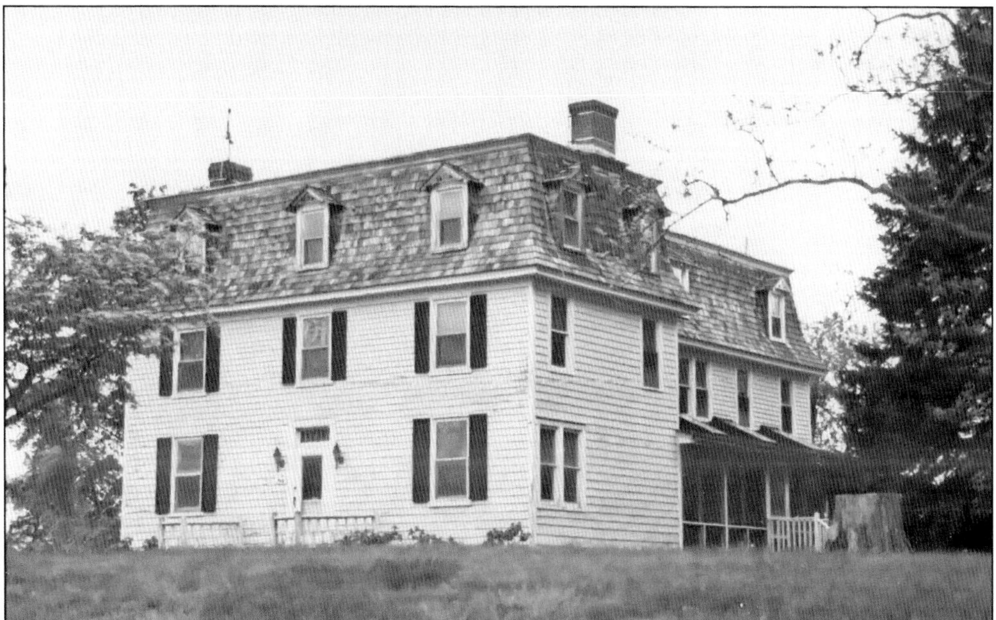

This photograph shows the main house at the top of Mill Hill, still watching over the land and waters first settled more than three centuries ago by John Townsend. Though the area has changed greatly over the years, the fields and meadows and waters of Magnolia Lake compel travelers passing through to reflect, even briefly, on a quieter, slower-paced time before they speed ahead to the seashore resorts. The tale about original Ocean View settler John Townsend and the wrestling match with local Indians has been passed down and appears in a number of books written about Cape May County. Louisa Van Gilder mentions it in her book, but according to Alma George, the story might not be entirely true. However, it suffices as the stuff of legend.

Nine

Ocean View and Clermont "Smell the Ocean, You're Almost There"

Like most of Dennis Township, Ocean View struggled with its name until the intervention of the Post Office Department. It was called Townsend's Inlet, Seaville, Seaside, or South Seaville until 1872, when the mailman arrived and the issue was settled once and for all.

Ocean View's story begins with John Townsend, the 17th-century Quaker outcast from Long Island in 1696. Townsend was a larger-than-life type within Colonial history. A man of many talents, he built his own dam and gristmill, cultivated crops, cut lumber, and built and operated ships. When he was not busy working with his hands, Townsend performed assorted legal and spiritual tasks for his fledgling community.

The road he built is still in use. Today's Ocean View is better known to summer visitors as a busy intersection where traffic bound for seashore resorts bottlenecks. South of Ocean View, Clermont was one of the last settled places in Dennis Township. The mainland stretch from Seaville to Cape May Court House, as well as the barrier islands that are today's Sea Isle City and Avalon, was once called Townsend's Inlet, named for the family that first settled the region.

As population along the Shore Road grew, new names were given if for no other reason than to expedite the workings of the postal service. Townsend's Inlet acquired a post office in 1849. Part of that area eventually became Swainton in Middle Township. The portion located just to the north of Swainton became Clermont in 1886.

Unlike other hamlets in Dennis Township, heavily wooded and marshy Clermont did not experience boom growth during the 19th century. Subsistence fishing, hunting, and agriculture were the main livelihoods of the locals. The railroad's arrival in neighboring South Seaville allowed rail shipments of clams and oysters from Clermont's shellfish beds. In addition, a small tourism industry developed utilizing the area's proximity to good fishing grounds.

Today, the hamlet of Clermont is known for antique shops, campgrounds, and mom-and-pop businesses along the Route 9 corridor. But not far away, the Great Cedar Swamp and a string of wild cranberry bogs that lace through the center of the area serve as reminders that Clermont was once a wild place.

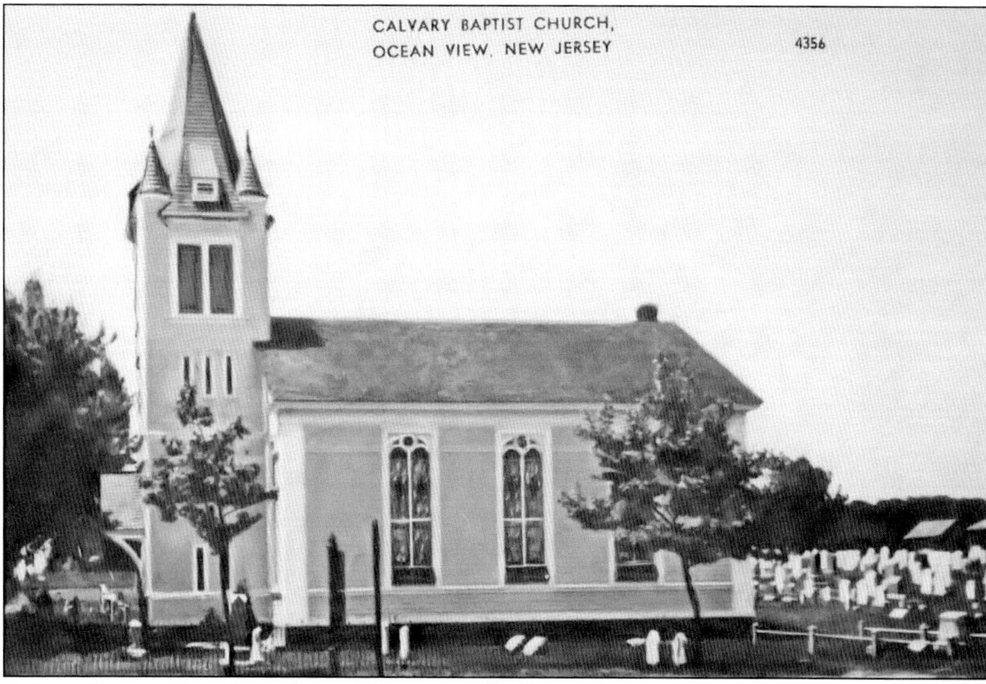

Calvary Baptist Church, built in 1855, was founded by Anabaptists as a meetinghouse. It acquired its current name in 1863. The cemetery holds the remains of Revolutionary War veteran Shamgar Hewitt along with three men who served in the War of 1812—Barker Cole, Joshua Swain, and Joshua Townsend.

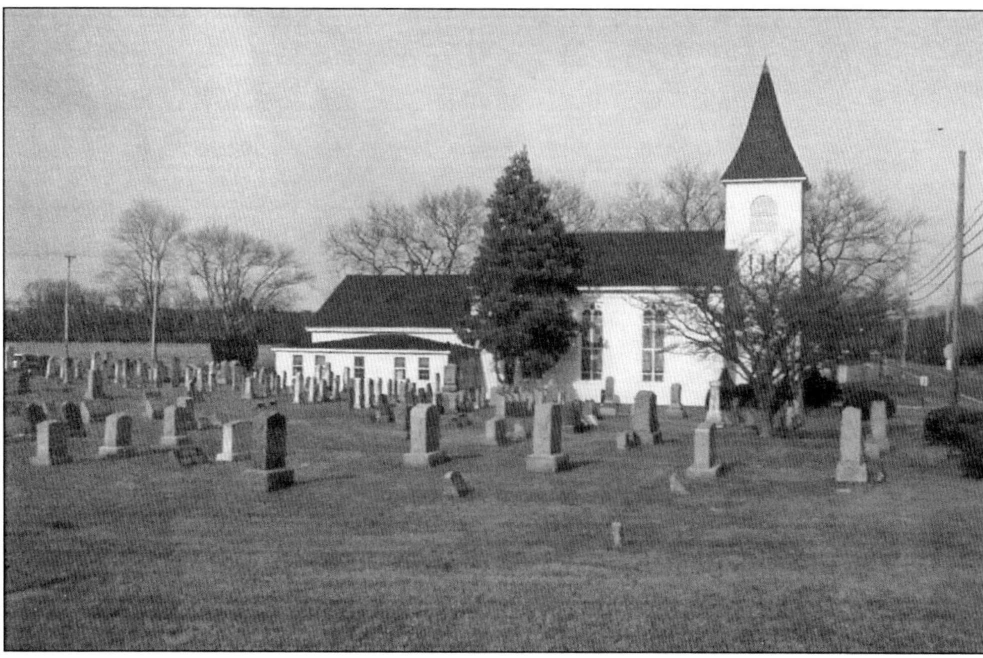

This more modern view of the church was taken from the south with Route 9 to the far right. The church was added to the National Register of Historic Places in 1980. The church and cemetery cover over six acres. The Gothic-style church was designed by Daniel Hand.

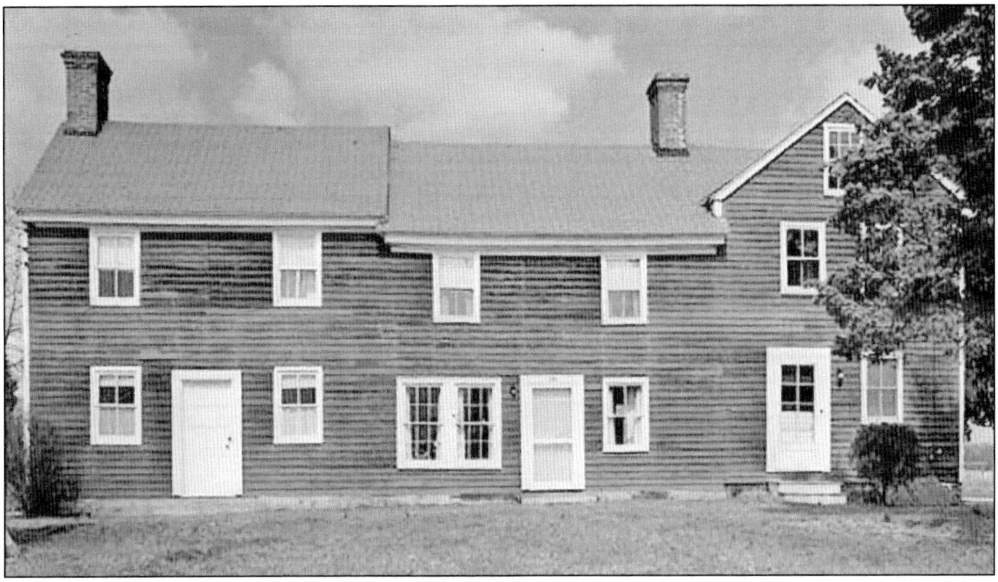

Pictured is the Rising Sun Inn, an important stop for stagecoaches traveling from Philadelphia to Cape Island (Cape May). The three doors are from three separate buildings built in the mid-1820s. The inn operated until 1876, when the growing popularity of rail travel took away most of the lodging's trade.

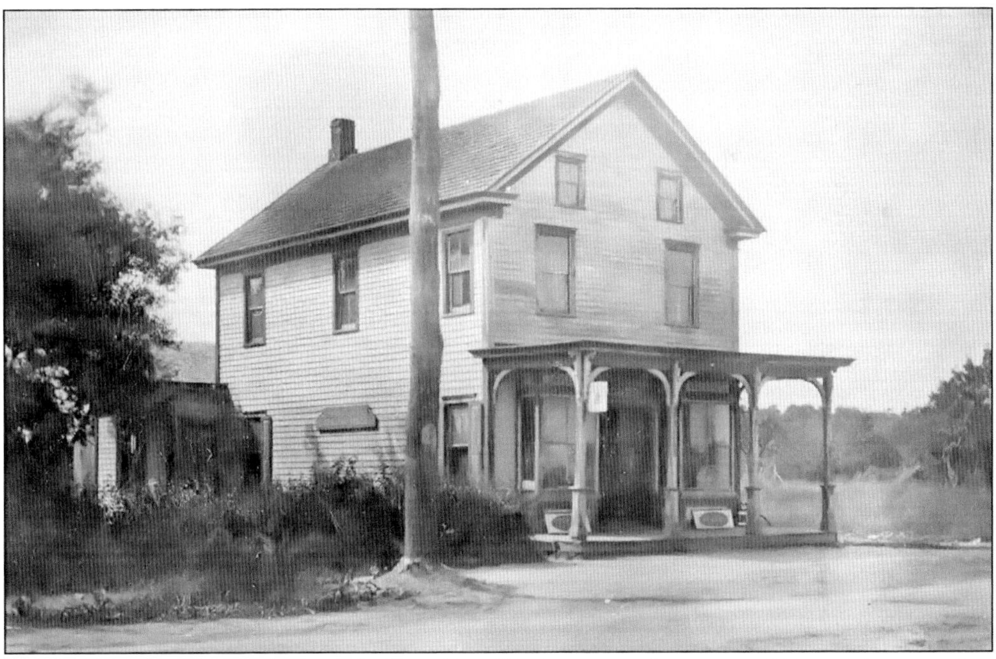

This early 20th-century photograph shows Bert Way's store in the center of Ocean View, on what is today the intersection of Route 9 and Sea Isle Boulevard. At the time of this photograph, the Sea Isle train passed to the right of the store.

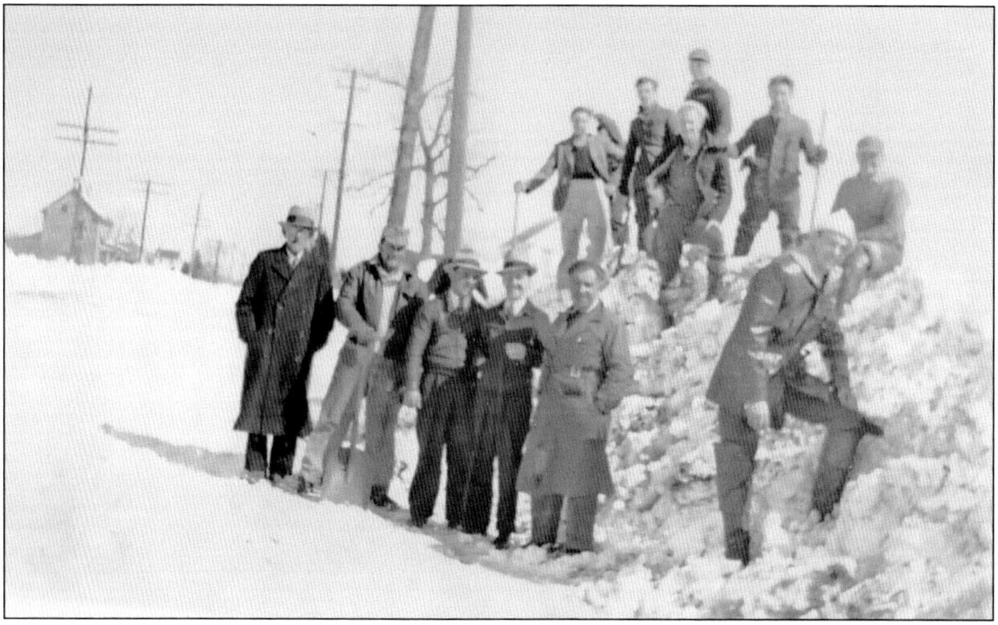

Locals gather on a rare "mountain" along Route 9 in front of Canuso's Service Station in this 1941 photograph. Snow started falling at 11:00 p.m. on February 27 and ended at 10:00 a.m. on March 1.

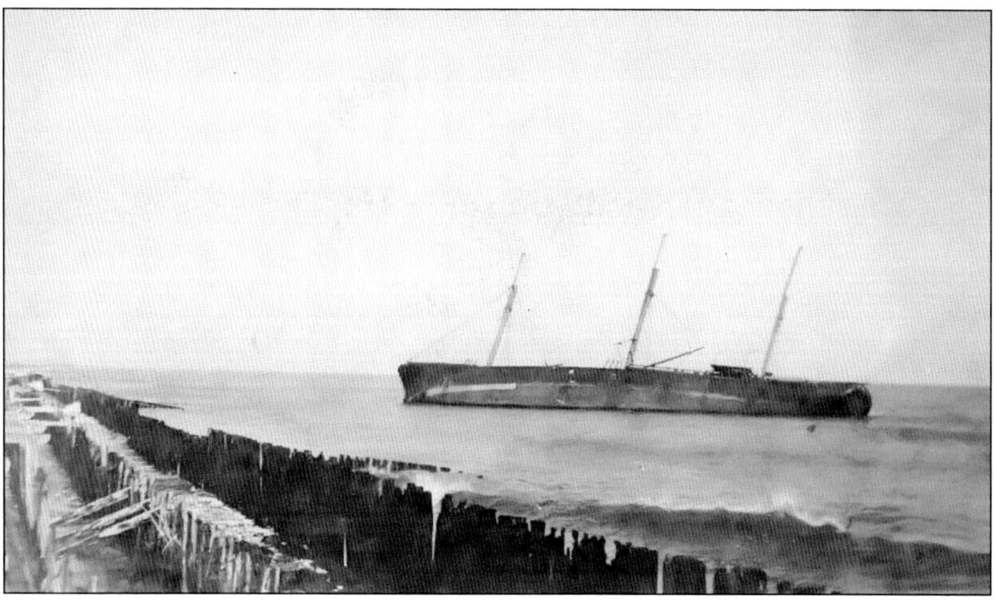

Pictured is a shipwreck off the beach near Townsend's Inlet. Shipwrecks typically meant scavenging for washed-up goodies, a time-honored activity along the New Jersey coast in the 18th and 19th centuries. A barrier island, Sea Isle was originally part of Dennis Township until 1882, when it became a separate political entity.

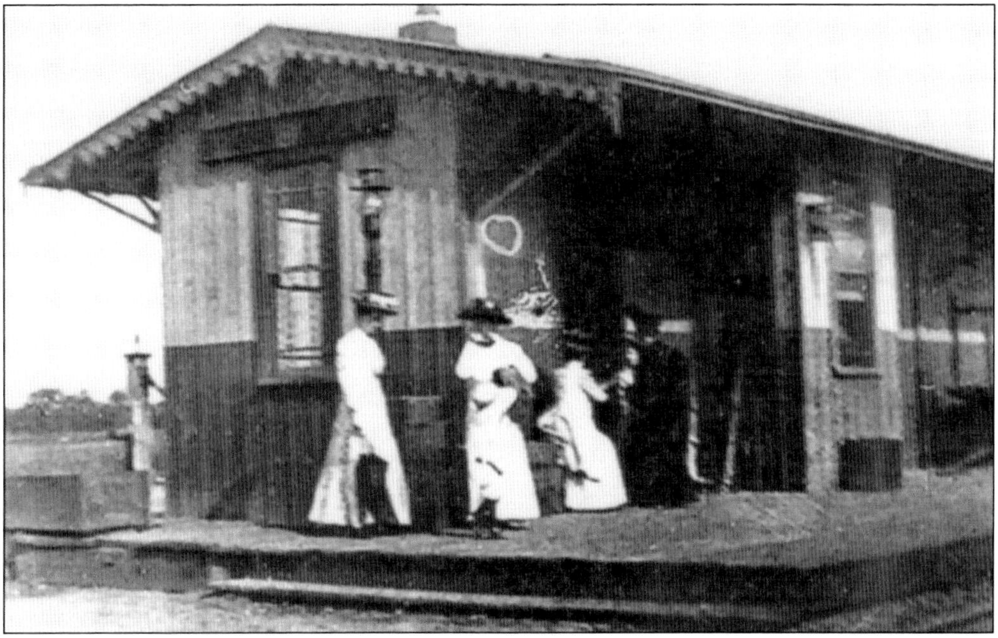

Fashionably dressed ladies wait at Ocean View Station to board a train to Sea Isle. The first connecting road from Ocean View to Sea Isle was corduroy, a type of road with logs as the surface. Logs gave way to rails in the mid-1880s when the Philadelphia and Reading Railroad brought tracks through the area.

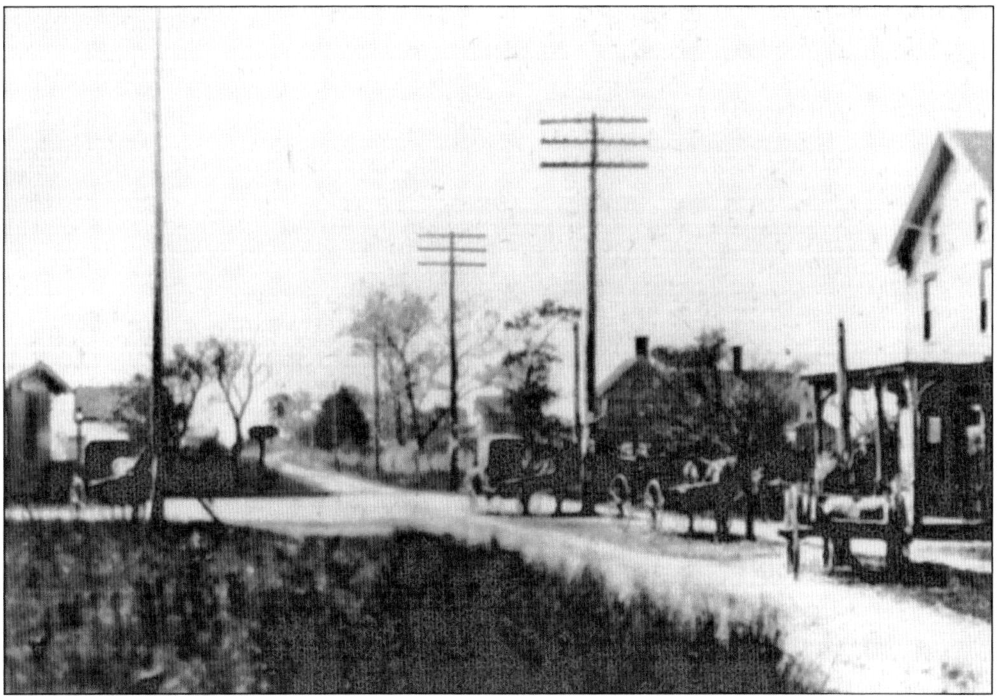

The traffic is heavy in this pre-automobile photograph of a dirt road that would soon be paved by the state. Those traveling south (away from the camera) pass Mill Hill. Those turning left most likely ended up in Townsend's Inlet.

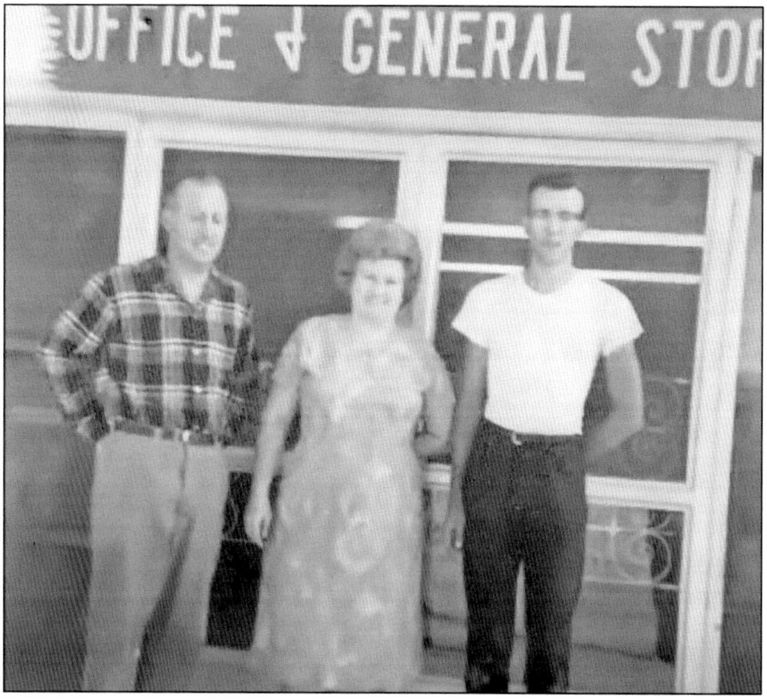

John T. Turner Jr. (left) poses with his wife, Dorothy, and son John T. III in front of the office at their Ocean View Campground in this 1960s-era photograph. John Jr. and Dorothy opened the campground in 1960.

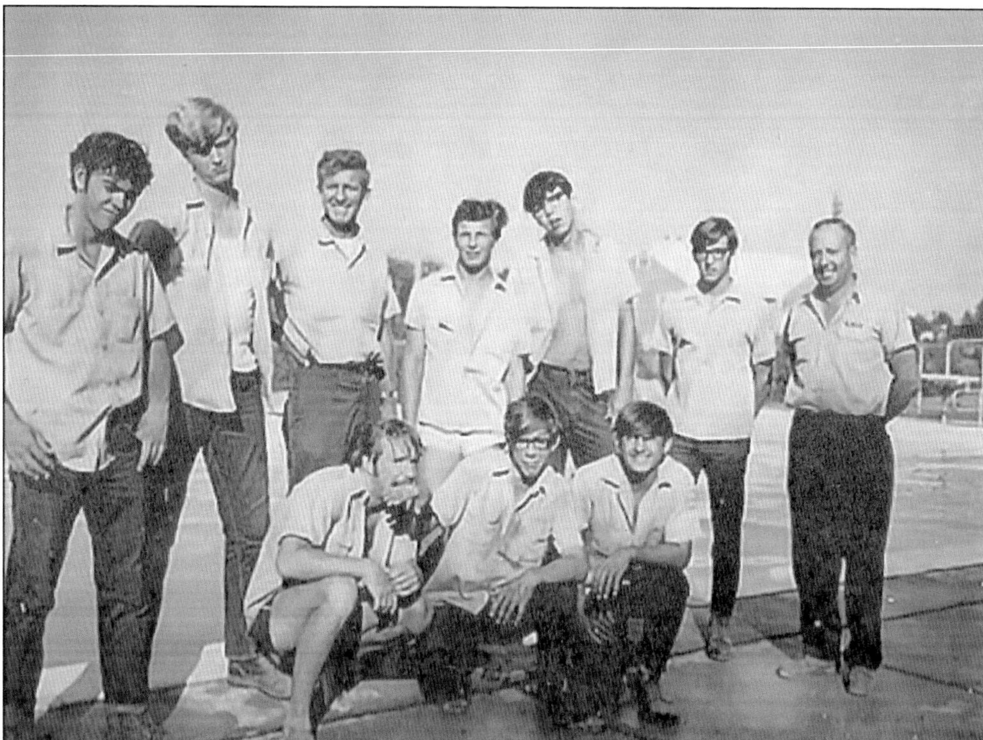

The maintenance crew at Ocean View Campground takes a photograph break with the boss, John Turner Jr. (right). Several members of the Turner family initially worked at the campground, which offered 35 sites on 27 acres for tents and recreational vehicles.

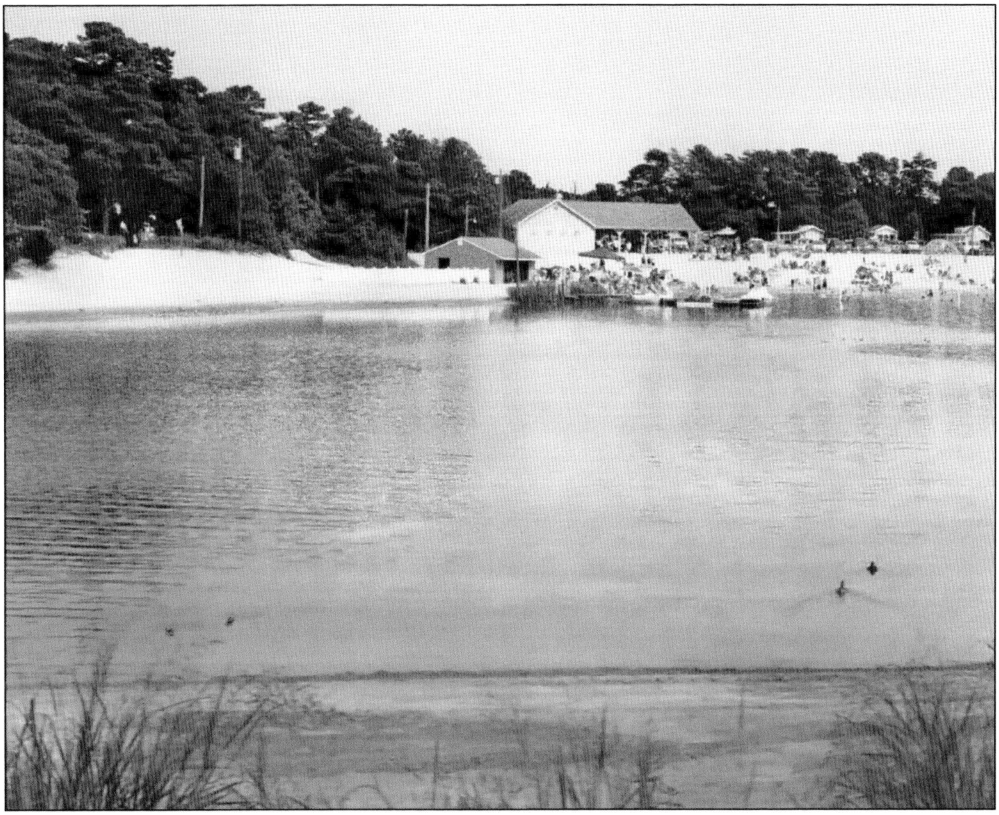

The photograph shows the lake at Ocean View Campground. In 1978, the Turners expanded, opening the Greenbriar section of the campground. Now with 1,175 sites on over 180 acres, Ocean View is the largest privately owned campground in the Northeast.

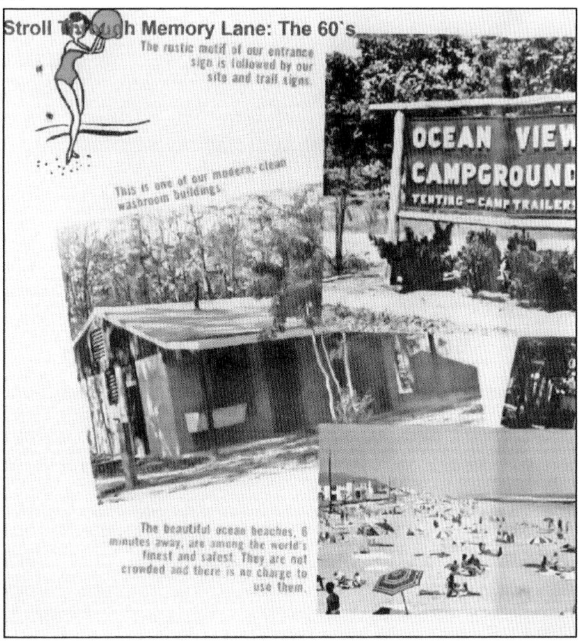

This photograph shows a 1960s-era brochure advertising the campground when proximity to area beaches was the primary selling point. No longer the primitive tent campgrounds of old, facilities like Ocean View have become self-contained resorts, offering just about any of the modern amenities today's traveler has come to expect. With 16 campgrounds in Dennis Township alone, competition is steep.

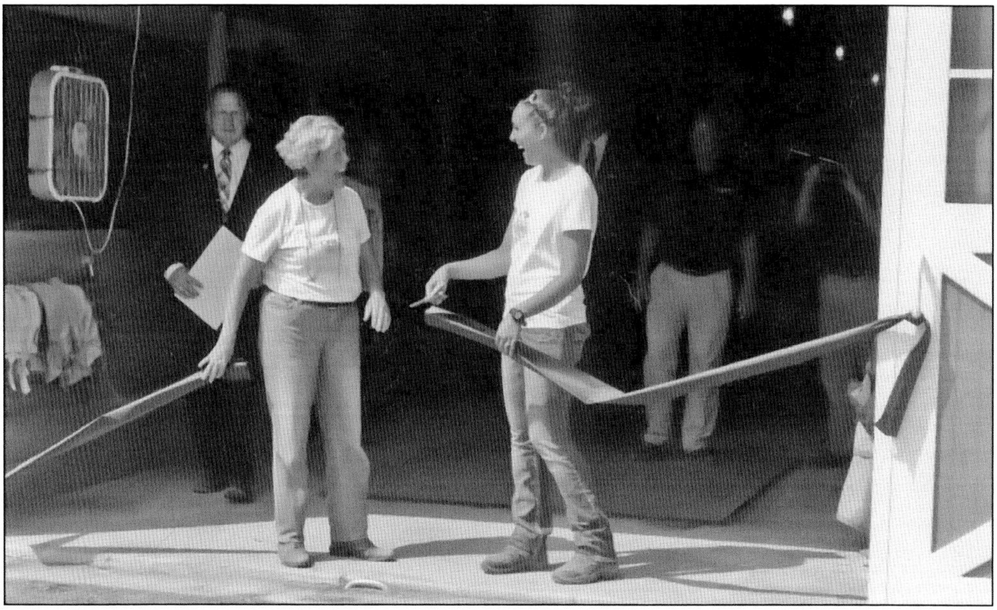

Is it Clermont or South Dennis? This 2013 photograph shows the grand opening of the new barn at Star Hollows Stables, which, among other services, offers equine therapy for disabled individuals. Shown snipping the ribbon are owner Pat Moran (left) and stable manager Abby Revoir. To the left is New Jersey state assemblyman Bob Andrzejczak.

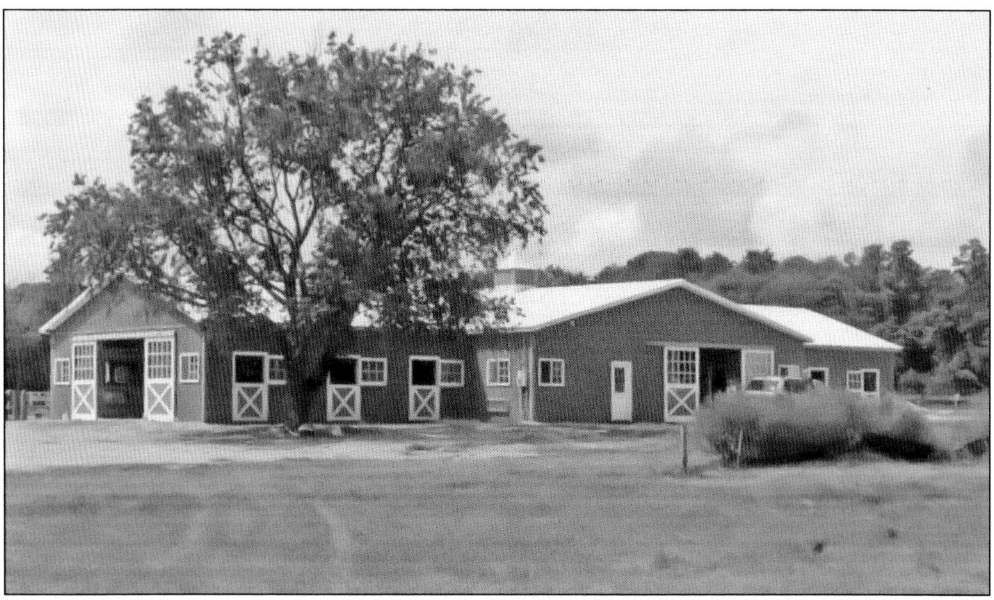

The photograph shows the brand-new barn at Star Hollows Stables. The stables are used to board horses as well as provide room to work with clients for the SELF (Seaview Equine Learning Facility). Part of the program includes therapeutic riding, always carefully monitored by qualified staff.

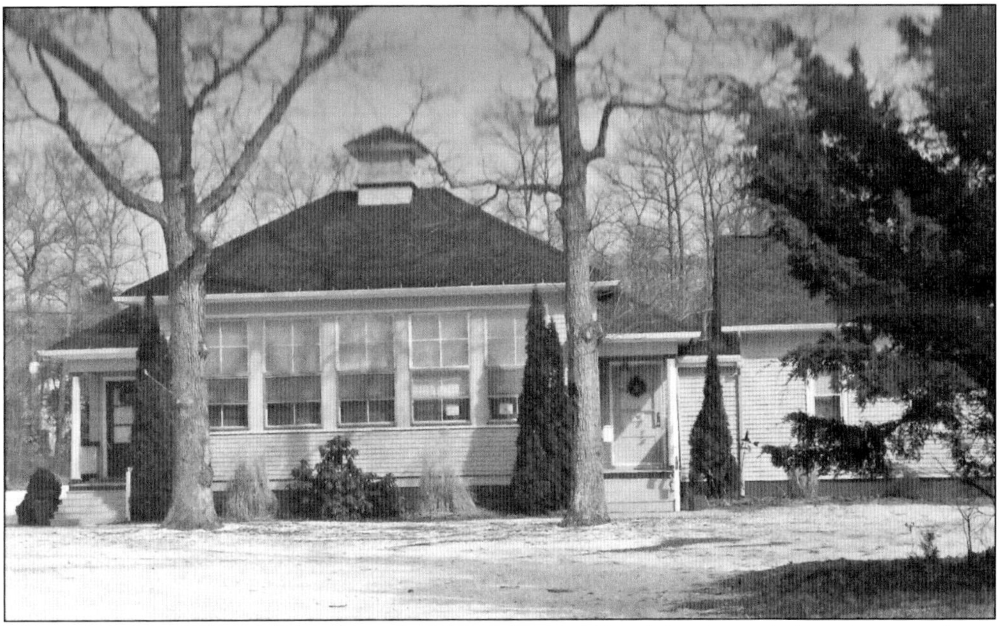

This is the old Clermont schoolhouse, still standing on King's Highway. It has also served as a church, and is a private residence today. According to one former student, the teacher's duties included making quill pens for students using goose quills. The school had insufficient space for an outside play area, so recess was held on the nearby highway.

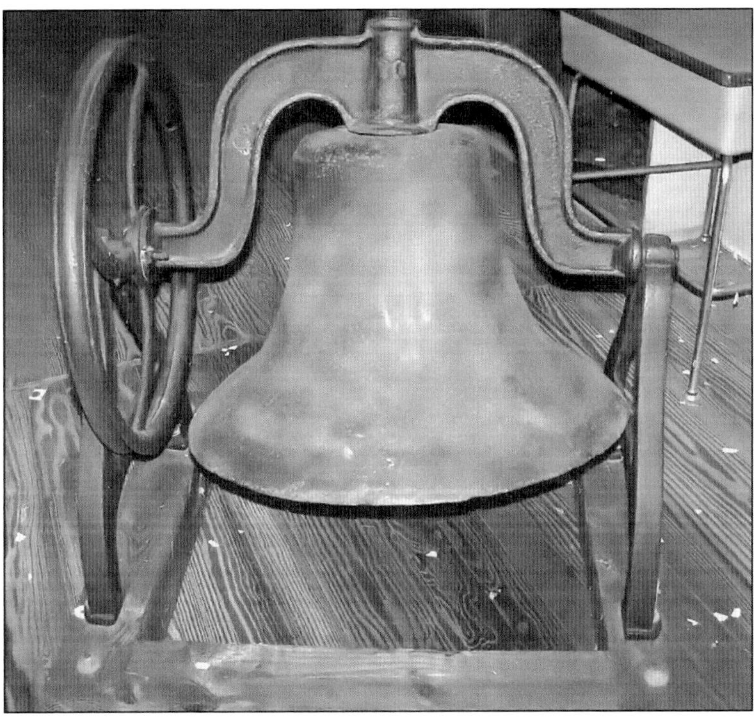

Found locked away in storage at the Ludlam School, the bell for the former Clermont School (now a private residence) is located on King's Highway. It may ring once more after it has been set up on display at the local museum. The bell was originally donated by the Mattifords, onetime owners of the former Clermont School property.

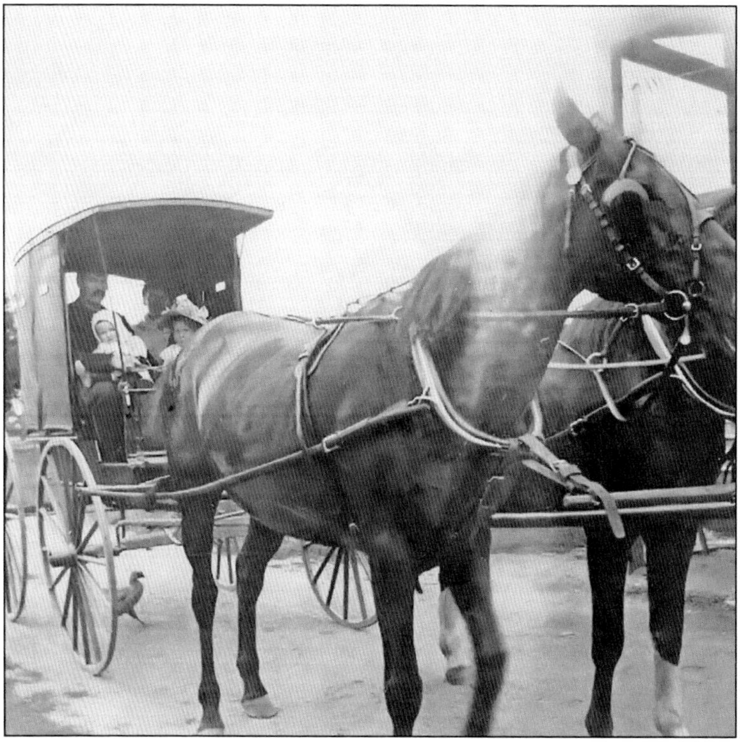

The Holly Tree Inn was built in 1872. At the time, the building was valued at $5,000, with its contents valued at $2,500. The inn was kept by a blind man named Sherman Todd. Tourists traveling by train from Philadelphia who stopped at South Seaville were conveyed to the inn by carriage, as seen here. The price of a stay included daily fishing excursions out to nearby sounds. When the inn was destroyed by fire near the end of the 19th century, the horse barns were saved.

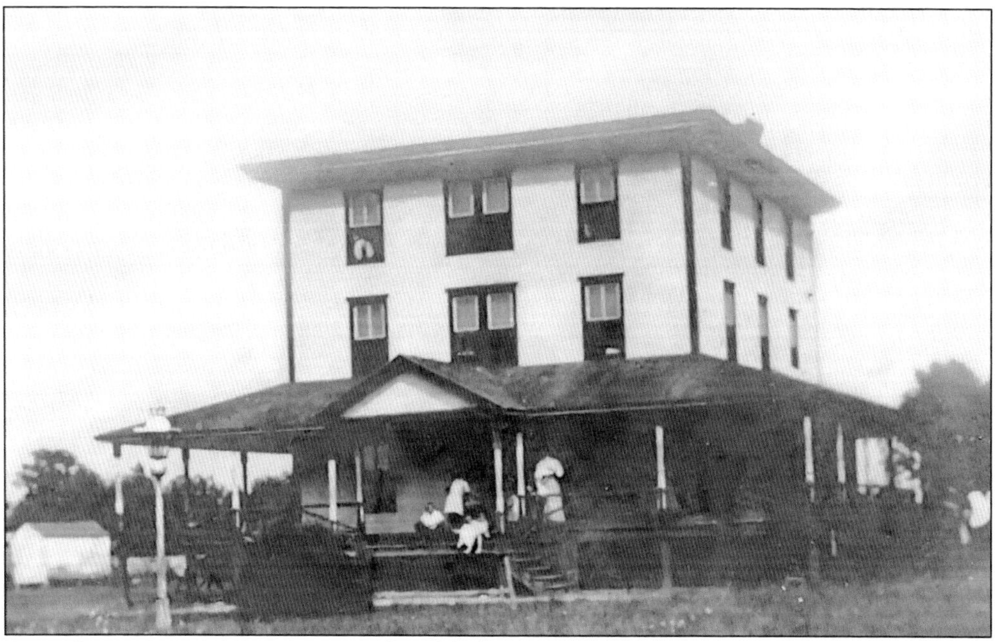

According to an item appearing in the *Philadelphia Inquirer* on March 2, 1897, the Holly Tree Inn was destroyed the previous evening as a result of fire in a defective chimney flue. The alarm was spread to the Asbury Methodist Episcopal Church (still active on Route 9), where the pastor closed services in order to battle the blaze with a bucket brigade.

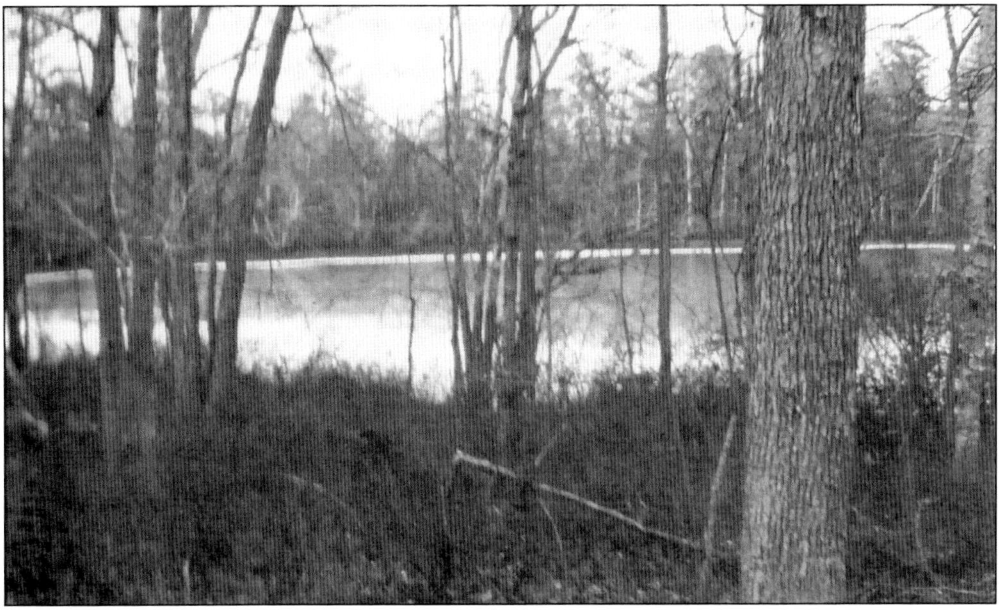

Pictured is one of seven remaining freshwater bogs in Clermont. The stretch of road between Clermont and South Seaville was once called Squeedunk. People living in this area earned their livelihood from nearby bays, harvesting shellfish such as clams and oysters. Before being shipped by train to Philadelphia, the catch was rinsed with freshwater, wrapped in burlap, and then packed in barrels. City folks celebrated their flavor, naming them Cape May Salts.

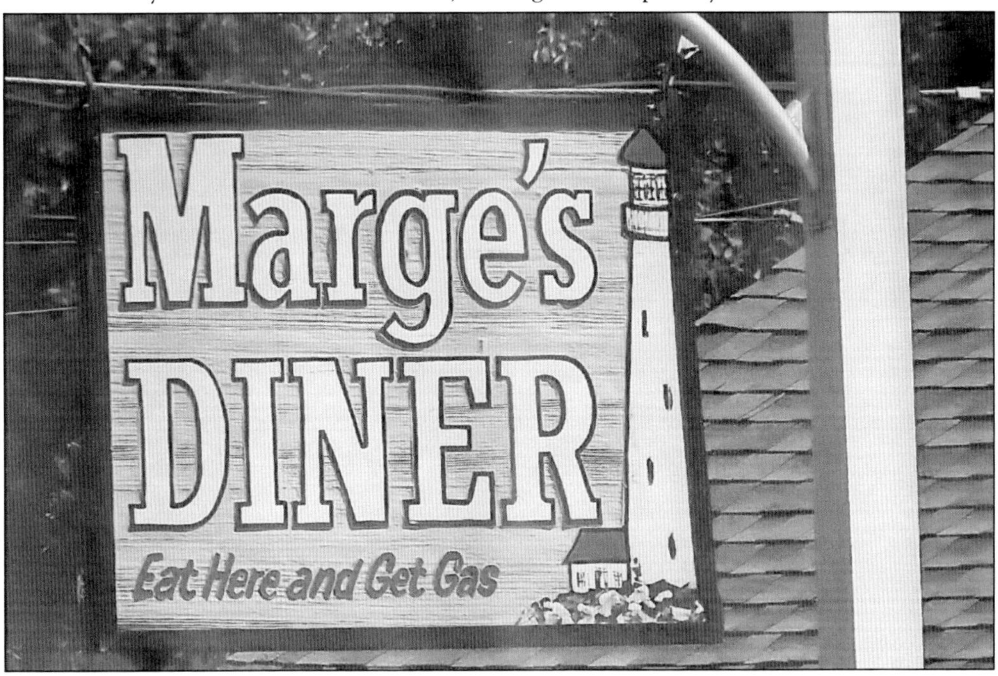

Speaking of eating, this iconic sign over Marge's Diner, the small eatery that has been serving locals and campers for more than 50 years, is bound to elicit chuckles even after it is explained that, at one time, the business also sold fuel for thirsty automobiles. The sign does not deter the lines of customers one sees every Sunday morning in summertime.

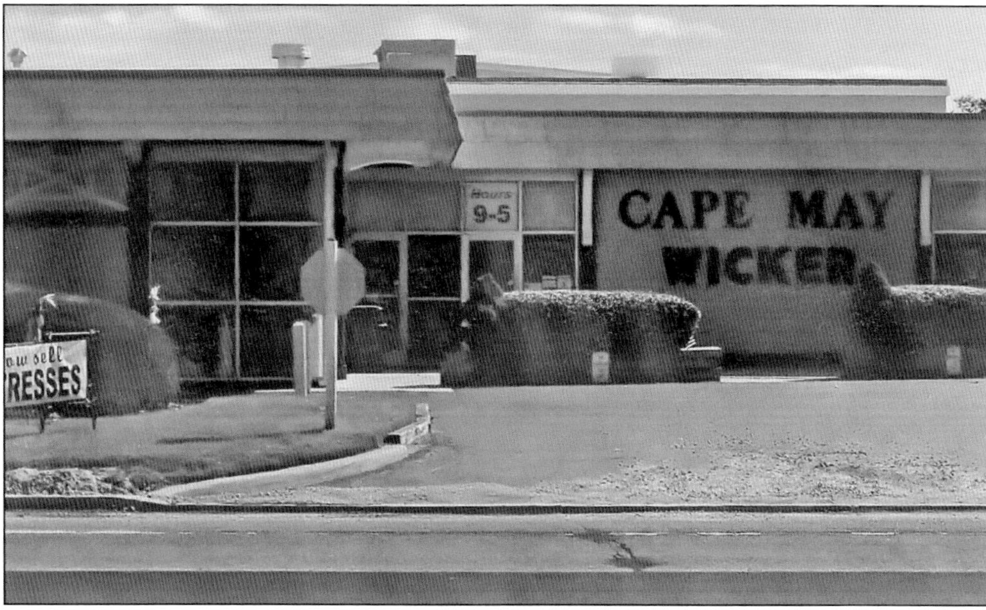

People come from all over New Jersey to Cape May to buy wicker. From its humble origins as a one-man operation selling wicker at flea markets, this business has evolved into a Clermont landmark for decades and is a key business in Dennis Township's Route 9 commercial district.

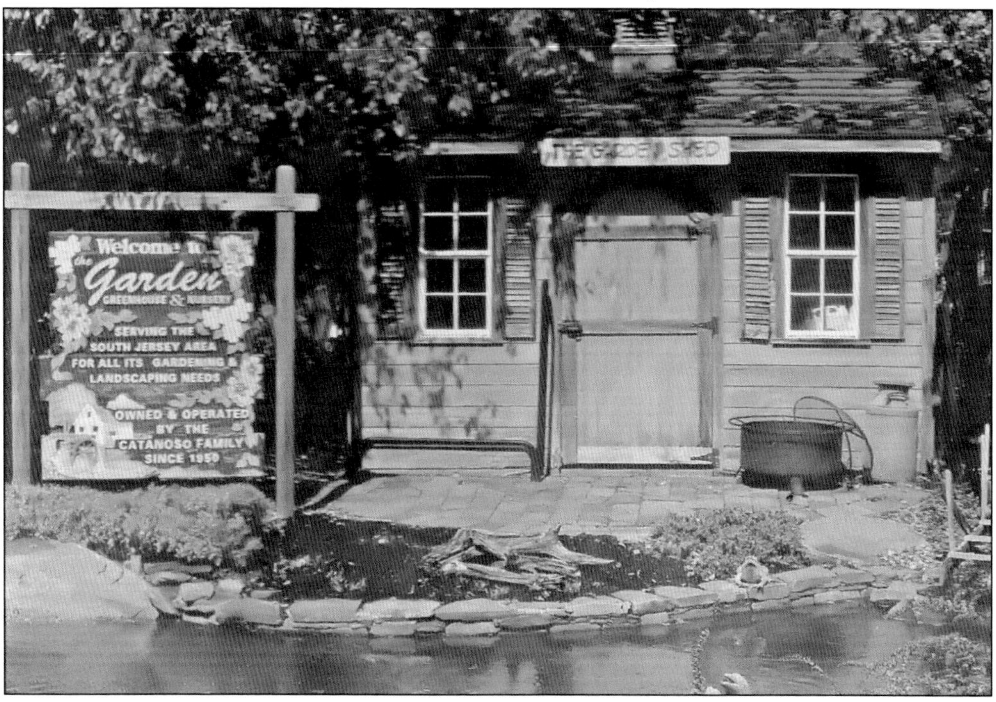

Another long-standing business is Garden Greenhouse. Since relocating from North Wildwood, three generations of the Catanoso family have expanded their landscaping and garden supply company to include a unique retail attraction in the area: Woodland Village. The village offers 17 shops, each self-contained in its own unique structure, and they sell everything from toys to perfume to homemade jellies.

Bibliography

Anderson, Richard. "John Townsend's Mill." *Cape May County Magazine of History and Genealogy*, June 1976.

Beelsey, Maurice. *Sketch of Early History of Cape May County*. Office of the True American, 1857.

Boyer, George. *Cape May County Story*. Egg Harbor City, NJ: Laureate Press, 1975.

Hand, Roy. "Life at West Creek (Eldora) 1875–1925." *Cape May County Magazine of History and Genealogy*, June 1976.

Dickinson, Karl. "The Dennisville Mill." *Cape May County Magazine of History and Genealogy*, June 1976.

Directional Guide for Touring the Eight Villages of Dennis Township, A. Dennis Township School House Museum, Historical and Genealogical Society, Dennisville, NJ, 1997.

Dorwart, Jeffrey. *Cape May County Story*. New Brunswick, NJ: Rutgers University Press, 1992.

Hughes, Mrs. Walter. "Clermont." *Cape May County Magazine of History and Genealogy*, June 1976.

Hunter, Garrison W. "Calvary Baptist Church." *Cape May County Magazine of History and Genealogy*, June 1976.

Hunter, William Garrison. *A History of Education in Dennis Township, 1664–1964*. Glassboro, NJ, 1965.

Lewis, Frances Carroll. "The Gatzmer House." *Cape May County Magazine of History and Genealogy*, June 1976.

McGuigan, Alice. *Historic Dennisville, A Walking Tour*. Seaside, NJ: Atlantic Printing, 2005.

McMahon, William. *South Jersey Towns: History and Legends*. New Brunswick, NJ: Rutgers University Press, 1973.

Robinson, William. *Cape May Datelines*. Dennisville, NJ, 1992.

Ross, Edgar. "The South Dennis School." *Cape May County Magazine of History and Genealogy*, June 1976.

Stevens, Lewis Townsend. *The History of Cape May County, New Jersey, 1638–1897.* Cape May City, NJ: Lewis T. Stevens, 1897.

Tomlin, Charles. *Cape May Spray*. Philadelphia: Bradley Brothers, 1913.

Van Gilder, Louisa. *The Story of "Mill Hill."* Self-published, 1982.

South Seaville Methodist Camp Newspapers:
Star of the Cape, Cape May County Gazette, Cape May Ocean Wave, Atlantic City Press